1760

22 January	Colonel Coote defeats Lally at Wandewash
8 September	Amherst captures Montreal
25 October	Death of King George II

1761

15 January	Lally surrenders Pondicherr
8 June	Belle Ile captured
22 September	Coronation of King George

1762

4 January	Britain declares war on Spain
6 January	Cabinet decides to attack Havana and Manila
16 February	Martinique captured
5 March	'Secret expedition' sails for Havana
26 May	Earl of Bute becomes Prime Minister
6 June	Pocock's fleet appears off Havana Admiral of the Fleet Lord Anson dies
30 July	Fortress of El Morro stormed at Havana
13 August	Surrender of Havana
23 September	Admiral Cornish and General Draper attack Manila
7 October	Manila surrenders

1763

10 February	Treaty of Paris ends the Seven Years War
16 April	News of the capture of Manila reaches London
7 May	Chief Pontiac's Indian rebellion in North America

Introduction

The conflict that began in 1756, ended in 1763 and is generally known as the Seven Years War – or, in America, as the French and Indian War – was, in fact, the very first world war. The international fighting that preceded it, which became known as the War of the Austrian Succession, lasting for eight years from 1740, had included attacks by the British on Louisbourg in North America and by the French on Madras in India and might be considered a dress rehearsal for a war in which the grand strategy and the prizes were global.

In the Seven Years War, the combatants were Britain, allied with Prussia and Portugal against France, Austria and, latterly, Spain. It was to consist of a formal, slow-moving confrontation in Europe and far-flung campaigns of extraordinary vigour and, indeed, exoticism around the world. There were campaigns in both hemispheres and on every continent and ocean. A sailor, or soldier, who survived, might have fought in the North Atlantic and the China Sea, or in northern forests and tropical jungle. One admiral fought battles in the Indian Ocean and the Caribbean and a senior soldier did so on an island in the Atlantic, on the coast of India and in the Philippines. This book concentrates on those campaigns beyond the traditional European battlegrounds.

The Seven Years War is sometimes seen as the war that laid the foundations of the British Empire. When it ended, the whole eastern seaboard of North America was British; Britain dominated India and the rich Caribbean islands were secure – and yet for most people it is a forgotten war. When it is remembered, it is usually just a few images that remain in the memory from history lessons at school: Clive facing the war-elephants in Bengal, Hawke chasing the French fleet among the rocks of Quiberon Bay in a gale, or Wolfe on the Heights of Abraham at Quebec.

History lessons that I remember concentrated on these moments of high drama and ignored other aspects that suffuse the first-hand accounts of that war: the fear of disease in the Caribbean and, if taken prisoner in North America, the fear of torture by Indians; the cunning and duplicity with which campaigns were conducted in India; the courage of the soldiers who tried to storm the heights of Ticonderoga and Montmorency.

These thoughts and emotions swim to the surface in archives and libraries, where they are recorded. I personally became aware of other scenes through

Table of Contents

Chronology

1755

9 July	General Braddock's force ambushed before Fort Duquesne, North America

1756

14 February	Admiral Watson and Colonel Clive capture Geriah, India
6 April	Admiral Byng sails for the Mediterranean
17 May	Britain declares war on France
20 May	Byng's action off Minorca
20 June	Calcutta captured by Surajah Dowlah
26 July	Byng arrested
27 December	Court-martial of Byng opens

1757

2 January	Watson and Clive recapture Calcutta
14 March	Byng executed
23 March	Watson and Clive capture Chandernagore
23 June	Clive defeats Surajah Dowlah at Plassey
15 August	Watson dies, Pocock succeeds him

1758

29 April	Admiral Pocock's first action with Comte d'Aché
8 July	Abercromby's defeat at Ticonderoga
26 July	British capture Louisbourg
3 August	Pocock's second action with d'Aché
14 December	Comte de Lally besieges Madras

1759

16 February	Captain Kempenfelt relieves Madras
27 July	General Amherst captures Ticonderoga
1 August	British and Prussians defeat the French at Minden
18 August	Admiral Boscawen's victory off Lagos
10 September	Pocock's third action with d'Aché
13 September	General Wolfe's victory at Quebec
20 November	Admiral Hawke's victory in Quiberon Bay

tenuous family links. The bloodstone in my grandfather's signet ring, I learned, commemorated the wounds suffered by our collateral ancestor Admiral Pocock at the taking of Chandernagore. An aunt by marriage gave us an unsigned manuscript account of a fearful battle in a forest, written in anger, but not naming the place or the general the author blamed so furiously. Research identified it as Ticonderoga; the author was first supposed to be one of the Townshends, who had fought in North America, because that had been my aunt's maiden name, but he turned out to have been Captain Charles Lee of the 44th Regiment, who had also fought before Fort Duquesne.

Tangible reminders for me of that first world war include a box of Havana snuff brought home by Admiral Pocock in 1762 that is it now considered unwise to sniff because of the high lead content; a beautifully turned wooden rigging truck – now used as my pen-holder – from the rigger's store of the *Invincible* and salvaged from her wreck in the Solent more than two centuries after she sank; a fragment of pale limestone from the ramparts of El Morro.

Symptomatic of the limbo into which memories of the Seven Years War had fallen is the fate of Admiral Pocock's statue by Peter Scheemakers. Commissioned, together with one of Clive, by the East India Company to celebrate his achievements in India, it adorned East India House, then the India Office and finally the Commonwealth Office; there it was moved from the entrance hall to the porters' lobby (where it could sometimes be seen wearing a porter's cap) and was then immured behind the wall of a poky office until rescued. It is now displayed within the India Office entrance to the Foreign Office.

As a journalist, assignments took me to several of the battlefields, amongst them Louisbourg, Ticonderoga, Quebec, Madras, Havana and Manila. At Havana, just before Castro's revolution, I was arrested as a suspected spy while studying, as closely as my ancestor had done, the great dry moat of El Morro; at Ticonderoga, I walked through the woods and up that blood-soaked hill in the footsteps of Captain Lee. As a young man, I came to know Portsmouth harbour and the anchorage at Spithead intimately. When, in the third quarter of the twentieth century, I reported to newspapers on the campaigns brought about by the unravelling of the British Empire, my thoughts sometimes turned to those who had been involved in its foundation; this book is dedicated to those who brought to a close two centuries of history with as little violence as possible.

No great figure from the war has become recognised as a national icon on the scale of Nelson. The nearest is Wolfe, whose memory Nelson was to revere; in 1962, when I was reporting the war in Algeria, I was reminded of him – jokily but effectively – by a journalist friend, the late, ever-lamented Siriol Hugh-Jones, who sent me a postcard of his odd face from the National Portrait Gallery, on which she had written, 'Dear Child, you do not seem to be in a very *healthy* spot. I send you this inspiring profile to cheer you on.'

But, as documentary research for this book began, unfamiliar characters stepped from the shadows: men such as Able Seaman Strahan, who took the fort at Baj-Baj on the Hooghly river single-handed; Captain Speke and his son Billy, who were so brave at Chandernagore; Mr. Kendrick, the navigating master, bantering as he conned his ship up the uncharted St Lawrence; Lieutenant Daniel Holroyd, who had worried about his muddled love-life before storming El Morro. Among the men who directed events, three stand out as underestimated: Major-General Viscount Howe, the most remarkable soldier of his time, who might have changed North American history but for what happened on the shore of Lake George; Vice-Admiral Sir George Pocock, who swept the French from the Indian Ocean, so making Clive's achievements possible, and then conducted what was perhaps the most successful large amphibious operation to achieve total surprise until the D-Day landings off Normandy in 1944, both events taking place on 6 June; Major-General William Draper, who captured Manila and would write *The Laws of Cricket*. A few seem like our contemporaries and, surely, Augustus Hervey and George Townshend would still feel at home, drink in hand, at White's, their club in St James's Street, and Draper, at Lord's cricket ground.

The field research has, as always, been enjoyable and enhanced by those who volunteered to guide and explain. Tom and Penny Treadwell, with whom I stayed on the shores of Lake Champlain, showed me the forts at Ticonderoga and Crown Point. I am grateful to Juliet Barclay for advice on Havana, to Julian Barrow for his account of Calcutta and to James Dreaper for giving me nuggets from his own research into his ancestor General Draper, the captor of Manila. The Hon. Mrs W.A.C. Keppel, the Marquess Townshend and Sir Peter Thorne kindly showed me relevant paintings in their collections. Mrs Scilla Lonsdale and Mr Roy Stimpson arranged for me to see Townshend caricatures at Raynham Hall in Norfolk, and Michael Nash advised on sources. Elizabeth Woodward generously gave me books from the library of her father, my friend, the late David Woodward. Admiral of the Fleet Lord Lewin gave useful advice on sources.

I must thank David Roberts and Andrew Lownie for their encouragement and Richard Ollard for reading and commenting upon the typescript; Ian Hessenberg for photography; Stephanie Cooke and Jackie Gumpert for their parts in preparing for publication; and my wife, Penny, for her help with the index.

My gratitude is also due to librarians and archivists at the National Maritime Museum, the Royal Naval Museum, the National Army Museum, the National Portrait Gallery, the British Library, the London Library, the Norfolk Record Office and the Courtauld Institute of Art, for their help with research involving printed sources, manuscripts and pictures; in North America, those at the McCord Museum, Montreal; the New York Public Library; the Huntington Library, California; the Thompson-Pell Research Center, Ticonderoga; the William L. Clements Library of the University of Michigan; and the Massachusetts Historical Society. The manuscripts departments of Christie's and Sotheby's have, over the years, helpfully shown me documents that have passed through their hands.

I am grateful to Jack Golding, who introduced me to Quebec; to Michael Robinson, for mounting the bicentennial exhibition of the Havana campaign at the National Maritime Museum; and to my father, Guy Pocock, who once taught history at the Royal Naval College, Dartmouth, for first telling me some of these stories.

Tom Pocock
Chelsea, January 1998

'Bashful of Blows'

On the afternoon of Saturday, 5 March, 1757, a string of horses came trotting down the Portsmouth Road. Twenty-five miles from London, they were clear of the bare, wintry branches of the Surrey woods, where the highroad widened as it reached the coaching village of Ripley. Wheeling off the road and between the fluted pilasters of the high archway leading to the stable yard of the Talbot Arms, the cavalcade halted, hooves stamping, flanks steaming. A tall man swung from his saddle and stooped to enter the inn, while the groom, who had accompanied him, also dismounted to help the waiting ostler lead the horses to their stalls.

The tall man was wearing thick woollen clothes as befits a traveller on wintry roads, but he had an easy air of command as might be expected of the naval officer he was. The landlord showed him to a chair by the fire and Captain the Honourable Augustus Hervey ordered dinner and a room for the night. He was a strongly built man aged thirty-two, with a round, lively face, cleft chin, a firm but sensual mouth and candid, humorous eyes. Had he appeared less humorous, his manner might have been seen as arrogant rather than supremely self-confident, as was appropriate to the landed aristocracy accustomed to money and the expectation of a great estate to be inherited from his father, the second Earl of Bristol. His interests were navigation and fighting at sea; his recreations, philandering and convivial evenings at White's Club in London, or with brother-officers at sea.

Captain Hervey had an air of purpose about him and indeed, he was on a mission; yet one with no direct connection with a naval command or operation, although war with France had broken out in the previous May. Next morning he hired a fresh set of horses, leaving those he had brought from London in the care of the ostler, who was instructed to keep them ready for instant departure on his return to Ripley. Thereupon he and his groom again rode south-west, through Liphook to another coaching town, Petersfield, where they stopped at the Red Lion. The halt was brief, just giving Captain Hervey time to arrange for four good horses to be kept ready for him day and night until further notice, quickly agreeing to the charge of £3 a day. He then wrote to his servant in London, William Craddock, requiring him to have his own horses kept saddled, again by day and night, ready for an immediate departure. He also ordered him to go down to the Thames near Billingsgate Dock in the Pool of London and charter a Dutch fishing-boat, instructing her skipper to remain at his moorings until further notice because he was to take a servant to France on urgent business and at short notice.

Leaving Petersfield for Portsmouth, Captain Hervey rode across the ridge of downland that separates the wide hinterland of Hampshire from the Channel coast. Having completed all but the final and most vital arrangements of his mission, he now had time to consider the friend he was riding to meet. This was an unlikely friend, although from the same stratum of English society as himself. A bachelor of fifty-four, overweight, pompous, and reputed to have homosexual tendencies, he seemed the antithesis of Captain Hervey excepting their shared profession. What gave such high drama to the latter's journey to Portsmouth was that his friend was under sentence of death and Hervey intended to rescue him.

Vice-Admiral the Honourable John Byng was this friend and, for months past, he had been the talk of the ruling and executive classes from drawing-rooms to quarterdecks and amongst ordinary folk in coffee-house and taproom. Yet only a year before he had been only one of many admirals, occasionally called to active service by the Royal Navy but otherwise passing their time quietly on their country estates and in their town houses between Hyde Park and Charing Cross. Perhaps, if John Byng's father had not been such a successful and admired admiral himself, his son would still be passing quiet hours at Wrotham Park, or at 41 Berkeley Square. He had, indeed, spent the preceding eight years in both places and occasionally at the House of Commons, where he represented Rochester, a Parliamentary seat comfortably in the Admiralty's pocket because of the influence generated by the neighbouring naval dockyard at Chatham. His father had been George Byng, raised to the peerage as Viscount Torrington in recognition of his victory over the Spanish off Cape Passaro in the Mediterranean in 1718, when his son John had first heard a broadside rumble across the sea.

He had been taken to sea with his brother Jack and his first cousin, George Pocock. The latter did not enjoy the same social advantages as the Byngs, since his father was a naval chaplain, the Reverend Thomas Pocock, who had married John Byng's maternal aunt, Joyce Master. Naval service had since separated them but Pocock had been an executor of John Byng's elder brother, Pattee, who had succeeded their father as Lord Torrington; now, only John's sister Sarah survived of his five brothers and sisters.

When Hervey and Byng had first met, the latter was commanding a ship of the line – as captain, isolated by his rank and by temperament from the rest of the ship's company – and Hervey was an acting lieutenant of seventeen. In 1714, he had been appointed to Byng's ship, the *Sutherland*, outward bound for a cruise in the Newfoundland fishing-grounds, his father's political and social influence helping to promote his career as a naval officer.

Patronage was the recognised path to advancement, which was sought for financial reward as much as professional glory. A naval officer could expect a harvest of prize money in wartime from his share of the proceeds of selling enemy ships in whose capture he had been involved or, better still, for which he had been responsible. There was also money to be made from carrying, or escorting, valuable cargoes – notably bullion – on commission in peacetime. Byng, unlike his cousin, had, when a lieutenant, used his family's influence to avoid service in the unhealthy West Indies, choosing the more agreeable, if less challenging and rewarding, Mediterranean instead. There he had commanded a frigate, then a stationary guardship at Port Mahon, the naval harbour of Minorca, and finally, in 1747, begun a year as the senior officer in the Mediterranean.

Augustus Hervey was quite different. For him, a career at sea offered adventure, the chance to augment the fortune he would eventually inherit and to philander ashore in foreign countries, where the proprieties of home could be disregarded. The Army might be more fashionable for a young man-about-town, but it offered no such enticement: commissions were purchased; no training was necessary, nor was it obligatory to spend much time with one's regiment in peace, or even in war; only a minority of young officers developed into dedicated professionals. If Hervey's motive was excitement, Byng's had been the emulation of his father and a life away from the routines of country estate and town house. Middle-aged and overweight from years of good living ashore, Byng was no longer handsome and his customary expression combined arrogance and defensiveness. He had not married, and, although he was said to have a mistress older than himself, some said that she was more of a housekeeper and her presence served to distract attention from his homosexuality. Were his inclinations such, they were well concealed, for homosexuality was illegal and its practice was a capital offence in the Navy.

In London society, Byng was not popular. Horace Walpole, the tireless chronicler of his time and himself homosexual, only saw him in the House of Commons, or in the street, but thought 'his carriage haughty and disgusting'. [1] Fanny Boscawen, the bluestocking wife of an admiral and member of the

Board of Admiralty, was more explicit, writing in her journal: 'I met Admiral Byng, who seems to me a mixture of coxcomb and f——[*], if you'll allow a judgement upon an admiral. He had an undressed frock [coat], very richly embroidered with silver, which in my eyes is a strange dress, and his discourse and manner pleased me no better than his garb.'[2] Her husband, who had admired Byng's father, considered him 'a degenerate son'.[3] Yet Byng could command the close friendship of Hervey, himself the essence of heterosexuality.

The two unlikely friends – the extrovert captain and the introvert admiral – had had another bond in their dislike of the ruling politicians. This had begun with a general distaste for an irresolute administration led by the Duke of Newcastle, now in his sixties, as neurotic and querulous as he was energetic in political intrigue. Within the duke's inner circle were Henry Fox, who had been Secretary for War and was now Secretary of State, and was valuable for his understanding of their fellow-politicians and for his ability in the House of Commons; a suave, ambitious politician, with a quizzical, yet knowing, look. Another was Lord Granville, the Lord President, an urbane and cultivated man of the world with skills in diplomacy; and the Earl of Hardwicke, the Lord Chancellor, a judge with a cold, detached legal air.

Of more interest to Hervey and Byng was Lord Hardwicke's son-in-law, George Anson, the most famous member of their own profession, who was now not only an admiral and a peer but First Lord of the Admiralty. Anson had become the most famous sailor of his age after his four-year cruise around the world in command of a small squadron ordered to harass the most distant and lucrative Spanish colonies and their trade. It had been an extraordinary achievement in the face of appalling difficulties and hardship but had ended with his triumphal procession through London when the Spanish treasure he had taken was paraded in 32 wagons. Since then he had been an ardent reformer of the Royal Navy, giving it a new structure, standards and sense of purpose, establishing the corps of marines, increasing efficiency and reducing corruption in the dockyards, and for the first time dressing naval officers in uniforms.

Yet there was something strange about Anson. For all his brilliance, he was a withdrawn, taciturn man – like Byng, rumoured to be bisexual, at least – as ruthless in politics as he was successful at sea. In 1748, he had married Lady Elizabeth Yorke, the daughter of Lord Hardwicke, and, through him, exercised political influence. Indeed, while at the Admiralty, he virtually controlled a cabal of 15 Members of Parliament, mostly through the selection of suitable candidates to represent naval ports. Like his father-in-law, he was fascinated by naval and military strategy. It was Anson who, as First Lord of the Admiralty, had advised the Government – notably Newcastle and Fox – on moves to counter the mounting hostility between the British and an increasingly self-confident France in the closing months of 1755 as they blundered into open war.

The preliminary shocks of the war that had been formally declared in 1756 had been rumbling for years in European capitals and in distant seas and territories. At its epicentre was the rivalry between the two dominant European states, Britain and France, the latter with a population of 25 million, double that of the former, the French army twice the size of the British, though Britain's navy was double that of the French. Both increasingly depended upon the economic support of global trade.

Britain, an island naturally looking to the sea as a means of trade, communication and defence, was, however, tied to continental Europe by a monarch of German descent in the Protestant succession. King George II was also Elector of Hanover and felt at least as much responsibility for his little inheritance embedded in the patch-work of German states as he did for the islanders who were also his subjects.

The French and English had been rivals, if not enemies, for centuries, despite the successful Norman invasion and colonisation of 1066. Protestant England faced Catholic France in repeated wars of dynasty, religion and territory not only across the Channel but in North America, the Caribbean and India, where both traded and sometimes settled.

King Louis XV of France had, at the age of five, succeeded his great-grandfather, *Le Roi Soleil*, inheriting the concept of absolute monarchy and, unlike King George, personal power unbridled by parliamentary politicians. Among the other monarchs with designs on Europe was the forceful, cultivated King Frederick II of Prussia, who, although his territories were far smaller, had inherited a well-trained army and was determined to expand the borders of Prussia. Others with their own territorial ambitions were the Empress Maria Theresa of Austria and the Empress Elizabeth of Russia, daughter of Peter the Great, who introduced the French language and culture into her court at St Petersburg.

Alliances were forged, broken and reversed, but the constant factor was the enmity between Britain and France. While King George's electorate of

Hanover remained a potential hostage in the heart of continental Europe, Frederick was now the ally and Louis, Maria Theresa and Elizabeth the enemies. Yet the dominant British politician of the coming conflict – as Secretary of State and Prime Minister – the able, imaginative, but depressive William Pitt, the future Earl of Chatham, had his own eyes on far more distant horizons. While the King fussed about Hanover, Pitt's imagination ranged across the forests, mountains and plains of North America, the sugar islands of the Caribbean and the hot expanses of India. There, Britain and France confronted one another more immediately than in Europe, and there, both knew, lay the key to future wealth and power. Pitt, and those who thought as he did, were convinced that the destiny of Europe would be decided in the limitless expanses of the world beyond the oceans.

Britain and France had fought each other in 1740 for eight years, mostly on the Continent, in what came to be known as the War of the Austrian Succession, when France had supported Prussia against Britain and Austria. Then the European fighting had spilled over into the distant, disputed territories and the British had taken Louisbourg in North America from the French and the French had taken the Indian trading city of Madras from the British; both had been returned under the peace treaty.

Since then, the two nations had come to rely more upon global trade and developed imperialist ambitions. Now the distant possessions, existing and potential, themselves became a cause worth fighting for. Spasmodic clashes in North America and India drew military and economic resources from the disputes in Europe and those, it was being said, might be decided on the banks of the St Lawrence and the Ganges.

The immediate vortex of conflicting interests was in North America, where both Britain and France dominated huge territories with seemingly limitless economic potential. The British had settled most of the Atlantic seaboard with 13 colonies stretching as far west as the Appalachian ranges that ran parallel with it, some 200 miles inland. But whereas the British had settled to farm, the French had explored, traded and begun to open up the central prairies and the wild western deserts and mountains. Only in the north-east had they settled the St Lawrence Valley, where the riverside city of Quebec had been built and fortified. This had become the capital of the boundless territory they named New France, and a second fortress-city, Louisbourg, commanded the wide mouth of the river opening into the Atlantic and to France beyond.

At first it had not been a question of fighting for land but of occupying it and hoisting national flags over forts built of logs, rocks and heaped earth to command a pass, ford, or the junction of rivers, which usually offered the only means of travel through thickly wooded country. Every so often, reports would reach London, or Paris, that the rival was about to send more troops to garrison such forts, and the threat would be countered by sending a larger convoy of troopships to New York, or Quebec. Occasionally, British and French would collide and fight at sea, or deep in the American wilderness. Such a collision could, it was realised, light a long fuse that would explode in a European war.

Negotiations for a peaceful compromise began in 1755, but it was already too late. The critical moment came on 9 July of that year, deep in the wilds of forest, rock and swamp between British territory on the Atlantic seaboard and French around the Great Lakes. Both sides had been reinforcing and, when news reached the British that the French were constructing a chain of forts, designed to contain British expansion, at the junction of the Ohio and Monongahela rivers, further blocking westward expansion of the British settlements, action was taken. An expeditionary force, commanded by Major-General Edward Braddock, formerly of the Coldstream Guards, was shipped to America. A pre-emptive strike was ordered against the French by British columns advancing westward from Maryland, New York and Nova Scotia. Braddock's column, marching from Maryland, was to attack the new Fort Duquesne at the fork of the two rivers. His slow progress through the wilds was reported to the French by Indian scouts; Braddock was ambushed and routed, leaving more than 500 dead amongst the trees. He himself was killed, but among the fugitives who lived to fight again was a Colonel George Washington, already seen as an American officer of promise.

One Sunday morning in March 1757, Hervey breasted the long chalk ridge of Portsdown and looked south over a panorama of land and sea. Below him to the south-west, the keep of Portchester Castle rose above its Roman ramparts, washed by the tides of the great harbour. This had been the original naval base from which King Richard I had sailed for the Crusades and King Henry V for the campaign of Agincourt, two centuries before the present naval dockyard had been built closer to the harbour mouth at Portsmouth.

Between Portchester and Portsmouth spread the harbour, running from creeks winding from Fareham and Gosport, widening into a great anchorage serving the fortified dockyard at Portsea, a few hundred yards from the bastions and earthworks defending the town of Portsmouth itself. There, the narrow mouth of the harbour was defended by forts and batteries on either shore and, beyond, lay the open water of the Spithead roadstead and the wide Solent channel between Hampshire and the hills of the Isle of Wight.

Riding down the southern slopes of Portsdown, Hervey crossed the wooden bridge to Hilsea island and its flat, desolate farmland to where the cupola of Portsmouth church and the russet rooftops of the town showed above the grassy embankments and stone ramparts of the surrounding fortifications. Beyond could be seen the masts and yards of ships rising behind the dockyard buildings like the bare trunks and branches of woods in winter.

His horses' hooves drummed on the wooden bridges over the moat to the ravelin and then the Landport Gate and clattered on the cobbles of the High Street. This was quiet but for those going to church and potboys and ostlers sluicing the stable yards of the inns. Not wishing his movements to attract attention, Hervey did not choose to stay at his usual lodgings in the house where Edward Hutchins, the boatswain of the dockyard, rented rooms to transient naval officers. Instead, he took more discreet quarters and stabling from which his horses could be taken to a rendezvous on the shore of the harbour outside the walls without questions being asked. Here he learned that Admiral Byng was confined on board the *Monarch* (as Hervey spelled the name of the former French prize, *Monarque*), which was moored at the head of the harbour. He at once applied for permission to visit him and, next morning, a note arrived from Byng himself, inviting him aboard.

The sequence of events that had brought Hervey to Portsmouth had begun early in the preceding year, 1756. Now that open war had broken out in America, tension between the rich and expanding British and French trading settlements in India was increasing and the French seemed to be looking upon Hanover as a possible hostage in their rivalry with Britain. The formal declaration of war was bound to follow, but the British Government was unprepared.

Intelligence reports had started arriving from the courts of Europe – seemingly based on rumour rather than specific evidence – that the French were planning to invade England. This had been a recurrent nightmare since it had actually taken place seven centuries before; it eclipsed all other possible disasters in the minds of politicians. In 1756, the talk might be of invasion but the factual reports were of a French army and fleet assembling at Toulon, under command of the Duc de Richelieu, with 12 ships of the line preparing to attack the British base in the Mediterranean, the island of Minorca.

While the Duke of Newcastle ordered panicky defensive moves against invasion, the more likely contingency was met only by a fleet of ten ships of the line; a sixth of those available on home waters or close to the British Isles and 'the very worst of the fleet', as Hervey described them.[4] Undermanned by often sickly crews and mostly commanded by inexperienced or second-rate captains, the ramshackle fleet lacked a hospital ship and the auxiliary warships essential to a major naval operation; the ships' marines had been replaced by an infantry regiment to reinforce Minorca. This collection of ships – many scarcely seaworthy, let along battleworthy – was then ordered to the Mediterranean under the command of Vice-Admiral the Honourable John Byng.

The composition of the fleet and the choice of its admiral were curious decisions, based as they were upon Anson's professional advice. Perhaps he regarded Minorca as being of marginal strategic importance, given that the British held Gibraltar; perhaps he kept more ships than seemed necessary in home waters to descend upon French merchant shipping off their ports on the outbreak of war. Byng, who was neither popular nor energetic, was a curious choice for the command, but it had been decided that two admirals should be sent to the Mediterranean – the second-in-command being Rear-Admiral Temple West – and Byng was the only available officer of sufficient rank for the command and had had experience of Minorca and the surrounding sea.

Sailing on 6 April, the fleet reached Gibraltar on 2 May, where it was joined by three more ships of the line. However, the admiral was given the news that he was too late because the _ French had already landed 15,000 troops on Minorca and were besieging the fortress of St Philip, which commanded the long fjord of a harbour. Gibraltar itself seemed vulnerable, too: it was so weakly defended that the Governor was not only unable to supply more troops for the relief of Minorca but considered it pointless, if not impossible, to land there those Byng had brought with him. The admiral at once sailed for Minorca, arriving off its rocky shore to see the British flag still flying above the fortress and the smoke of French guns.

Now he was met by the small frigate *Phoenix*, commanded by Captain Augustus Hervey, who reported a French fleet, similar in size to his own, cruising off Majorca and commanded by the Marquis de la Galissonnière. Early in the morning of 20 May, the two fleets were in sight and Byng did not hesitate to attack. But he was not an inspiring commander and his captains had not been trained to react quickly in action. Indeed, some seemed less than enthusiastic about joining battle with the French fleet, which, although numbering 12 against Byng's 13, mounted heavier guns, including 42- and 36-pounders on their lower gun-decks, against the British 32- and 24-pounders. The British formed a line of battle, the essence of which was that the ships sailed in line ahead and in a prearranged sequence according to weight of armament so as to concentrate gunfire most effectively. But their approach to the enemy's line was oblique, the van closing before the centre and rear and so coming under concentrated French fire. Aiming for the masts, spars and rigging, as was the French custom, they brought down the foretopmast of the *Intrepid*, the sixth ship in the British line. Swinging into the wind, the ship's sails were taken aback and she slewed to a stop, forcing the ships astern to veer away to avoid collision. The British line was now in disarray. Byng tried vainly to restore order and did not take the bold decision to order all ships to steer for the enemy line and a pitched battle, ship to ship. By the time he had shepherded his command into some semblance of a line of battle, the French had turned away. La Galissonnière had given priority to the support of the French invasion of Minorca rather than victory over a British fleet, however vulnerable that appeared. Next morning, the two fleets were out of each other's sight.

Byng had to decide on his next move. His ships had suffered damage and casualties – 42 killed and 165 wounded – in the action and he had no hospital ship to take the latter or the more than 400 men sick in his fleet. It would be difficult, if not impossible, to land his few hundred soldiers on Minorca and, even if he did, they could do little against 15,000 French. So should he return to Gibraltar, which might be the next objective of the French, to defend it and refit his damaged ships and land his wounded? Instead of taking an immediate decision himself, he summoned his second-in-command and captains to a council of war. Having considered all options, they decided that the most prudent course would be to set course for Gibraltar. His fleet arrived there on 19 June and found five ships of the line – belated reinforcements sent by Anson – awaiting him. So he landed the wounded and sick, repaired battle-damage and prepared to sail back to Minorca.

But it was too late: Fort St Philip surrendered on 29 June. Next day, a letter reached Gibraltar overland from London, reporting that Byng was to be recalled to London in disgrace. So it was no surprise when, three days later, a ship of the line, the *Antelope*, sailed into the bay, flying the flag of Vice-Admiral Sir Edward Hawke, bringing with him an order from the Admiralty for Byng's immediate recall. What was particularly shocking was that the order had been signed and sent before the Admiralty had received Byng's own despatch, reporting his action with the French. The order had been based solely on French claims of victory, which had reached London from Paris.

Byng could only comply, angrily changing his uniform for civilian clothes as he began to prepare himself for the humiliation of having to explain the reasons for his actions when he reached London. But when the *Antelope* anchored at Spithead on 26 July, the senior naval officer came out from Portsmouth, which seemed a good sign because he was Vice-Admiral Henry Osborn, whose brother was married to Byng's sister, Sarah. Yet Osborn had been given the task and the embarrassment of showing his brother-in-law the order for his immediate arrest on a charge of cowardice.

It was only then that Byng became aware of the hysteria his encounter with the French had generated. He had thought he had done his best under difficult circumstances: it had been too late to relieve Minorca, and his fleet had been inadequate for that, or to defeat the French at sea. He could not have risked the additional loss of Gibraltar and he had not done so. His move, agreed by his captains, had been to safeguard Gibraltar and prepare for a second engagement with the enemy. This had been disappointing but not shameful.

But the loss of Minorca, and Byng's failure to win such a victory as his father's in the Mediterranean, had shocked and humiliated the British. As Horace Walpole (the younger son and eventual heir to Sir Robert Walpole, who had been the first prime minister) put it, 'At this moment we are all perplexity! When we were expecting every moment that Byng would send … Marshal Richelieu's head to be placed upon Temple Bar … Byng … notified his intention of retiring under the cannon of Gibraltar in case he found it dangerous to attempt the relief of Minorca!'[5] Realising that the fault had been their own in sending Byng to the Mediterranean too late and with inadequate force, the Government sought to shift the blame. Now even more fearful of invasion, they needed a scapegoat, and Byng seemed ideal. He had few friends and was regarded as a remote, pompous figure who was disposable. Foundation for a campaign of defamation was to hand when much naval opinion seemed against him and as distinguished an officer as

Admiral Boscawen, who disliked Byng, could suggest that his failure had been due to cowardice, writing to his wife: 'I found courage of more worth than I thought it but, if a chief does not show example, the cause will hardly ever succeed ... Indeed Byng's letters would have written him coward before any jury in the world.'[6]

Newcastle, Fox and the rest manipulated the evidence, and Byng's own despatch was edited and distorted before publication. As Horace Walpole put it, 'The impression against Mr Byng was no sooner taken, than every art and incident that could inflame it were industriously used and adopted.'[7] Pamphlets and broadsides accusing and lampooning him were circulated. A typical ballad ran thus:

If you believe what Frenchmen say,
B—g came, was beat and run away.
Believe what B—g himself had said,
He fought and conquered and he fled.
To fly when beat is no new thing;
Thousands have done it, as well as B—g:
But no man did, before B—g, say,
He conquered and then run away.
B—g therefore is, without a fable,
An Admiral most admirable.[8]

Word went out that Byng was a coward, and that was enough to inflame tempers. Around the country mobs burned and hanged effigies of the admiral, who had been unknown to them hitherto. The King entered into the spirit of the persecution, telling a party of London merchants who raised the matter, 'Oh! indeed he shall be tried immediately – he shall be hanged directly.'[9]

A month after Byng's arrival at Portsmouth, he was sent, under close escort of 50 dragoons, to the Tower of London, but was diverted at the last moment from the prison for traitors to a small, barred and guarded room on the top floor of the Royal Hospital at Greenwich. It was rumoured that an attempt at rescue was to be made so the fireplace was bricked up; one cartoon showed him trying to escape after asking to go to the lavatory while dressed as a woman. It was there that Augustus Hervey had last seen his friend, heavily guarded and forbidden to receive guests after dark. Yet he had found Byng, as he recorded, in 'his usual good spirits and speaking with a manly contempt of all the ill-treatment he received'.[10] That had been on 20 November 1756; a month later Byng was taken back to Portsmouth where his court-martial was to be held. Even now the caricaturists continued to mock, deriding his supposed effeminacy; one drawing showed the coming court-martial as composed entirely of women with Byng himself dressed as a courtesan. Even his taste – including the design of the handsome country house, Wrotham Park, he had built – was lampooned:

That B—g is an Admiral all the world knows
Of great taste in building but bashful of blows …[11]

Yet all were aware that a charge of cowardice in the face of the enemy could mean the death sentence.

From the moment Hervey stepped into the boat that was to take him across to Portsmouth harbour to the ship in which his friend was now imprisoned, he looked about for possible means and routes for the rescue he planned. But, as he neared the *Monarch*, he could see that this would be even more difficult than he had imagined: boats manned by armed marines were moored at the ship's bow and stern, and soon he could see sentries in the open galleries on to which opened the windows of the cabins in the stern, where he assumed Byng to be held.

Hauling himself up the ship's side, he found more armed marines on the quarterdeck and more sentries outside the door of the admiral's quarters. Within sat a naval officer, who showed him into the cabin beyond where Byng, dressed in a grey suit and wearing a large, old-fashioned wig, rose to greet him. 'I found him very composed, cheerful and seemed quite rejoiced to see me', Hervey wrote afterwards in his journal. 'He told me 'twas hard he should pay for the crimes of others with his blood that had never before been stained.'[12]

Byng and Hervey discussed the court-martial, at which the latter had been a witness for the defence. It had been held on board the *St George* and had lasted a month. The court had been composed of three admirals and nine captains, many of whom had known Byng for many years, although not necessarily as friends. Indeed, he had already become aware of the unreliability of expressed opinion when his own captains, who had jointly taken the decision to return to Gibraltar rather than seek out the enemy, had turned against him on realising that he was to be made a scapegoat.

Most of his judges were friends, or favourites, of Lord Anson, but one of them was Captain the Honourable Augustus Keppel, who had sailed with him on his voyage round the world, and he was to prove an exception to the others' reflection of their patron's opinions. A brother of the Earl of Albemarle, a soldier with dose connections with the Court and Government, Keppel was a tough, fair-minded officer, who seemed unlikely to join a vindictive persecution.

Another ally was, of course, Augustus Hervey, who had been one of more than 50 witnesses who were asked to describe the events of the preceding May. He had been vigorous and meticulous in presenting detailed evidence, particularly in giving the exact times of each stage of the battle off Minorca. 'About five or six minutes after three, I saw the *Ramillies*'s topsails aback ... about six or seven minutes afterwards a red ensign was hoisted at the mizzen topmast-head'[13] was typical of this detail. Indeed, so exact was his recall, that one of Mrs Boscawen's friends, the sharp-tongued Mrs Montagu, wrote to her after reading a report of the proceedings: 'I admire Captain Hervey's method of watching the battle. I have known people boil an egg with a watch in their hand, counting the minutes, but I never heard we were to do so when we basted the French.' In fact, Hervey had noted the time and content of each of the flagship's signals because his frigate had had to repeat them. Like others who were instinctively hostile towards Byng, Mrs Montagu thought Hervey's evidence too strongly supportive, adding sarcastically: 'By this noble gentleman's evidence, I conceive Mr Byng's to have been the most bloody engagement that ever happened. The Blakes, Van Tromps and de Ruyters, though men of some courage, must strike the flag to Admiral Byng.'[14]

The court was reasonably fair, listening to evidence from officers and senior ratings who had been in the battle. Byng claimed in his defence that he had, in fact, defeated the French as they had withdrawn from the action; yet this had only been a tactical withdrawal and Byng's own retreat to Gibraltar had left the enemy in command of the sea surrounding Minorca and that was a strategic defeat. In conclusion, they had cleared Byng of cowardice or disaffection but, bearing in mind the Government's hostility to Byng and their obvious desire to make a scapegoat and example of him, they had found him guilty on a seemingly lesser charge. This was that the court was

unanimously of opinion that he did not do his utmost to relieve St Philip's castle; and also that, during the Engagement between His Majesty's Fleet under his Command and the Fleet of the French King, on 20 May last, he did not do his utmost to take, seize and destroy the Ships of the French King, which it was his duty to have engaged …[15]

This seemed enough to warrant a severe reprimand, or that he might be cashiered; certainly it would mean the end of Byng's naval career. But there had been a recent amendment to the law governing penalties which stated baldly that this verdict carried the death penalty, the qualifying words offering as an alternative 'such other punishment as the nature and degree of the offence should be found to deserve' having been dropped seven years earlier after another court-martial following a failure in action at sea. Yet nobody thought that the sentence would be carried out, and in order to make sure of this, the court added the unanimous rider that Byng's failure had not arisen 'either from Cowardice or Disaffection and to therefore unanimously think it their Duty most earnestly to recommend him as a proper Object of Mercy'.[16]

It was assumed that King George would show mercy, commuting the sentence to a professional penalty. But to the surprise and horror of most, including many who disliked Byng, he did not do so. Even Fox put on a show of compassion now that the blame for the Minorca fiasco had been safely pinned on Byng, and, seeing Hervey at White's, tried to pass responsibility to the court-martial, remarking that he would rather be Byng than one of his judges. At this, Hervey, who described Fox as 'that infernal black demon',[17] made no reply and turned away.

Admiral Forbes, a new member of the Board of Admiralty, declared that the sentence was illegal, and refused to sign the death warrant. Admiral Osborn, realising that he, as the senior officer at Portsmouth, would be responsible for carrying out his brother-in-law's execution, immediately applied to the Admiralty for leave, which was granted, while his wife wrote letters pleading for mercy to those in authority or positions of influence. There were no other close relations to help: Rear-Admiral George Pocock, Byng's first cousin, was at sea off India. Horace Walpole, although he had taken an instinctive dislike to Byng, lobbied Members of Parliament both from his sense of outrage and from his hatred of Newcastle and Fox; as a result, Byng was granted a reprieve of a fortnight, during which, it was hoped, a life-saving formula might be found.

Hervey had been intensely active, lobbying and writing pamphlets in Byng's defence. One of his most effective allies was Captain Keppel, who had sat on the court-martial and could not believe that their recommendation of mercy could be ignored. The King, whom Hervey described as 'a hardened brute',[18] seemed adamant, but when he was told that Keppel, as a Member of Parliament, had said, on behalf of several members of the court-martial, that they wished to be released from their oath of confidentiality in order to re-open Byng's case, in the hope of changing the verdict, he reluctantly agreed.

The Bill to allow this was eventually steered through the House of Commons, despite complications arising from the absence, or quibbling, of some members of the court-martial. Even worse confusion arose in the House of Lords, where the debate was manipulated for the Government by Lord Hardwicke. Over-awed, or confused by legal flummery and cunningly phrased questions, Byng's support crumbled, only Keppel, and one other, remaining adamant that the case must be re-opened. So the Bill was rejected and nothing but a royal pardon stood between Byng and his execution. Already it had been announced that 'His Majesty is determined still to let this sentence be carried into execution unless it shall appear, from the said examination, that Admiral Byng was unjustly condemned'.[19]

Now there was to be no re-examination of the evidence. A petition to the King asking for the sentence to be commuted to one of banishment brought no response. It was this that had prompted Hervey to plan his rescue attempt. The chartering of a small, fast ship in the Thames and the placing of horses along the Portsmouth Road had presented no problems; escape from a strongly guarded warship anchored as far as possible from shore in Portsmouth harbour would be otherwise. However, after considering possibilities that could include bribery, false documents, disguise and even force, Hervey now presented them to Byng in the cabin of the *Monarch* when his officer-gaolers were out of earshot. Later, he wrote in his journal: 'I offered my services to him and shewed him two or three schemes for his escape but he told me that he thanked me but would never think of it. He would rather die than fly from death that way.'[20]

Byng seemed to have attained a serenity, Hervey finding him 'very composed and cheerful ... His only happiness was that the court-martial could not with all their endeavours charge him with cowardice and disaffection and was acquitted of both. He often repeated the very harsh manner he had been treated with, which he freely forgave.'[21] Now it seemed that even if he had been offered a chance to escape with the connivance of the authorities, as had been rumoured, he would have refused it. All who saw him were moved by Byng's serenity and courage. Once, when he was talking easily with a group of naval officers, one of them stood up and asked, 'Which of us is tallest?' 'Why this ceremony?' replied the admiral. 'I know what it means. Let the man come and measure me for my coffin.'[22]

There was nothing more to be done for him and, Hervey recorded, 'I left him in the evening and had determined to go off no more as it really hurt me too much to see a man so treated.'[23] But Byng sent a note to him in Portsmouth asking him to return and, next day, he did so. There was no more talk of rescue, whether legal or not, and Byng only asked him to witness bequests 'in case he suffered'; Hervey himself was to be left a clock encased in Dresden porcelain painted with flowers. Then, when Byng and his lawyer were out of earshot and sight in the sleeping-cabin, Hervey could stand the emotional strain no more and explained this to the *Monarch*'s officers, later writing: 'I stole away and begged of them to tell him I could not bear the taking leave of him and only prayed earnestly that I might see him again, which I own I never expected, knowing the hard heart of the King and his old ministry ever revengeful. I set off therefore that evening for London.'[24] As soon as he arrived on 11 March, he asked the Admiralty if he could immediately rejoin his command, the *Hampton Court*, which was at Gibraltar.

'The fatal morning arrived but was by no means met by the Admiral with reluctance', recorded Horace Walpole. 'The whole tenor of his behaviour had been cheerful, steady, dignified, sensible. While he felt like a victim, he acted like a hero.'[25] At noon on 14 March, as a gale dashed rain across Portsmouth harbour, he stepped calmly from his cabin onto the open quarterdeck, dressed in his customary grey suit and thick, unfashionable wig. Across the wind-whipped water, the other ships at anchor could be seen crowded with spectators, who had climbed the rigging for a view of the distant spectacle.

The *Monarch*'s officers and ratings had been mustered on the upper deck and nine marines in red coats, white cross-belts and mitre-shaped caps were drawn up in three ranks of three. Byng had prepared himself for this moment. Horace Walpole wrote:

Of his fate, he talked with indifference, and neither shunned to hear the necessary dispositions, nor affected to parade in them. For the last fortnight he constantly declared that he would not suffer a handkerchief over his face, that it might be seen whether he betrayed the least symptom of fear; and when the minute arrived, adhered to this purpose.

He took an easy leave of his friends, detained the officers not a moment, went directly to the deck and placed himself in a chair[*] with neither ceremony nor lightness. Some of the more humane officers represented to him that his face being uncovered might throw reluctance into the executioners; and besought him to suffer a handkerchief. He replied with the same unconcern, 'If it will frighten *them*, let it be done; they would not frighten me.' His eyes were bound ...[26]

Blindfolded, Byng faced his executioners, another handkerchief held unfolded in his hand. At an order, the front file of marines knelt on one knee, the muzzles of their muskets 2 feet from his chest and the second rank presented their muskets over their shoulders; the third, stood with muskets at the port, ready to administer a *coup de grâce*. He remained for a moment in silence, then, according to the arranged signal, dropped the handkerchief. Six muskets fired and Byng 'sank down motionless, gently falling on his side, as if still assiduous to preserve decency and dignity in his fall',[27] a shot through the heart. The master of the *Monarch*, John Paynter, thereupon wrote in the ship's log: 'At 12 Mr Byng was shot dead by 6 Marines and put into his coffin.'[28]

Not long afterwards, the novel *Candide* was published by François de Voltaire, who had taken an interest in the case. Having heard from his friend the Maréchal Duc de Richelieu, who had commanded the invasion of Minorca, that Byng's 'reputation ought not to be attacked for being worsted, after having done everything that could be expected.... All the measures taken by Admiral Byng were admirable ...',[29] he had written to the imprisoned admiral to tell him so. In his book, the hero, Candide, visits Portsmouth and, surprised to see an admiral facing a firing squad on his quarterdeck, asks what is happening. He is told: 'In this country it is thought well to kill an admiral from time to time to encourage the others.'[30]

The nation was shocked by its own savagery and by its victim's courage. 'Do cowards live or die thus?' asked Walpole. 'Can that man want spirit who only fears to terrify his executioners? Has the aspen Duke of Newcastle lived thus? Would my Lord Hardwicke die thus, even supposing he had nothing on his conscience? This scene is over! what will be the next is matter of great uncertainty.'[31]

.

'Heaps of Gold and Silver'

On 14 August, 1757, a despatch vessel slowly made her way against the muddy swirl of the Hooghly river (an arm of the great Ganges), steered between the mud banks and finally moored off the fortifications and mercantile palaces of Calcutta. At once the mail and despatches from London, which had been forwarded by George Pigot, the Governor of Madras, were sent ashore for Vice-Admiral Charles Watson, the officer commanding the squadron of ships of the line belonging to the Royal Navy and the frigates and sloops owned by the East India Company.

Watson was aged forty-three, florid and overweight but with 'a manly, commanding countenance'. He could be touchy and quick-tempered but also generous, was popular and 'made no scruple at his own table to promote a free circulation of the glass'.[1] As a captain, he had served under the successful admirals Anson and Hawke and, when himself commanding the North American station, had also been Governor of Newfoundland. Appointed to command in the East Indies, as all that lay east of the Cape of Good Hope was described, he had arrived in Bombay at the end of 1755.

Admiral Watson was unwell. Ashore at his country house outside the city, he was recovering from a recurrent tropical illness, inducing lassitude, occasional vomiting and a hot, dry skin. Watson had always appeared robust but had been liable to fever and digestive troubles, particularly during the summer heat and humidity when the air over the coast and rivers of Bengal seemed like hot water. But now emetics and draughts of sherbert prescribed by the naval surgeon, Edward Ives, were beginning to take effect.

He received the packets from London in the high-ceilinged room where heavy cloth *punkahs* stirred the hot air. Too tired to go through his correspondence himself, he asked Surgeon Ives to read the letters aloud. Usually, those from the Board of Admiralty, sealed and stamped with the fouled anchor insignia, would give him the intelligence of expected French dispositions and what the chances were of reinforcement for his own squadron. But today there was shocking news, which lost none of its impact because a rumour had already reached this most distant squadron of the Royal Navy.

'He desired me to read some letters', Ives recorded in his journal. 'They related chiefly to the conduct of Admiral Byng ... He reflected, and reasoned much, on the uncertain basis on which an officer's conduct stands and concluded with observing how much more hazardous it was for him to err on the cautious, than the desperate, side.'[2]

The admiral's duty was now to pass this news to Byng's cousin, his own second-in-command, Rear-Admiral George Pocock. But first he ordered Ives to go to the hospital – already crowded with more than 600 cases of 'putrid fevers' and 'fluxes' from the British ships' companies and garrison – and send Mr Bevis, the surgeon of the *Blaze*, now working ashore, to see him. That evening Ives returned to find the admiral cooler and more relaxed, although his bowels were still upset and his eyes 'a little yellow'. Dutifully, Ives noted: 'To the saline draughts (of which he took one every two hours), I added six grains of rhubarb' as an emetic and prescribed 'acidulated gruels, chicken-water and whey.'[3]

Next day, Watson was better and Ives told Bevis to continue the treatment. While the admiral was unwell, he could confidently leave the command of his squadron to Pocock, who was accustomed to such a climate from long service in the Caribbean and nearly two years in the Indian Ocean. The two men had become friends; both were easy in manner and popular in the Navy, and, unlike his cousin John Byng, George Pocock, one of a naval chaplain's 11 children, had never felt privileged, nor been reluctant to serve on unhealthy stations, like the Caribbean. This had been as prudent as it was brave, because that sea could make a naval officer rich if it did not kill him with tropical disease. Eight years older than Watson, Pocock's friendly, particularly English, looks with a blunt nose and cleft chin had been lined and weathered by the tropics, and the climate of the Ganges delta presented him with no problems. Also a bachelor, he was calmer by temperament than his superior, and, perhaps because of his father's calling, was never known to swear, even on his own quarterdeck.

In the Caribbean and the Atlantic, the collecting of a fortune, which was part of every naval officer's ambition, had come easily to Pocock since it involved the capture of enemy ships and the claim for prize-money. Indeed, he had been lucky, efficient and successful in this, particularly in 1742 with his capture of two Spanish bullion ships from South America and again six years later with his capture of nearly 40 merchant ships in a French convoy after Admiral Hawke had attacked their escort. This had brought him so much prize-money that he had been able to live well above a captain's station.

George Pocock's introduction to the exotic world east of the Cape of Good

Hope had come in 1745 when he had escorted four East Indiamen – the big, armed merchant ships that carried the East India Company's trade to and from the mercantile settlements of Madras and Calcutta – to the Indian Ocean. He now had himself painted by Thomas Hudson, the most fashionable portrait-painter in London. He had been a boyish-looking captain then, wearing the newly designed officers' uniform, to which the artist could add further touches of paint as his rise through the higher ranks increased the amount of gold lace on his blue coat. Nine years later he sailed east again, commanding the 56-gun *Cumberland*, as a commodore and second-in-command to Rear-Admiral Watson, whose small squadron was ordered to protect British trade. They had escorted a troop convoy carrying the first regular regiment of infantry to be sent to India to reinforce 'The Company's' own little army of mercenaries.

The squadron's presence had been dictated by more than a decade of active antagonism and, occasionally, fighting between the British and French, who had succeeded the Portuguese and Dutch as the principal traders with the Indian sub-continent. Since the forceful Joseph François Dupleix had been appointed Governor-General of the Indies by King Louis XV, both nations had prepared for armed confrontation, if not war. The British had fortified Madras and Calcutta, the capitals of their two east coast 'presidencies', and the French had done likewise at Pondicherry and Chandernagore.

There was currently no immediate French threat on the Coromandel coast – the south-eastern shores of the Indian Peninsula – where the winter monsoon storms would soon start to blow. Watson's ships were in need of refitting, so he sailed for Bombay, the capital of the west coast presidency, arriving on 10 November. This was different from the eastern settlements in that there was no separate European quarter within the fortress walls, a 'black town' for the Indians outside and the Europeans' country houses beyond. In Bombay, both communities lived together in harmony within a steamy, sprawling, ramshackle trading town around a castle built on a low-lying peninsula.

The size of Watson's squadron impressed the merchants. Under his command were four ships of the line – the *Kent, Cumberland, Tyger* and *Salisbury* – together with the sloops *Bridgewater* and *Kingfisher*. Added to these were the East India Company's 44-gun ship *Protector,* the frigates *Revenge* and *Bombay,* a sloop, and four bomb-ketches mounting mortars for shore bombardment. At the end of 1755, there were no French ships to fight, so the governing councils of the East India Company decided to send a military expedition to Hyderabad and Mysore on the wide Deccan plateau above the steep coastal ranges. The French, under their military commander, the Marquis de Bussy, had been active there, trying to establish themselves inland of the British coastal settlements, as they had in North America, and the East India Company had decided to ally themselves with the Mahrattas of the hinterland to move against them. For this purpose three more companies of regular infantry and artillery had been shipped from England and the second-in-command of the expedition was sailing at the same time, returning from home leave with his bride. This was Lieutenant-Colonel Robert Clive.

Service with the East India Company sometimes transformed young men, sent from England to work as 'writers', into fortune-hunters, eccentrics, or soldiers, and Robert Clive became all three. The son of a Shropshire squire, he had had a difficult childhood to which he had reacted with aggression. Before he had reached the age of seven, his uncle had declared: 'I am satisfied that his fighting (to which he is out of measure addicted) gives his temper a fierceness and imperiousness, that he flies out upon every trifling occasion: for this reason I do what I can to suppress the hero, that I may forward the more valuable qualities of meekness, benevolence and patience.'[4]

In this he had failed and, when fighting had broken out between the British and French in 1746, Clive had exchanged his pen for a sword, showing himself to be as brave and imaginative a soldier as he was touchy and truculent a man: a manic depressive, his moods swung between inspiring leadership and suicidal despair. Amongst his feats of arms, the most celebrated had been the successful defence of Arcot, a town inland from Madras, when outnumbered 50 to one.

While on leave in England Clive had tried and failed to enter Parliament, but he had married and was now returning to command the little expeditionary force at Bombay before taking up the Governorship of Fort St David on the Coromandel coast. Aged thirty, his was a powerful, brooding presence; he was not a conventionally handsome man – resolute mouth, short upper lip, pugilist's nose, dark, brooding eyes and a high forehead – but sometimes he dressed as a dandy, and his moods were unpredictable. He reached Bombay in October, a month before the little army arrived, after a voyage of 36 weeks.

At the beginning of December, Clive inspected his command, which was in a poor state after the voyage, many being 'very bad with the scurvy and flux', to be followed by the despatch of 'a great many of our men every day to the hospital occasioned by their drinking new arrack'.[*][5] But the arrival of so much artillery had significant potential, both in possible attacks upon fortified French settlements and in defence against the vast Indian armies that could be mustered by rulers allied with them.

The expedition into the Deccan was now unnecessary: the expansionist Dupleix had been recalled to Paris for an enquiry into allegations of corruption and personal ambition made by his political enemies in France. So peace now reigned, however temporarily, between the *Compagnie des Indes* and the East India Company. However, a new plan had been conceived to make use of the force to eliminate another, albeit lesser, enemy – a pirate.

For years, the Malabar coast south of Bombay and the trade plying to and from that port had been plagued by a marauding fleet commanded by an hereditary pirate chieftain named Tulagee Angria. Not only had his galleys swept up local trade but they had even attacked and occasionally taken big, armed East Indiamen, both British and French, and had even attacked ships of the line. Several attempts to suppress him had failed, but in March 1755 Commodore William James, commanding the East India Company's ships, had succeeded in capturing Angria's offshore island base of Severndroog and a small port on the mainland. However, the main base was so strongly fortified that only now could an attack be contemplated. The plan was for an amphibious attack to be mounted by the British in alliance with the Mahrattas, Hindus to whom Geriah had originally belonged; indeed, Angria himself was a Mahratta by birth. The price of the alliance would be the return of Geriah to the Mahrattas once the pirates had been destroyed.

On the last day of January, 1756, James Wood, a cadet gunner in the Royal Artillery and a potential officer, who had just arrived from England, noted in his diary:

> The King's and Company's artillery with one company of infantry were reviewed by Governor Bourchier, the two admirals, Watson and Pocock, and Colonel Clive. After the review, all the officers breakfasted with the Governor and Admirals in camp … This afternoon it was in orders for the detachment of the Royal Artillery to hold themselves in readiness to embark at an hour's warning.[6]

They were to take part in the first amphibious operation of the global war that was about to begin.

The pirates' lair lay some 150 miles south of Bombay in the mouth of an estuary divided and dominated by a rocky headland on which Angria had built his stronghold, commanding both the harbour and the busy market-town of Geriah. In this secluded harbour lay his fleet, which now consisted of one deep-sea ship, the merchantman *Restoration*, which Angria had captured from the East India Company, eight three-masted galleys, or 'grabs', eight ketches, and more than a dozen oared 'gallivat' gunboats. The fortress itself was said to be impregnable and comparable with a great European castle.

While Watson's ships had been careening,[⁶] Commodore James had been sent to reconnoitre Geriah. He described in his report

a large mass of buildings and I believe the walls may be thick … and quite irregular with round towers and long curtains in the eastern manner and … thirty-two embrasures below and fifteen above. On the west side of the harbour is a fine flat table-land opposite the fort … I am sure within distance for bombarding and from whence a very good diversion might be made, while the principal attack is carried on by ships … It is also very plain from our depth of water that the ships can go near enough for battering and consequently for throwing shells.[7]

As the squadron completed its repairs at Bombay, a meeting was called to arrange the distribution of the prize-money that was expected to be a consequence of a successful operation. 'It was settled at this council', noted Surgeon Ives, 'that Admiral Watson, as Commander-in-Chief of the King's squadron, should have two-thirds of one eighth. Lieutenant-Colonel Clive and Major Chambers were to share equally with the captains of the King's ships …'[8]

This was agreed but, soon afterwards, Clive complained to Watson that his own officers thought the division unfair, since he was commander of the land forces and should be accorded a share equal to Pocock's. The admiral replied that it was too late to renegotiate the division of spoils but that he personally would increase Clive's share to match Pocock's, an offer which the former declared he would 'come into with great cheerfulness'.[9]

Finally, the expeditionary force of 1,300 men under Clive's command was embarked. It was made up of 700 Europeans (including five companies of artillery, three regular and two raised by 'The Company'), 300 *topaze* Indo-Portuguese and 300 Indian sepoy infantrymen. On 7 February, 1756, the fleet of six sail of the line, five bomb-ketches and smaller warships sailed, James Wood noting in his diary: 'Sailed by Bombay Fort with a pleasant land breeze.'[10]

Four days later, the squadron entered the wide estuary sheltered by low, wooded hills and palm-groves. Standing on its heights, the fortress of Geriah – its walls, ten feet thick, seeming to grow from the solid rock, powerfully bastioned and turreted and flying Angria's standard from a tall flagstaff – looked as formidable as expected. They could also see, some distance away, out of range and sight of the ramparts, about 50 grabs and gallivats belonging to their allies, the Mahrattas, lying in a secluded creek. The operation of war that was about to begin was already demonstrating the characteristics that divided battles fought in India from those fought in other parts of the world. The division of spoils between Government and Company forces, which had already been arranged, was one of them; another was the political intrigue that was always conducted in parallel with military operations and was sometimes more decisive. In this case, the British imagined the Mahrattas to be their allies, with a fleet of small galleys and an army of some 12,000 – half cavalry, half infantry – ready to attack Geriah from the landward side; but were they to be trusted?

The Mahratta commander, Ramajee Punt, was rowed in his barge to the *Kent* for a formal visit to Admiral Watson. As the smoke of saluting guns billowed, the general was received on deck with ceremony and taken on a tour of the ship, when 'at the sight of its batteries he appeared greatly astonished'.[11] This was probably polite play-acting, because the Mahratta leadership was also negotiating with Angria in the hope of occupying Geriah and keeping its loot themselves.

As soon as his ships were off Geriah, Watson sent a boat ashore under a flag of truce, summoning Angria to surrender. As expected, this was rejected and the admiral began to deploy his forces for an attack. Angria had quickly realised that he might be able to defend his fortress against the British for a few days but not indefinitely. So, leaving his brother in command of the fortress, he himself had gone to the headquarters of the Mahratta army with his own terms for an alliance, inviting Ramajee Punt to enter and occupy Geriah in return for his own safety and freedom. The Mahrattas had expressed interest; the first indication to Watson that his supposed allies might not be as staunch as they proclaimed came when next morning, boats came out from shore carrying both members of Angria's family and officers of the Mahratta army on what they insisted was another formal, diplomatic visit.

Warned of their duplicity by a deserter from Geriah, Watson ordered that his visitors be shown round the ship and then called them into his cabin. Repeating his demand for surrender, he assured them that, if this was immediately agreed, they could personally count on his protection. Their reply was that Angria must be consulted and that that might take a few days. So Watson announced that, in that case, he would enter the anchorage below the fortress to await the outcome and would not fire unless fired upon himself.

There was nothing more to be said but, as a reminder that his guns were the final arbiters of negotiation, the admiral 'ordered that a thirty-two pound ball should be put into their hands, which he desired them to carry as a present to their master and then dismissed them'.[12] So, laden with the cannonball, the visitors scrambled down the ship's side into their boat.

Early that afternoon, the British ships made sail and a light breeze carried them towards the fortress. Each ship of the line, cleared for action, took position to cover the bomb-ketches and smaller ships from enemy fire. This began at two o'clock, when a shot was fired from the shore batteries at the *Kingfisher*, and at once Watson made the signal to anchor ready for the bombardment to begin. Each ship was to signal as she anchored, but the *Tyger's* flags were not seen on board the flagship, the *Kent*, which rammed her bows, carrying away the bowsprit. Finally, the ships were all at anchor, another signal was hoisted and the broadsides threw out flame and smoke in rolling clouds until only their upper masts and yards could be seen.

As the battleships concentrated on the fortress walls, the bomb-ketches tossed shells into the moored mass of Angria's warships, lying with blue, green and white pennants fluttering from their mastheads. One shot set fire to the *Restoration* and

she driving among the rest of the enemy's shipping, which were lashed together, set them all in flames; so that in a few hours almost the whole of Angria's fleet was destroyed. The fire also communicated to a large ship lying on the shore and from her to several smaller vessels that were building; and from these last it was conveyed to the arsenal, storehouse, suburbs and city and even to several parts of the fort, particularly to a square tower, where it continued burning all the night with such violence that the stone walls appeared like red-hot iron.[13]

The bombardment continued, the burning keep glowing in the darkness – an aiming-point for the mortar crews in the bomb-ketches – while Colonel Clive led his soldiers down the sides of the ships into waiting boats to be rowed ashore. They landed to the east of the fortress soon after nine and Watson ordered his ships to warp closer to the shore, ready to batter a breach that could be stormed at daybreak. As the light grew, Clive saw a crowd of armed men, drawn upon high ground inland, which he took to be the Mahratta army, waiting for a signal from Angria to enter Geriah before the British.

As the sun rose on the smoking ruin ashore and afloat, the bombardment ceased and Watson sent an officer under a flag of truce with another summons to surrender, this time within the hour. After more delay, Angria's brother replied that he could not comply without higher authority, for which he would have to wait until next day. Realising that he was prevaricating in order to allow the Mahrattas to occupy the fortress, Watson ordered his ships to open fire again. Within half an hour, a white flag was hung from the walls, but Angria's standard remained flying from its staff. This was not surrender, so the admiral ordered his ships to warp closer inshore to within a cable's length (200 yards) and open the maximum rate of fire. This was so effective that 'the garrison cried out for mercy, which our troops were near enough to hear distinctly'.[14]

Then the magazine exploded and another white flag was waved from the walls. Watson sent a lieutenant ashore to demand that British troops should be allowed immediate entry to the fortress and that, as a sign of final submission, a British flag should be flown. Angria's brother agreed to hoist the colours and that five or six British officers should be allowed to enter at once, but he insisted that the final surrender could not take place until the next morning. So the guns of the squadron again opened fire.

Ashore, meanwhile, Clive had sited his field-guns and had also opened fire, realising that he had not only to besiege the fortress but also to keep the Mahrattas away from it. This became fully apparent when Ramajee Punt offered two of his captains, Forbes and Buchanan, a bribe of 50,000 rupees to allow the Mahrattas through the British lines. So indignant were they that they threatened to behead the general if his men advanced a step.

There were to be no more delays and the defenders were told that, unless the gates were opened immediately, they could expect no quarter. So Geriah fell. Within were found some 250 guns, six brass mortars and huge stocks of ammunition. Ten British and three Dutch slaves – all captured seamen – were released, but when the booty was assessed it was found to be worth £140,000, a large amount but far less than had been expected.

Angria himself had escaped, having remained within the Mahratta lines and, seeing his fortress overwhelmed, left for their capital, Poona. There, it was reported, he was able to buy a pardon for his annexation of Geriah with the bulk of his treasure, which he had managed to save. His brother and family were captured, however, and found to be suffering from smallpox. Surgeon Ives was summoned and prescribed the usual medicines, which they refused to take, preferring their own traditional method of covering their bodies with wood ash. They all recovered, but not before the infection had spread to their captors; those British who had not hitherto been exposed to the disease were immediately sent away from the town, or on board ship, but, as Cadet Wood noted, 'our men dying very fast with the smallpox'.[15]

Visited by Admiral Watson, Angria's family threw themselves on his mercy, his mother bewailing that 'the people had had no king, she no son, her daughters no husbands, the children no father'. Watson, a sentimental man, thereupon said that they must look upon him as their father and friend. At this, her six-year-old grandson – doubtless well-rehearsed – burst into tears and, taking the admiral by the hand, sobbed, 'Then you shall be my father.' Whereupon, as Surgeon Ives reported, 'This action of the child's was so very affecting, it quite overpowered that brave, that good man's heart and he found himself under a necessity of turning from the innocent youth for a while to prevent the falling of those tears, which stood ready to gush from his eyes.'[16]

The cost to the British of this successful little operation had been about 20 killed and wounded. This had been a small price for ridding the coast of piracy and providing the British with useful training but Clive wrote sarcastically to his superiors in Bombay: 'I make no doubt but the newspapers will be swelled with a pompous account of the taking of this place (which proved a very easy conquest) and of the immense riches found within.'[17] It had also been a demonstration of warfare as it was to be expected on the sub-continent, involving diplomacy, duplicity and venality as much as martial activity.

On the return of the squadron to Bombay in mid-March, the prize-money was distributed, Clive's share being £5,000. When Watson offered him an extra £1,000 from his own portion to bring it up to the level of Pocock's, Clive declined, saying that his protest had only been a point of principle, urged on him by his officers. Prize-money, sharply diminishing in portions as it descended through the ranks to the lowest, which was 20 rupees for each sepoy, was then distributed. The smallpox abated and, in April, an amateur theatrical troupe of naval and military officers performed for the amusement of Bombay society the play, *The Fair Penitent*, which Nicholas Rowe had written at the beginning of the century.

In April, Watson and his ships had sailed for the Coromandel coast to escape the west coast monsoon, arriving off Fort St David two months later. (While they were on passage, Admiral Byng had fought his inconclusive action off Minorca, but news of that and what followed could not reach India for several months.) Orders from the Admiralty to hand over command to Pocock and return home were waiting for the admiral. He was delighted since, as his surgeon put it, 'the heat of the climate had, ever since his first arrival, been greatly distressful to Mr Watson, whose constitution was sanguine and whose habit was rather corpulent'.[18]

His pleasure was brief, for the East India Company had just received a report that six French ships of the line and six large merchantmen of the *Compagnie des Indes*, which could be easily converted into warships, had embarked 6,000 regular troops and were bound for India. Watson immediately abandoned his plans to return home. More up-to-date news of this was soon to reach Bombay, which had been suffering the monsoon gales and thunderstorms. There, Cadet Wood noted in his diary on 1 September, 1756: 'Mustered the 3 companies, R.A. Seventy of our men died since arrival. We have lately received accounts privately that the French are preparing a large fleet at the Mauritius: it is supposed in order to lay siege to Bombay, on which information all the troops off duty were told off to repairing the works and fortifications and making some additions.'[19] While the alarmed officers and merchants of Bombay assumed that their city was the French objective, those on the Coromandel coast and in Bengal felt as vulnerable and hoped that Admiral Watson's little squadron was strong enough to defend them.

Although it was known that war had broken out with France on 17 May, there did not seem cause for alarm in Bombay, or in the Carnatic to the south-east, or in Bengal in the north. The British and French settlements appeared balanced militarily with small garrisons of European mercenaries and locally recruited sepoys, neither seeming to threaten the other. Even on the rich plains of Bengal, the French could only muster some 300 regular troops, and these would hardly be enough to march down the banks of the Hooghly river against Calcutta. There the British could muster about the same number of mercenaries, mostly Portuguese – although a third of them were sick, or absent – and 250 militiamen, mostly seamen, who might be called away to their ships; or assorted Europeans, who often had difficulty understanding orders in English.

So it came as a wholly unexpected shock when, on 16 August, news reached Watson, Pocock and Clive at Madras that Calcutta had already been lost to an invader. The merchants on the Hooghly had become complacent and accustomed to living within a day's journey of their French rivals at Chandernagore, with their lesser rivals, the Dutch, nearby at Chinsura. They had also got used to living in the realm of the Nawab of Bengal and the limitless army he could summon if the mood took him.

The old Nawab, Alivardi Khan, one of the three viceroys ruling the Mogul Empire under the Emperor, had died in April, after a reign of 14 years, and his successor – his twenty-seven-year-old grandson, Surajah Dowlah – was less predictable. True, Alivardi had resented the Europeans as Calcutta became as prosperous and populous as his own capital, likening Europeans to bees, whose honey could be enjoyed but who could sting if upset. So he tolerated them, taking what honey he could in the form of taxation. Yet his underlying fear was the knowledge that, elsewhere in India, the Europeans had reduced the indigenous princes to puppet rulers and enriched themselves at will.

The new Nawab was a weak, spoilt young man whose soft looks – almond eyes and small, curled moustache – suggested a petulance that, combined with power, could be dangerous. He had inherited his grandfather's suspicions, also suspecting that the British were intriguing against him with other Indian rulers. Resenting the Europeans and coveting the wealth that, he imagined, filled the warehouses of Calcutta, he found two pretexts to move against the city. One was that the British were strengthening their defences against a possible attack by the French from Chandernagore, 21 miles up the river, which he chose to see as a breach of their undertaking to limit the fortifications. The other was that the British had arrested a Sikh merchant whom the Nawab had accused of stealing treasure from his court; when they denied finding this treasure, he assumed that they had confiscated and kept it themselves. So he mobilised his army – rumours running through the city's bazaar put it at anything up to 70,000, including 30,000 cavalry, 400 war-elephants and artillery with European gunners – and advanced on Calcutta. Trouble broke out within the city when a principal contractor was arrested on suspicion of being the Nawab's spy; his guards resisted, one of whom escaped to tell Surajah Dowlah that the British were slaughtering Indians.

When news of the Nawab's approach reached the city, there was alarm and despair. The Europeans knew that Calcutta was not defensible. After the governing council had been admonished by their superiors in the East India Company – 'We hear you make a very pompous show to the water side by high turrets and lofty buildings, which have the appearance but not the benefit of a fortification'[20] – the rebuilding of Fort William and the digging of a deep defensive ditch around the whole city had been authorised but not carried out. Now some frantic digging of trenches began, but everyone knew that time had run out. So Calcutta awaited its fate: the East India Company's imposing, pedimented Factory House standing within the rectangular walls of Fort William and, outside them and wholly vulnerable, the two-storey mansions and warehouses in elegant, classical style of the administrators and merchants.

Only about 300 Europeans capable of bearing arms could be found to man what defences there were. A collection of East India Company soldiers, militiamen of mixed nationality and armed civilians could do little against the horde that advanced against the city. Beneath a pall of dust hanging in the hot, still air, it moved across the plain like a tide to the beat of drums, clash of cymbals and the braying of trumpets. After two attacks on the outer defences had been repulsed, the Nawab's army swarmed into the town on 18 June and the surviving defenders fell back on Fort William, where the magazine held ammunition for less than three days' fighting. At this point, the Governor, Roger Drake, the governing council, senior army officers, most of the principal merchants and their families scrambled into boats to be rowed out to ships anchored in the river, which spread, half a mile wide, brown and swirling, towards the sea and safety. Once aboard, they sailed downstream, abandoning several hundred more Europeans ashore with no hope of escape.

For three days Fort William held out in the heavy summer heat, its defenders under fire from the nearby ruins of the residences and warehouses. Finally, John Holwell, a member of the ruling council who had stayed behind, was told that there was only enough ammunition for two hours' more firing, so he agreed to discuss terms for surrender and hung out a white flag of truce. He had hoped to negotiate an evacuation by river but all the ships, loaded with fugitives, had dropped several miles downstream, not even leaving a rowing-boat. While the outcome of the first contacts was awaited, a Dutch sergeant – probably in collusion with Dutch deserters outside the walls – knocked a lock off a postern gate and the Indians burst into the fort. A few officers fought bravely, refused to surrender and were struck down. Ensign Blagg fought until 'cut to pieces on a bastion',[21] and a lieutenant and a civilian had already shot themselves rather than be taken prisoner. Most, exhausted by heat and thirst, dropped their weapons and hoped for mercy.

Smoke gathered in a dark cloud that seemed to press the stifling heat upon the smouldering city. When all was quiet, the Nawab himself entered Fort William to inspect the treasure in the vaults, only to find that it had been carried out to the ships and was now miles down-river. Then some European soldiers – believed to be the Dutch deserters – discovered a cache of alcohol and rampaged drunkenly, attacking the victors, who had piled their arms. They were dispersed but the incident was reported to the Nawab, who asked where the British had imprisoned their unruly soldiers. He was told that they were locked in the guardroom by the main gate of Fort William, known as 'The Black Hole'. This was a room 18 feet square, almost dark because its two small, barred windows opened onto a wide, shaded verandah.

So, at seven o'clock in the evening, it was into this room that the European prisoners were pushed. Estimates of numbers varied from 39 to 146 but, even if the lowest was accurate, the men – and one woman, the wife of a British prisoner – were packed so tightly that they could hardly breathe, and the heat was suffocating. Holwell was thrust through the door first and positioned himself by a window, where he could inhale a little hot air and plead for water. Some guards mocked but one took pity and poured water into a prisoner's upturned hat that had been thrust through the bars; this was soon spilled in the struggle to drink. In the darkness of the long, hot night some died and others went mad. Holwell pleaded for release but was told that that could only be sanctioned by the Nawab and he was asleep and could not be disturbed. Finally, at six o'clock next morning, the door was opened and a few gasping survivors staggered into the light; behind them, 'The Black Hole' was heaped with bodies, a few showing signs of life.

Holwell, who had survived, claimed that 146 people had been shut into the Black Hole, and that 143 had died. But he may have assessed this from the total number of European casualties in the defence of Calcutta; a more likely total is that 48 died and 23 survived. The survivors included the woman, the half-Portuguese Mary Carey, who had chosen to remain with her English husband; both lived through the night. The horror of 'the Black Hole of Calcutta' had not been a deliberate atrocity; it was rather the outcome of the literal interpretation of orders from the Nawab that had to be obeyed to the letter, and the prevailing indifference to suffering.

News of the fall of Calcutta reached Madras on 16 August, 1756, and Colonel Clive was at once summoned from Fort St David to attend a council of war. Watson had just heard from the Admiralty that he had been promoted to vice-admiral and had again received permission to return to England on sick leave, but he disregarded it and placed his squadron at the disposal of the council. They decided to counterattack, though the admiral advised a delay of two months until the end of the rainy season before embarking all available troops in the warships and sailing for the Hooghly. This would mean accepting the risk to Madras should the French then advance north from Pondicherry.

Preparations for the expedition continued and the ships – the *Kent, Cumberland, Tyger* and *Salisbury*, the frigate *Bridgewater* and five of the Company's warships – were each victualled for 15 days. Finally, the troops were embarked: 250 regular infantry, 700 Europeans and 1,200 sepoys in the East India Company's service. These were divided between the ships, most of the artillery, the regular troops and more than 400 sepoys being allocated to Pocock's ship, the *Cumberland*, and the Company's ship, *Marlborough*. They eventually sailed for the mouth of the Hooghly on 16 October, although this was now the season of gales and strong currents as storm water from monsoon rains swept from the mouth of the Ganges into the Bay of Bengal. At once, gales struck the squadron, driving it almost as far south as Ceylon. 'The monsoon this year was uncommonly tempestuous', noted Surgeon Ives, adding, 'at length, however, by great perseverance and unwearied industry the whole squadron reached the mouth of the Ganges.'[22] One ship, the *Salisbury*, sprang a leak in her bows, and to lift them so that they could be plugged with oakum, her guns had to be moved aft; the leaking continued and the ship wallowed in Watson's wake.

Worse followed. In the night, the *Cumberland* – Pocock's ship – ran aground on a sandbank as the squadron reached Palmyras Point to the west of the Ganges delta. Next morning, the whole squadron found itself among shoals, Pocock flying a red flag from his grounded ship to warn of the danger. The *Cumberland* was re-floated but both she and the *Marlborough* were in a bad state; both were crowded with troops and running short of food and water. As the rest of the squadron worked into the mouth of the Hooghly – a principal branch of the Ganges on which Calcutta lay – the two ships were separated, Pocock trying to beat against wind and current to reach the river. After ten days without progress, 266 men – nearly half of the *Cumberland*'s sailors and soldiers – were sick and the ship only had enough food and water for a few more days. Reluctantly, the admiral put his ship about and ran south to Vizagapatam, north of Madras, to replenish. So when Watson's squadron entered the estuary he lacked half of Clive's best troops and most of his artillery.

After awaiting a high tide to carry them over the mudbanks, Watson and Clive had sailed 50 miles up the Hooghly by 15 December. There, off the swampy shores around the village of Fulta, they found the refugees from Calcutta, who had been joined by survivors of the Black Hole, on board the ships that had saved them, many sick with malaria. Here they heard the latest news from the lost city upstream.

Calcutta was now governed on the Nawab's behalf by the Rajah Manikchand, who was said to be preparing to intercept the British expedition. But he was a Hindu and rumoured to be wavering in his loyalty to his Moslem master, so he might be open to overtures. Watson and Clive were prepared for any eventuality, the latter sending a letter for forwarding to the Nawab which combined threats and flattery, like a stiletto wrapped in a silken scarf. 'I have brought with me a larger military force than has ever appeared in Bengal', he wrote.

> You will judge it therefore prudent … to consider maturely how injuriously the English settled in the province have been treated by your people … These are acts of violence, which I hope you do not approve of, and I expect you will take care to have them severely punished. Your power and personal bravery are universally known; my reputation in war is likewise established … and I trust in God I shall be as fortunate in these parts. Should necessity oblige me to proceed to those extremities one of us must be overthrown, we cannot both be victorious and I leave you to reflect how uncertain the fortune of war is.

He then listed the restitution and compensation required at Calcutta, concluding: 'By doing this piece of justice you will make me a sincere friend and get eternal honour for yourself ... What can I say more?' On the same day, Watson wrote a similar letter, announcing that 'The King, my master (whose name is revered among the monarchs of the world) sent me to these parts with a great fleet to protect the East India Company's trade, rights and privileges ...', explaining his intentions and also ending, 'What can I say more?'[23]

On Christmas Day, Clive wrote to the Nawab again:

I know you are a great prince and a great warrior. I likewise for these ten years past have been constantly fighting in these parts and it has pleased God Almighty always to make me successful. The like success may attend me in Bengal, it may attend your Excellency. Why should the soldiers on either side run the risque of war, when all things may be made up in a friendly manner by restoring to the Company and to the poor inhabitants what they have been plundered?[24]

Meanwhile, Watson and Clive pressed on with plans to retake Calcutta, despite the continuing absence of the best troops in the two missing ships. Reports from the city estimated Manikchand's total remaining force at only 2,000 and that his artillery was in a poor state. First, a fort on the river at Baj-Baj, halfway between Fulta and Calcutta, had to be taken by Watson's ships and by Clive making a night march through swamps to cut off the enemy's retreat. Here, disagreement over tactics and friction arose between Watson and Clive, and not for the first or last time. The former regarded the Company's forces as mercenaries and the latter thought the former lacked experience of war.

All was resolved by a drunken sailor from the *Kent* named Strahan. He, recalled Ives, 'having just been served with a quantity of grog [arrack mixed with water] ... strayed by himself towards the fort and imperceptibly got under the walls'.[25] One of Strahan's officers reported:

This sailor had a very hoarse voice and when he hallowed one would have thought there were several voices. The passage to this battery was very narrow and so deep with mud and water, that the Moors, thinking the passage of it impracticable, had left it unguarded. This the sailor observing, immediately entered it, and holding his pistols in his hands above his head, waded almost up to the chin to the foot of the battery and, getting up halfway without being seen by the Moors, he fired one of his pistols, crying out, 'One and all, my boys, one and all, Huzza!' Mounting the bastion, he fired his other pistol and killed one man; then drawing his cutlass, huzza'd and charged three more, one of whom he cut down, one ran away and the other broke his cutlass in two by a blow aimed at his head with a scymetar, which Jack parried, and throwing his right fist into his face, just as he was recovering his weapon, knocked him down, took his scymetar, cut his throat and so got possession of the battery.[26]

Then, standing on the ramparts, Strahan gave 'several loud huzzas, cried out, "The place is mine"' so loudly that it was heard by several other sailors outside the walls. 'They, hearing Strahan's huzzas, immediately scaled the breach likewise and, echoing the triumphant sound, roused the whole army, who, taking the alarm, presently fell on pell-mell without orders and without discipline, following the example of the sailors.'

The fort fell, together with 18 guns, and next morning they were fired to salute Admiral Watson. He, however, was not pleased and sent for the sailor and demanded, 'Mr Strahan, what is this you have been doing?' Then, noted Ives,

the fellow, after having made his bow, scratched his head and with one hand twirling his hat upon the other, replied, 'Why, to be sure, sir, it was I who took the fort *but I hope there was no harm in it.*' The admiral with difficulty was prevented from smiling ... then with a severe rebuke dismissed him but not before he had given the fellow some distant hints that at a proper opportunity he should certainly be punished for his temerity. Strahan, amazed to find himself blamed, where he expected praise, had no sooner gone from the admiral's cabin, than he muttered these words, 'If I am flogged for this here action, I will never take another fort as long as I live, by G-d.'

However, Watson, having to frown on drunkenness, was determined to promote Strahan, 'but unfortunately for this brave fellow, the whole tenor of his conduct, both before and after the storming of the fort, was so very irregular as to render it impossible for the admiral to advance him from his old station to any higher rank'.[*][27]

The ships continued up the river and, on 2 January, 1757, came in sight of Calcutta. At a distance, with the sun behind it, the city appeared quiet and normal except for the river being empty of shipping. As they came nearer, they could see that the merchants' palaces along the waterfront had been blackened and gutted by fire and the great classical façade of the Factory House within Fort William fronted a hollow shell. Then, a cannon fired from the bank, then others and the water spouted with falling shot. 'The Europeans in the Nawab's service made the round and partridge shot fly very thick about us,' wrote an officer on board the flagship. 'We lay within pistol-shot of the Fort and made prodigious havoc with our small arms. My little musket was fired so often that broke the lock; the barrel must certainly be a good one since I fired fifty cartridges with two balls each in the space of an hour and a half.'[28]

Clive and his troops scrambled into boats to be pulled ashore, form and advance on the city from the south. But when they entered the empty streets lined with burned, sacked houses, they saw the enemy had fled. After more than six months, Calcutta had been retaken. It was soon back to life, and, as one of its liberators reported, 'The Moors, ... destroyed all the fine furniture and set fire to several dwelling houses, which are now repairing ... The houses are all large and grand with fine balconies all round them ... The people are all agreeable and very obliging to everybody; once introduced, you are always known to them and you dine and sup where you please.'[29]

The fruits of victory were soured when Watson, without reference to Clive, appointed a regular British Army officer, Captain Eyre Coote, to command Fort William. Considering it to be the Company's property, Clive entered, was ordered by Coote to leave, refused, and Watson's arbitration was invoked. The admiral resented the manner of an East India Company officer towards a King's officer and sent him a note, ordering, 'If you still persist in continuing in the Fort, you will force me to take such measures as will be as disagreeable to me as they possibly can be to you.'[30] His flag captain, Captain Henry Speke, spelled out his meaning, telling Clive that, if necessary, the Navy would 'fire him out'.[31] The deadlock was broken when a more diplomatic naval captain arranged that Watson himself would assume command of Fort William and then hand it over to the Company. The incident illustrated Watson's distrust of Clive and his officers as the mercenaries of a commercial organisation and Clive complained to Pigot of 'the mortifications I have received from Mr Watson and the gentlemen of the squadron'.[32]

As might have been expected, there was friction between Clive and Governor Drake, who had abandoned the city so precipitately with most of his councillors. The former loathed them as they concentrated on recovering what they could of their personal wealth, writing to the Governor of Madras: 'these gentlemen … are bad subjects and rotten at heart … the riches of Peru and Mexico should not induce me to dwell among them'.[33]

Although all was quiet, the threat remained. The Nawab had withdrawn from the city but might return, and the most dangerous possibility was that he might be joined by some 300 regular French troops from their main settlement upstream at Chandernagore. In the middle of January, the *Marlborough* arrived with most of Clive's artillery but the *Cumberland* was still missing. So, still without his best troops, Clive set about preparing to fight the Nawab outside the city, with Fort William as the final bastion of defence.

Meanwhile two of Watson's ships managed to sail farther up the river, passing Chandernagore and the small Dutch settlement at Chinsura to bombard and burn the town of Hooghly, belonging to the Nawab, in the hope of deterring another attack. It had, however, the opposite effect and the Nawab, who had been angered by the tone of Clive's letters, ordered his army to march south, towards Calcutta. Yet on reaching Hooghly, the devastation had a sobering effect, the Indians imagining that British cannon could devastate anywhere on the banks of the river, even as far up it as the Nawab's capital, Murshidibad. Also, Surajah Dowlah distrusted some of his officers and allies, notably his paymaster-general, Mir Jaffir, a great-uncle by marriage, who had plotted against him in the past.

So the Nawab began to keep other options open, renewing his correspondence with Clive with the declared object of negotiating a settlement. He even offered the resumption of trading rights to the East India Company on condition that Drake was replaced as Governor of Calcutta, to which Clive would have been happy to agree had he had the power. Yet, while the Nawab talked of peace, he prepared for renewed war, moving his army – rumoured to number anything up to 100,000 – closer to Calcutta. As the threat grew more tangible, another evacuation of European women and children began and the tragedy of the preceding June seemed about to be repeated.

Clive marched his own modest force of 800 Europeans, 100 artillerymen with 14 small field-guns and 1,300 sepoys 4 miles north of the city to await a confrontation in open country near the river. Watson and Clive had patched up their quarrel and, on 2 February, were dining together in the latter's tent when the Nawab's army was reported in sight. Sure enough, a mile distant the horde again appeared beneath its cloud of dust, shaking the ground with the tread of what scouts now reported to be 15,000 infantry, 18,000 mounted warriors and 50 war-elephants, passing inland to take up position east of the city.

Dinner was abandoned, Watson hurrying to his boat to rejoin his flagship. Clive ordered his men to arms, then marched towards the long, heaving flank of the enemy. Once within range, shots were fired, followed by a brief cannonade, but, as darkness fell, Clive decided that this was not the moment to fight and ordered a withdrawal to the camp. Tempting as it was to take the enemy in the flank, he still hoped that the *Cumberland* would arrive with his best troops to give him the decisive advantage.

The great Indian host took two days to pass Clive's camp but the *Cumberland* did not arrive. Despite the skirmish, he and the Nawab continued their flowery exchanges. Both could be duplicitous: the Nawab wrote to assure Clive that his army was only moving to a more convenient site for its camp, sending him a gift of fruit and vegetables; and Clive wrote to the Nawab: 'I esteem your Excellency in the place of my father and mother and myself as your son and I should think myself happy to lay down my life for the preservation of yourself.'[34] At the same time, Clive was writing to Governor Pigot in Madras that he planned 'to finish everything by a decisive stroke'.[35]

Had the Nawab decided to blockade Calcutta, another pell-mell evacuation would have been followed by surrender because food was already short. Clive had sent two emissaries to the Nawab; they found him in the country house of the Sikh merchant whose arrest had been the excuse for the first attack on Calcutta. They were kept waiting but invited to stay the night in a tent. That evening they heard reports that the Nawab was intent on attacking the city in a day or two, so after dark, they escaped, made for the British camp and urged Clive to launch an immediate attack.

This he ordered, asking Watson for 600 sailors to drag his guns. His plan was to thrust through the enemy's main camp that night to seize the Nawab himself and capture his guns. The sailors did not arrive until two in the morning so, although Clive then advanced, he was not in action until dawn. Yet he was not concerned because the thick morning mist, prevalent at this season, thickly wrapped the enemy camp. The British and the sepoys attacked as planned, firing to left and right as they tramped between the tents and bivouacs, hardly able to see their targets but hearing the commotion they caused. Then 300 Indian horsemen came charging out of the mist, to be driven off by well-drilled volleys. The British pressed onward but had lost their direction and, instead of cutting through the camp to the headquarters, advanced into the centre of the great camp itself.

The sun was up, burning the mist away, so that suddenly the British found themselves exposed to view in the midst of the enemy. No attack on the Nawab's headquarters was now possible as the British, pounded by cannon-shot, fought off cavalry charges. Outnumbered and outgunned and seeing his men cut down, Clive ordered a retreat on the city. With difficulty but with discipline, the little force fought their way back to the walls. They had lost 57 killed, including Clive's aide-de-camp and secretary, but the Nawab had lost 1,300 killed, amongst them some of his best officers. Both sides held their fire to await the other's next move.

On 6 February, Clive wrote to the Nawab again:

> This action sufficiently shows you meant only to amuse me, but … your firing on my people … puts it out of all doubt that you intended to carry on the war. I therefore made a tour through your camp to show you what I was capable of effecting. I cautiously hurt none but those that opposed me. If you still think meanly of my force, I assure you upon the faith of a soldier, that I shall shortly receive a supply of English soldiers equal to my present number. If these should not prove sufficient to procure us satisfaction from you, let me further assure you that when the great King of England shall have heard of the treatment his subjects have received in this kingdom he will certainly send forces sufficient to destroy the whole province.[36]

The debonair threats were effective and the Nawab cautiously withdrew his army. Clive had planned another attack to cut the enemy's line of retreat but concluded that diplomacy might be more effective, at least until the arrival of the *Cumberland*. Even if the attack succeeded it might only serve to forge an alliance between the Nawab and the French in Chandernagore, who had so far withheld direct support against the British. So Clive sent a draft agreement to the Nawab and he agreed to the terms, allowing trading to continue through Calcutta unmolested and to pay some compensation. To seal the treaty, Surajah Dowlah sent a present to Clive, Watson and Drake of a jewel, a robe and an elephant. Watson, as a King's officer, returned the presents but received the Nawab's delegation on board the *Kent*, took them on a tour of her gun-decks and 'displayed to them his lower tier of thirty-two pounders, of which they made a dreadful report to their master'.[37] More effective than diplomacy was news of an Afghan invasion of northern Bengal; the Nawab knew that he could not survive a war on two fronts, even with French help.

Despite the onset of calm, the Nawab was not to be trusted. The final battle outside Calcutta had been close-run, and he would certainly have won had he had the support of regular French troops. This might be the case next time, so, Watson decided, a pre-emptive strike against Chandernagore was necessary even though the British still awaited the troops, presumed to be with Admiral Pocock, aboard the *Cumberland* somewhere in the Indian Ocean. But, while nothing had been heard of him, disquieting news about his cousin Admiral Byng – that he was under arrest and to be tried by court-martial for his failure off Minorca – had reached Watson, via Madras, in the middle of January. 'I hope the news you write me with regard to Mr Byng ... is not true', he replied to the governing committee at Fort George. 'It comes from Paris, therefore the less to be credited.'[38]

At last, news arrived of the missing Pocock. After his failure to defeat the Nawab in the field, Clive had written to the Select Committee at Madras that 'the absence of the *Cumberland* is another disappointment'.[39] At the end of January, Watson wrote to Cleveland, the Secretary of the Admiralty, telling him that about a week beforehand

I received a letter from Mr Pocock acquainting me that he had used his utmost efforts to get round Point Palmyras but his provisions and water being almost expended and his people very sickly, he was at last obliged to bear up for Vizagapatam, where he arrived on 14 December. As there are near 300 troops on board the *Cumberland*, I thought it proper to send Mr Pocock orders to make the best of his way to Bengal and proceed up the river as high as Kedgeree and to disembark the troops without any loss of time and send them to Calcutta, it being at this vital juncture of the utmost importance our land force should be augmented.[40]

But another crisis had developed in the Carnatic, for, on his arrival, Pocock had heard that the French, under the command of the Marquis de Bussy, intended to take the offensive there while the main British force was absent in Bengal. Indeed, as Clive later recognised, Pocock's unexpected arrival seemed to have deterred an attack on Vizagapatam, for he had reported to Watson that de Bussy might be heading northward in that direction and towards Bengal.

Having received no orders from Watson, Pocock left 90 East India Company troops at Vizagapatam and, on 5 February, sailed for Madras, where he arrived on the 21st and landed 100 more for the defence of Fort St George. There, Pocock received his orders to sail for Bengal and did so at once, first embarking 100 sailors, who had been ashore in hospital, and taking with him the remaining 90 officers and men of the regular Aldercron's Regiment, so named after their colonel. But on 24 February, Watson was again writing to Cleveland: 'I have heard nothing from Mr Pocock but am in expectation of his arriving … every day and can't help being a little surprised at his not being in the river long ago.'[41]

Despite the absence of the *Cumberland* and her soldiers, Watson and Clive decided that their attack on Chandernagore must go ahead. The operation would be dangerous without the awaited regulars in the face of a well-trained French garrison – said to number 1,200, half of them French, and nearly 200 guns – and with the possibility of the Nawab again taking the field. So the main attack would be made from the river by ships which would have to pick their way between the shoals, against the current and, certainly in the final stages, under fire from shore batteries.

Finally, the *Cumberland* reached the Hooghly and, at the village of Ingelee, Pocock heard that Watson had already left Calcutta for Chandernagore. For a relatively big, 66-gun ship like the *Cumberland*, the river could only be ascended under the guidance of a relay of Indian pilots, and these were not to be found; nor were boats available to carry the infantry upriver. Even if his ship could not join the attack on the French, the admiral might be able to, and there were pressing reasons for doing so. One was, of course, that it was his duty to be there. Another was that a successful campaign should result in large amounts of prize-money, in which he would want to share. Finally, there was the disquieting news from Paris about John Byng, who, if the report was to be believed, was to be tried – and might already have been court-martialled – for failing to do his utmost against a French fleet, if not for actual cowardice in the face of the enemy; it would be prudent that no such slur could be cast on his cousin. Therefore, wrote a contemporary, 'Mr

Pocock with the spirit worthy of an English admiral, took the *Cumberland's* barge and, rowing night and day, joined Mr Watson a few hours before the morning of the attack.'[42]

The reason for the urgency in mounting the attack was the instability of Surajah Dowlah and the uncertainty of his intentions. Both French and British were making diplomatic enticements to him and his rivals, while he himself was not sure whether the British or the French might offer him the greater commercial reward and act as insurance against an Afghan invasion. So intense was the intrigue that when it seemed certain that the Nawab would throw in his lot with the French at Chandernagore, he was dissuaded by the very Sikh merchant whose arrest by the British had been the pretext for his first attack on Calcutta, who declared that only they were to be trusted. Meanwhile, the British had bought the services of the Nawab's chief of intelligence as their own spy in his camp.

When Surajah Dowlah appealed directly to Clive for military assistance against the Afghans, whom he knew were causing concern to the East India Company, the latter produced a characteristically disingenuous plan. On the excuse of complying, he would march his little army north from Calcutta towards the Nawab's camp and Chandernagore, so that, without interference from either, he could reach a position from which to attack the town. On 8 March he set out, marching along the flat, fertile riverside set with fine trees like oriental parkland. He kept his intentions secret and his options open, though Chandernagore was accorded the highest priority, writing to his friend Robert Orme of the East India Company, 'I am going to Patna, or Delhi, or somewhere.'[43] If the Nawab decided to support the French, he could switch plans to help him against the Afghans with a view to eventually taking over Bengal himself for the Company; if not, he could attack Chandernagore. The probability of the latter course was heightened when he heard that the Nawab had sent some of his army to face the Afghans and that the *Cumberland* had arrived in the Hooghly.

Clive took the march slowly, arriving before Chandernagore in three days, making camp two miles from its walls and telling the French, 'I have no intention of acting offensively against your nation at present; whenever I have, you may be assured I shall frankly acquaint you with it.'[44] On that same day, Watson ordered his three ships to sail upriver from Calcutta. The Hooghly was so treacherous with currents and shoals that the French were certain that it was not navigable by such big ships, but, to make sure, they sank four hulks filled with mud in the channels below Chandernagore, further blocking the deepest of them with a boom and chains. But the river was unusually high and the admiral, flying his flag in the 70-gun *Kent*, first sent two small ships, the *Bridgewater* and *Kingfisher*, up-river and then himself led the *Tyger*, of 60 guns, and the *Salisbury*, of 50 guns, in their wake.

Chandernagore was something like Calcutta. Around a massive fortification named Fort d'Orléans sprawled a town made up of the handsome quarters of the administrators of the *Compagnie des Indes*, merchants' palaces and warehouses and the houses of Indians who served, or traded with, the French. The fortress stood 130 yards square (about 119 metres square), with a bastion at each corner and mounting more than 50 heavy guns, with several more batteries nearby on the riverbank. The garrison was reduced by sickness but nominally consisted of nearly 250 well-trained French regular soldiers, about a 170 sepoys, 400 irregulars – including some British deserters – and 2,000 Indians sent to help by the Nawab when his dithering had favoured the French. This force was broadly equalled by Clive, who fielded some 2,500 men, including about 700 Europeans.

Next day, Clive made his first hostile move: having accused the French of harbouring British deserters, he sent the Governor of Chandernagore, Pierre Renault, a summons to surrender. No reply was received so, on the 14th, Clive read his declaration of war to his own troops and the fighting began. Without the heavy guns of Watson's ships to dismount the batteries on the ramparts, Clive did not intend to assault the walls and contented himself with the relatively easy task of clearing French outposts. This had the effect of demoralising the Indians loaned by the Nawab, whose officers announced that this was a European quarrel and abandoned the town. Thereupon Clive sealed the landward approaches so that the Nawab could not change his mind and send them back.

Clive made another shrewd move by getting word into the town – by notes attached to arrows – that British deserters who surrendered immediately would be pardoned and that any French officers who came over would be rewarded. One Frenchman who took advantage of the offer was a Lieutenant de Terraneau, who had quarrelled with Renault; he was a serious loss to the defenders because he was their only trained artillery officer. He was able to tell the British that his compatriots had been unable to sink two large ships in the remaining gaps in the deep channels of the river between the blockships already sunk. Clive sent word of this to the *Bridgewater* and the *Kingfisher*, lying three miles below the town, and that night a Lieutenant Bloomer cut the chains of the boom and towed away the moored sloop to which they had been fastened.

By 20 March, Watson's three big ships were within sight of the town but still below the blockships, so a Lieutenant Hey was sent by boat, rowed between the masts of the sunken ships, to deliver another summons to surrender. However, so little damage had Clive's small field-guns inflicted on the fortifications that, assuming the channel to be effectively blocked, Renault and his governing council dismissed it and, playing for time, suggested they negotiate a possible ransom for the settlement. This was rejected by Watson, and on the night of the 20th, the navigating master of the flagship, John Delamotte, buoyed a passage between the blockships. All was now ready for a coordinated attack on Chandernagore.

On the afternoon of Tuesday, 22 March, 1757, Watson ordered his three ships to clear for action: swinging the light bulkheads up to the beams to open the gun-decks from bow to stern; striking all unnecessary furniture and equipment into the holds; and preparing the guns and ammunition. At two o'clock a ship's barge appeared, pulling towards them from the direction of Calcutta; it was Admiral Pocock. He climbed aboard the *Kent* and reported to Watson, explaining the cause and outcome of his long absence. As second-in-command, he was entitled to hoist his flag in another of the ships and did so next morning, when the log of the *Tyger* recorded: 'At 8 we hoisted George Pocock Esquire's flag at our mizzen topmast head as Rear-Admiral of the White Squadron.' This dismayed Captain Thomas Latham, who commanded the ship and would now stand to lose in prize-money and renown.

Watson planned that, at sunrise next morning, Pocock should lead the attack and anchor off the north-west bastion of Fort d'Orléans, while the *Kent* would attack the forward ravelin (an outer defensive work) and the *Salisbury* the south-east bastion. Accordingly, as the sun came up over the plains of Bengal, Clive began the action ashore by opening fire on the fortress with his field-guns as the three ships slowly glided upstream under topsails, their mainsails clewed up to the yards to keep the upper decks clear. As the *Tyger* passed the ravelin, she fired a broadside at point-blank range, sweeping away the defenders, and then, at six o'clock, anchored in her appointed position. A French eyewitness recorded that the ships

with the aid of a strong south wind and the high waters of the Equinox, the strong tides of which moreover had displaced the sunken vessels, the squadron easily forced the passage and came before the Fort within pistol-shot. They bombarded us with all their artillery, to which was added that of the land forces. Accordingly for 3 hours the fire was as hot as we had ever seen.[45]

Watching the battle was a Dutch book-keeper, Johannes Ross, from Chinsura, who noted, as the ships came abreast of the town: 'On their arrival, they saluted Fort Orléans with three volleys each, whereupon the Admiral hoisted the red flag, the signal for general attack both on land and by the ships, which actually began with such a fearful cannonade that it really seemed as if both heaven and earth were doomed.'[46]

The 24-pounder guns on the ramparts replied, sweeping the deck of the Tyger to terrible effect, killing 15 and wounding 56. Pocock, standing on the quarterdeck, suffered 'a rap on the shins from the same ball that killed poor old Phillips, the master of the *Tyger* … the splinters flew so thick about him that he was scratched most shockingly and covered with blood from head to foot'.[47] One of her officers noted that 'we had all our lower masts, bowsprit, bell, coppers, several chain plates, anchors, several guns and gun carriages damaged as to be unfit for service, a most incredible number of shot in our hull'.[48]

The *Kent* suffered even more severely, from 142 heavy shot hitting her hull and six striking her masts, killing 37 – 'amongst them was Mr Perreau, the admiral's first lieutenant, who fell in the bloom of youth, unspeakably lamented by us all', recorded Surgeon Ives – and wounding 72. Watson was also on his quarterdeck, and when told that on the fortress walls 'an officer with a glass was giving directions to point a gun at him and that the gun was traversed for that purpose, he answered, "Why then, they shall have a fair shot"; stood still, smiled and went on after the ball had passed just by him'.[49]

He survived while all his officers but one, including both Captain Speke and his sixteen-year-old son, Billy, were hit. 'When Admiral Watson had the unhappiness of seeing both father and son fall in the same instant, he immediately went up to them and by the most tender and pathetic expressions tried to alleviate their distress', remembered Ives. 'The captain, who had observed his son's legs to be hanging only by the skin, said to the admiral, "Indeed, sir, this was a cruel shot, to knock down both the father and the son!" Mr Watson's heart was too full to make the least reply.' As both were carried down to the orlop deck, the quartermaster, who was carrying the boy, was killed by a cannon-ball. As Ives examined his leg, the boy turned to a wounded man next to him and said to Ives, 'Pray, sir, look to and dress this poor man, who is groaning so sadly beside me.' Then, of his own wound he said, 'Sir, I fear you must amputate above the joint', and Ives replied, 'My dear, I must.'[50]

Amid the whirring shot, splintering wood and crashing yards and rigging, the *Kent* drifted out of control and only managed to anchor in the position allocated to the *Salisbury* opposite the south-east bastion, so the latter ship was unable to get alongside the fort to join the action. After two hours, wrote Surgeon Ives,

> several of the enemy's shot struck the *Kent* at the same time; one entered near the foremast and set fire to two, or three thirty-two-pound cartridges of gunpowder as the boys held them in their hands ready to charge the guns. By the explosion, the wad-nets [ready-use wads to ram down gun barrels with the charges and shot] and other loose things took fire between decks and the whole ship was so filled with smoke that the men in their confusion cried out she was on fire in the gunner's store-room.

As the ship seemed likely to blow up,

> this notion struck panic into the greatest part of the crew and 70 or 80 jumped out of the port-holes into the boats that were alongside the ship. The French presently saw this confusion … and resolving to take the advantage, kept up as hot a fire as possible upon her during the whole time.
>
> Lieutenant Brereton [the only officer, other than Watson, still on his feet] however, with the assistance of some other brave men, soon extinguished the fire and then running to the ports, he begged the seamen to come in again, upbraiding them for deserting their quarters … and loudly exclaimed, 'Are you Britons! You Englishmen and fly from danger? For shame, for shame!' This reproach had the desired effect; to a man they immediately returned into the ship, repaired to their quarters and renewed a spirited fire on the enemy.[51]

The French had suffered, too. Both the riverside bastions had been battered into silence. After two hours and ten minutes' fighting, Renault ordered a white flag to be hung from the demolished battlements. He summoned a council meeting but there was disagreement, as the British were later told, between 'the Renaultians and the Anti-Renaultians, the former which they called the Great Wigged Gentry, or Councillors, were for giving up the Fort, but the others vowed they would die in the breach'.[52] Renault prevailed and he reported to the directors of the *Compagnie des Indes* that the bombardment had been so severe that the guns of the bastions – five, not ten, in each, they claimed – had been dismounted and 'everything threatened to crumble away to make a breach, which the exhaustion of our people and the small number which remained to us prevented us from hoping to defend, for … we had 200 men put *hors de combat*. Seeing the impossibility of holding out longer, I hoisted a white flag and the capitulation was signed that evening.'[53]

British deserters escaping to Chinsura from the garrison at Chandernagore reported that 500 had been killed in the fort and town, while other fugitives said that 'French ladies [were] in ignorance of what had become of their husbands and relations and whether, at the taking of the Fort, all of them would not be put to the sword'.[54] The terms of the surrender agreed that the lives of the British deserters would be spared, but one corporal of marines named Lee, who had deserted from the *Tyger* had, it was learned, 'pledged himself to the enemy that he would throw two shells out of three into the *Tyger*, but while he was bringing the mortars to bear for that purpose, he was disabled by a musket-bullet from the *Kent's* top. He was afterwards sent as a prisoner to England.'[55]

Clive's land forces had suffered few casualties but, when they marched into the town, they broke open a store of arrack and then 'the spirit of plundering was never more in vogue'.[56] Even the church was looted. Clive ordered three of his sepoys to be hanged immediately for looting and a British sergeant and private were sentenced to be shot for stealing 3,000 rupees from the treasury.

The Royal Navy had borne the brunt of the fighting and, as one eyewitness wrote, 'We have never yet obtained a victory at so dear a rate; perhaps you will hear of few instances where two ships have met with greater damage than the *Kent* and the *Tyger* in this engagement.'[57] While Watson was unhurt, a few days after the action 'Mr Pocock is still very lame and swelled above the legs'.[58][*] Captain Speke survived, but his son died of gangrene and lockjaw after nearly a fortnight. On being asked 'Well, Ives, how fares it with my boy?', Ives could not reply and later wrote in his diary: 'He immediately attributed my silence to the real cause. He cried bitterly, squeezed me by the hand and begged me to leave him for one half-hour … When I returned to him, he appeared, as he ever after did, perfectly calm and serene.' The British loss was not only human: the *Kent*, Watson's most powerful ship, was so badly damaged that she might have to be abandoned. For the first time in India, the British had fought the French in a costly battle.

Yet here, too, there was disputation among the victors. Some thought the terms of surrender too lenient, and there was even argument as to whether the Navy or the Army had contributed most to the victory. But it had not been profitable: the warehouses were mostly empty, the magazine had blown up when the French had started a fire just before surrendering, and there was little more booty than full-length portraits of King Louis XV and his Queen, which were carried off in triumph. Five small ships had been captured and five large ones scuttled above the town. French losses were lighter than expected: about 40 killed, 70 wounded and 300 taken prisoner; others might have escaped into the countryside. But the effect of the victory was devastating, Clive writing to the council at Madras that 'nothing could have happened more seasonable for the expeditious re-establishment of Calcutta than the reduction of Chandernagore … and the loss of it is an unexpressable blow to the French company'.[59] The French were now barred from the riches of Bengal, and it was from there that their settlements and even their naval base on the island of Mauritius – known to them as I'lle de France – imported much of their food. Watson, Pocock and Clive suggested that the Fort d'Orléans be demolished to complete their success.

Surajah Dowlah still cast a shadow across British dreams of prosperity in Bengal because, as soon as the monsoon season ended in the summer, their ships and troops would be needed to defend the settlements on the Coromandel coast against the French and Calcutta would again be at his mercy. With their customary disingenuousness, he and Clive exchanged flattery, the latter writing 'I am persuaded you will be pleased at my success' and the former declaring his 'inexpressible pleasure' and sending the colonel a gift of a pair of leopards trained to hunt deer. But, at the same time, the Nawab began a secret correspondence with the Marquis de Bussy with a view to establishing a military alliance against the British. This became known to Clive, who was neither surprised, nor daunted. He was willing to fight again, or to make an alliance with the Nawab against the Afghans, and meanwhile he began further intrigues of his own with other Indian rulers.

As the British and the Indians cast about warily for common objectives, it became increasingly apparent that, although betrayal and double-dealing were to be taken for granted, a pattern was beginning to emerge. The Nawab had no true friends and many rivals and enemies, who could be united in his overthrow. On 1 May, Clive and Drake joined a committee on future policy at Calcutta and unanimously decided to engineer the downfall of Surajah Dowlah in what could be described as a revolution. He would be replaced by Mir Jaffir, his kinsman and former paymaster, a wily, grey-bearded Moslem credited with influence amongst the majority of Indian rulers, who envied, or disliked, Surajah Dowlah. In gratitude for being installed as Nawab, Mir Jaffir would be expected to pay full compensation for the commercial and private losses of the previous year, make large grants to the Navy, Army and East India Company and cede more land to the Calcutta settlement. Meanwhile, Surajah Dowlah was to be lulled into a false sense of security with yet more flattery and a letter from Clive, telling him that 'I desire nothing so much as to live in peace and friendship with you.'[60]

So contorted did the intrigues become that the Sikh merchant whose arrest had been the Nawab's pretext for his attack on Calcutta became the vortex of double-dealing. He had been privy to the plotting with Mir Jaffir and threatened to betray the conspiracy to Surajah Dowlah unless huge financial benefit for himself was written into the secret agreement. This it was; but only into one of two near-identical documents, identified by coloured paper. One was regarded by the British as genuine; the other, written to the blackmailer's instructions and for his eyes only, was not. Both were signed by Clive and Drake, amongst others; Watson, as a King's officer, could not bring himself to put his name to such trickery and his signature was forged.

Clive's proposal was that he should lead his small army towards the Nawab's capital, Murshidibad, with aggressive intent. The Nawab would summon his supposed allies – including Mir Jaffir – and their armies to his aid but, when a confrontation was imminent, those Indians in league with the British would either turn on the Nawab, or 'stand neutral', while Clive used force.[61] All depended on them keeping their word to Clive rather than to the Nawab, otherwise the best the British could expect was a fighting retreat downriver to Calcutta, for Clive would be vastly outnumbered. He could field some 700 European troops and ten field-guns and just over 2,000 sepoys. They would have to face an Indian army of between 50,000 and 70,000, including Pathan cavalry, 50 guns and war-elephants clad in armour.

On 12 June, Clive's force at Chandernagore was joined by all available troops from Calcutta, and the next day they marched north. The Europeans travelled on the river by boat while the sepoys marched along the bank, through flat country broken by clumps of jungle, palm groves and tall, hardwood trees. There was some urgency because the rainy season had begun, flooding would follow and warfare become impossible. A week after the march began, the first heavy rain washed away Clive's camp and his sodden soldiers had to huddle in the little houses and huts of the nearby village of Katwa. But they had managed to keep their powder dry.

It was here that the extent of Clive's gamble became apparent as conflicting reports reached him. His agreement with Mir Jaffir was vague as to the latter's actual intentions. Clive had reason to expect he would bring his army over to the British when they reached Katwa and before a confrontation with the Nawab. But now a rumour reached him that Surajah Dowlah had been warned of the plot against him but had been reconciled with Mir Jaffir and the two had sworn friendship on the Koran. This seemed confirmed when news came from a British agent in Murshidibad to the effect that Mir Jaffir, having sworn friendship, would not turn against the Nawab on the battlefield but would 'stand neuter'. But would he even do that? There was the possibility that a counter-plot had been agreed amongst the Indians and that all would form a united front against the British.

On the night of 22 June, 1757, Clive led his little army through drenching rain to the village of Plassey on the east bank of the river and there occupied a hunting lodge belonging to the Nawab and a neighbouring mango grove surrounded by a bank with a ditch beyond. Even before first light, they could hear drumming, trumpets and cymbals from the Indian encampments to the north. When the sun came up and began to burn away the low, riverside mist, they saw a daunting panorama. As dark monsoon clouds drifted across a blue sky, the sun lit a wide, green plain and across it, one mile distant, stood the enemy, the sun catching the steel of sabres and spearheads, the colour of banners and the armoured humpbacks of the elephants among a heaving mass of soldiery. As Clive surveyed the enemy through his glass from the roof of the hunting lodge, he recognised that the army facing him was better organised than any he had faced hitherto. The infantry was, as usual, in vast, disorganised crowds, but the Pathan cavalry appeared to be in squadrons and the heavy guns were mounted together with their gunners and ammunition on juggernaut sledges, each hauled by 40 or more yoke of white oxen and pushed by an elephant.

With the bank and ditch as his front line, Clive's force faced north, with the river on its left flank. The Nawab's own army was directly opposite with the river on its right flank and his supposed allies adjoining its left and curving away inland in a wide arc so as to outflank Clive's position. If these allies proved to be such, the British could hardly survive, and even if they decided to 'stand neuter', it would be a close-run contest. Then with a rising cacophony of fanfares, drumming and clashing cymbals, the enemy began to advance. Turning to one of his officers, Clive remarked, 'We must make the best fight we can during the day and at night sling our muskets over our shoulders and march back to Calcutta.'[62] But such were the odds that it must have seemed unlikely that they would be able to manage even that.

To make a display of confidence, Clive ordered his men forward from the earthwork and took up position in the open. His guns opened fire at extreme range and the enemy fired, too, both heavy guns and modern field-guns manned by some 40 French artillerymen. At once, the British lost ten Europeans and 20 sepoys killed or wounded. After half an hour, Clive ordered his infantry back into the shelter of the bank and buildings, from which they could fire from cover; he seemed reconciled to holding out until dark, then either making a night attack, or retreating to Calcutta. At midday the sky darkened with storm clouds and another sudden downpour drenched both armies. The Indians' gunpowder was soaked; their cavalry charged the British in the expectation that they too would be unable to fire, but they were driven off by salvoes from the artillery and volleys from soldiers trained in keeping their ammunition dry under tarpaulins.

As the horsemen wheeled away, the commander, Mir Madan, the best general in the Nawab's service, was mortally wounded; another senior officer was also killed. These proved to be two of the three commanders out of eight upon whose loyalty Surajah Dowlah could rely. It had been their divisions – together with the French gunners – that had fought that morning, while three-quarters of that vast and intimidating array stood silently watching. This majority was commanded by Mir Jaffir and his fellow-conspirators, but Clive still did not know whether they would stand by their promises to himself, or to the Nawab. He showed what they could expect if it proved to be the latter by firing ranging shots at the Nawab's tent.

When the dying Mir Madan was carried before the Nawab, Surajah Dowlah despaired, sent for Mir Jaffir and urged him to attack. It was too late in the day to begin a general assault, replied Mir Jaffir, the army should be withdrawn to its encampment to advance again next morning; then, on his return to his own lines, he at last sent a message to Clive, urging him to attack. The message never arrived but it had been overtaken by events. Seeing the enemy's front falter and pull back, Clive himself advanced. This provoked the Nawab's warriors to rally and surge forward again, to be met by Clive's disciplined musketry and fire from his field-guns, which had been wheeled to the front. Four more of the Nawab's senior officers were killed, draught oxen were hit, bringing his artillery trains to a halt, and the elephants, their armour easily punctured by shot, stampeded.

For a moment Clive hesitated, seeing the mass of the enemy's battle-line appear to move forward. Then he saw that Mir Jaffir and the other conspirators were still not preparing to fight either side and he ordered a general assault on the Nawab's camp. Surajah Dowlah, with three-quarters of his host as spectators and his own army almost leaderless and beginning to panic, mounted a servant's camel and, escorted by Pathan horsemen, rode for Murshidibad. At five o'clock that afternoon the battle was over and Clive commanded the battlefield.

It had not been a particularly bloody encounter. The Nawab's army had lost about 500 men killed as against four Europeans killed and nine wounded and 14 sepoys killed and 36 wounded. The real victors of what came to be called the Battle of Plassey, who had not fired a shot or drawn a sword, were Mir Jaffir and the other Indian rulers. He and they had finally concluded that there was more to be gained by replacing the Nawab and allying themselves with the commercial empire and military capabilities of the British.

On the morning after the battle, Mir Jaffir and his retinue were invited to Clive's camp, arriving 'with anxiety as if he apprehended that the English resented his conduct in not having joined them'. As he alighted from his elephant, the guard was turned out in his honour and he took fright: 'not knowing the meaning of this compliment, he started back as if he thought it a preparation to his destruction; but Colonel Clive advancing hastily, embraced and saluted him Nabob of Bengal'.[63]

Surajah Dowlah fled to Murshidibad – arriving with the first news of his own defeat – followed by Mir Jaffir and finally by Clive, who entered on 29 March at the head of 200 British troops and 300 sepoys with colours flying to the music of fifes and drums. The defeated Nawab had escaped with his favourite concubine and a casket of jewels on the night of Mir Jaffir's arrival and was rowed by a harem eunuch upriver towards safety at Patna. Meanwhile Clive visited the treasury, finding it heaped with gold and silver but not stuffed with the expected treasure.[*][64] Then, while he made a show of refusing presents from other Indian grandees, he accepted a gift of £180,000 from Mir Jaffir as well as the grant made to him as army commander and a member of the Select Committee at Calcutta.

On the day of his entry into the capital, Clive saluted Mir Jaffir as the new Nawab in the audience hall of the palace. Next day, the details of the latter's indebtedness to those who had enthroned him were settled and boatloads of treasure began to make their way downstream to Calcutta, where Captain Thomas Latham of the *Tyger* expected 'a world of guns to be fired and the ladies all to get footsore from dancing'.[65] At the beginning of July, as the British ships were loading treasure, Surajah Dowlah returned to his former capital in chains, having been recognised by a holy man on the banks of the Ganges and arrested. Within hours of his arrival he was dead, hacked to death with swords. No explicit order for the execution had been given by Mir Jaffir, but his son knew that his father feared further double-crossing and had interpreted his wishes. The corpse was thrown onto the back of an elephant and paraded through the streets, dripping blood.

In August, Clive was reunited with his wife, Margaret, and their daughter at Calcutta in the midst of rejoicing over the collapse of all opposition to the East India Company in Bengal and the distribution of vast sums of 'bounty'. Yet the celebrations were soured by disagreements over the making of future policy. Again, Watson distrusted the Company's officers and administrators and asked Pocock to approach Clive to ensure the King's officers could play their rightful part. Pocock did so tactfully by first offering Clive passages home for himself and his family in a ship of the Royal Navy. But Clive replied that 'both my Circumstances and Inclinations make me wish to see Old England again as soon as possible but Gratitude to the Company will not permit my leaving the Management of their affairs under such wretched hands'.[66] Then, having implied his dislike of his Company colleagues, he put the naval officers in their place, too, adding, 'Certainly, Mr Watson's Rank and station, as well as yours, make it necessary you should be consulted on all Military transactions and, while the Committee can only consist of such as are in the Company's pay and service, your presence and advice will always merit their thanks.'[67]

It was then that the despatch-vessel arrived from Madras with the news of the trial and execution of Admiral Byng. The news of his cousin's public disgrace and death had to be broken to George Pocock and, amidst his grief, the lessons were not lost on him, as they would not have been on any other senior naval officer. Byng's fault had been in failing to control his line of battle in the face of the enemy; then spending too much time considering alternative options and choosing a cautious, rather than an aggressive, one. In hurrying up the river to join the attack on Chandernagore, Pocock had shown that he was of a more vigorous stamp, but Byng's failure at sea had been a lesson for all in command.

What the future might hold was suggested in other news from Madras, and Watson wrote to the Earl of Holderness, one of the Secretaries of State at the Foreign Office: 'The Governor of Madras informs me by some French Letters he has intercepted, he has great Reason to believe a French squadron is destined for the East Indies, but nothing is yet arrived in India ...'[68]

Just what the implications of this might be for Byng's cousin became apparent when Admiral Watson's fever suddenly worsened. He had seemed to be recovering on the day the mail arrived from Madras but the following day, the 15th, was, Ives noted in his diary, 'the most sultry day I ever experienced in India; not a breath of air was there for many hours; both man and beast and the very fowls of the air so sensibly felt it that some of each species fell down dead'.[69] By mid-morning, Watson was complaining of the heat and airlessness despite all the doors and windows being open. Ives applied hot fomentations to his back and arms and gave him more purgatives to expel bile. He became drowsy and 'stimulating poultices' were applied to his feet. 'The room was also fumigated with lemons and vinegar', recorded Ives, 'but, alas! all was to no purpose, for on Tuesday, the 16th between 8 and 9 in the morning, to our unspeakable grief, he died and a putrefaction came on to such a degree that in a few hours the body was in an entire state of corruption.'[70]

Admiral Watson was interred next day in the burial-ground of St John's Church,[*] his cortège followed by Admiral Pocock, who was to succeed to his command, and Colonel Clive, most of the British officers and merchants, military and civilian French prisoners and thousands of Indians and Armenians. 'Nor was there an individual among them all that did not shed a tear', wrote Ives. 'In a word, no man ever lived more esteemed, or died more regretted than Admiral Watson.'[71]

The admiral was said to have left a fortune of £600,000, amassed in India, while 'Admiral Pocock is also very rich and the other naval officers are also so in proportion',[72] and Clive was sending huge sums to London through Dutch merchants. Bengal was now secure for the production of wealth, be it for the East India Company or for individuals. It could only be threatened by French naval, or military, intervention, but the latter would involve long, dangerous, cross-country marches from the Carnatic past the British base at Madras. So it was from the sea that the threat would come.

Admiral Pocock hoisted his flag as Commander-in-Chief of His Majesty's Naval Forces in the East Indies, aware that a French fleet was soon likely to appear in the Indian Ocean. He assembled his officers and told those who had been Watson's protégés that they could now regard him as their patron. Yet the rivalry and venality that pervaded the European settlements arose again when Pocock heard that Watson's death would disqualify his heirs from his share in the huge payments that were to be made to senior officers by the Nawab they had installed. He wrote to Clive, who replied, putting the Navy into his own perspective: 'All the world acknowledges Mr Watson's great services and, if he has been the chief instrument in recovering the Company's settlements, give me leave, Sir, to say the land forces have been the Chief Instruments in effecting the late revolution.' As to the distribution of the booty, which was to be in two instalments, he continued: 'If this is to be looked on as a matter of Right, I am willing to let the Law decide it. If otherwise, I cannot command the property of others but, as far as I am concerned, I will readily give up for the service of Mr Watson's family as I always had a great esteem for that family.'[73]

Clive was as good as his word and he and four members of the Select Committee agreed to pay Watson's family 10 per cent of the 'Nawab's Bounty'. However, six other councillors decided that Watson was disqualified by his death and Governor Drake was only willing to pay the percentage from the first of the two instalments. Pocock was outraged, writing a detailed complaint to the Admiralty 'whereby their Lordships will see in what manner they have treated a man, who has all along acted with so much disinterestedness in giving up his share of everything taken at Calcutta belonging to the Company and individuals without appropriating one farthing for himself or the squadron'.[74]

Pocock went on to report that his squadron was hardly fit for sea, let alone action. He wrote:

The Seamen continue sickly and greatly reduced by Death; four hundred remain now at the Hospital. The *Cumberland's* Leak is increased much … She now makes 32 Inches [of] Water every two hours in this smooth River and I much doubt whether she will continue serviceable during the Summer Season and am very apprehensive that a Gale of Wind, or high Sea, would render her in very great danger.[75]

But the French would be in the Indian Ocean and all risks had to be accepted, so he embarked and gave the order to weigh anchor. His ships began to move down the river towards the open sea.

'Lions breaking from their chains'

Although Vice-Admiral the Honourable Edward Boscawen had, as a Lord Commissioner of the Admiralty, signed the order for the court-martial of Admiral Byng and, as Commander-in-Chief, Portsmouth, that for his execution, he had tried to distance himself from the tragedy. He had not liked Byng and had condemned his conduct off Minorca as unworthy, suspecting him of cowardice.

The son of the first Viscount Falmouth, who had won his peerage in politics, he was married to the charming, intellectual Fanny, a friend of David Garrick, Sir Joshua Reynolds and Dr Samuel Johnson, who had remarked, when dining with her and her friends, that life had no greater pleasure to offer. Boscawen was, after Anson, the most celebrated fighting admiral, with supreme self-confidence arising from his background. He had fought in the West and East Indies, the Mediterranean and the Atlantic; under Vernon at Porto Bello and in several successful actions; he had failed significantly, however, in the Indian Ocean when, in 1748, he had failed to take Pondicherry. In the action off Cape Finisterre he had been wounded in the neck, which caused him to hold his head slightly askew, earning him the nickname 'wry-necked Dick'. Appointed to the Board of Admiralty in 1751, he had, four years later, been given command of a squadron and the task of intercepting a troop convoy bound for Canada from France, with whom Britain was not then at war. The pre-emptive aggression had, as Lord Hardwicke had put it, been 'too little, or too much'.[1] Hampered by Atlantic fog, he had captured two French ships, which did not seriously affect the reinforcement but was more than enough to constitute an act of war. So he, too, had reason to welcome an opportunity to prove himself in the global opportunities for action that were offered once war was declared.

When operations were being planned, Boscawen would certainly be considered for the principal naval command, and in 1758 he was. The war had become almost global, from the Ohio to the Ganges. The main opponents were Britain and France, the former having enlisted the support of Prussia and the latter of Austria, Russia and Sweden; while Frederick the Great of Prussia was defending his own territories, the Germanic monarchy of Great Britain was trying to protect its homeland, the tiny state of Hanover, which had become a hostage, trapped in the centre of Europe. But while armies marched and counter-marched and occasionally fought on the Continent, the real cause of the conflict was the scramble for North America, and it suited the British with their long experience of sea power to choose that as the battleground. To this, the theatres of war in the West and East Indies, the Caribbean and the Indian Ocean, both vital to trade, were peripheral.

In North America, the conflict was over territory but the motivation differed. The British saw their colonies on the east coast as an extension of their own national life – William Pitt imagined a British nation spanning the Atlantic – and encouraged settlement. The French saw America – much as the British saw India – as primarily a territory to be harvested, particularly for furs; so, after initial government-sponsored emigration, settlement was neither encouraged nor discouraged. Their trappers and traders ventured far farther afield than the Anglo-Saxons, who were content to confine themselves between the Appalachian mountains and the sea, and they came to know and understand the indigenous Indians.

The consequence of this difference in attitude towards the New World was reflected in population. Whereas nearly half a million British settlers now lived in the east coast colonies and Canada, only about 70,000 French had settled in North America. While the British colonies grew in imitation of the urban and rural patterns that had bred them, the French were scattered along the banks of the St Lawrence river – notably in the city of Quebec – in isolated hamlets to the east and, far to the south, at New Orleans, where the Mississippi flowed into the Gulf of Mexico; elsewhere the French were itinerant, whether in commerce, or soldiering. Both sides raised militia: the French recruited trappers as sharpshooters and forest guerrillas; the British did likewise but were also able to raise regiments, drilled in battlefield tactics, from their well-populated colonies. Then there were the Indians, a million of whom were living across North America and with whom alliances could be made by diplomacy, bribery or coercion.

French enterprise in exploration, which reached west to the Rocky Mountains and north to Hudson Bay, had finally prompted the concept that, if the British could be contained between the mountains and the sea, the rest of that limitless and mostly unexplored territory could become theirs. This would be known as New France.

Already, means of travelling across North America from the Gulf of Mexico to Hudson Bay had been discovered by way of the great rivers, the Mississippi, the Ohio, the Hudson and the St Lawrence and the Great Lakes, with 'portages' for carrying boats and cargoes between the waterways.

Important confluences of rivers and key portages would have to be protected from the British and hostile Indians by the building of forts. The capital of New France was Quebec, a fortified city built on the headland at the junction of the great St Lawrence and the St Charles river, and the mouth of the former was guarded by another fortress-town and naval base at Louisbourg on Cape Breton Island.

All these fortifications would, of course, have to be garrisoned, so, during 1756, Louis-Joseph, Marquis de Montcalm-Gozon, arrived in the St Lawrence with a reinforcement of 3,000 regular troops from France. He was to take command of the armed forces of New France under its Governor-General, the Marquis de Vaudreuil, who had been born a *Quebecois* but seemed the antithesis of the tough, capable French-Canadian; now aged sixty, he was pompous, over-optimistic and, so Montcalm believed, ignorant of military matters. Montcalm himself was aged forty-six – his handsome, Mediterranean looks accentuated by a powdered wig – and a landowner at Candiac in southern France, who had left his château, wife and ten children to continue his military career, which had taken him to war at the age of fifteen. An able soldier and forceful leader, with experience of war in Europe, news of his arrival in America was taken seriously in London. There it was realised that the French, who, in Europe, could be held safely on the far side of the English Channel, could not only corral New England and the other colonies but might even overwhelm them from New France. Action had to be taken.

The British and the French had been fighting each other spasmodically in North America for more than a century. Neither government took backwoods scrimmages seriously but, occasionally, one side or the other took action that could not be ignored, whether or not it fell within the formalities of declared war. One of the two most significant actions had been the British capture of the newly built Louisbourg in 1745, only for it to be returned three years later under the Peace of Aix-la-Chapelle, which ended the eight years of the War of the Austrian Succession. The other, ten years later, was the sending of an expeditionary force from England and then inland from New York, to storm Fort Duquesne.[*] Commanded by a Guards officer, Major-General Edward Braddock, a hot-tempered duellist, a force of 1,300, including two regular battalions of East Anglian infantry, set out. They struggled for 100 miles through the forests and swamps and across mountains, hacking a path for their gun-limbers and wagon train, for 19 days, watched and reported to the French by unseen Indian scouts. Just short of their objective, they were ambushed by the French and the Indians and, floundering among the trees, trying to form tight ranks for a formal battle, nearly 500 of them were killed. Those captured by the Indians were tortured to death, including eight women; one of these was Braddock's mistress, who was seized from the French-Canadians who were trying to save her, stripped, used as a target for arrows and finally killed and eaten. Braddock himself was killed, but amongst the survivors was the efficient and ruthless militia officer from Virginia named George Washington.[*]

The possibilities of a worldwide theatre of war fired William Pitt's imagination and he began to surround himself with those who could share his global vision. To the west, his thoughts could reach across the Atlantic and beyond the Mississippi to the Great Plains and the far mountains; to the east, beyond the mountains and plains of India to the colonies of the Dutch and the Spanish – both potential enemies – on the way to China and even farther afield.

In mounting a global war, Pitt had as his naval and military chiefs of staff George Anson and Jean-Louis Ligonier. Lord Anson, now aged fifty and a sombre, silent man, had become famous for his global circumnavigation and was well suited to the planning of a world war, but the decisive part he had played in the persecution and execution of Admiral Byng had, in the eyes of many, left a stain on an otherwise brilliant career. General Ligonier, who was appointed Commander-in-Chief of the British Army and raised to the peerage in 1757, was, as his name implied, French, albeit of Huguenot descent, and a naturalised Englishman. He had been a dashing officer under the Dukes of Marlborough and Cumberland and had commanded the last-ditch defences that would have faced Prince Charles Edward and the Scottish invaders had they advanced beyond Derby in 'The Forty-Five' rebellion. He had never married but had had several children by a mistress and, although now aged nearly eighty, was known as a lively companion and an energetic, imaginative soldier. Importantly, he was not rigidly tied to the formalities of European soldiering, realising that this would often be inappropriate in the principal theatre of operations, North America, where there were almost no roads and most fighting would take place amongst trees. There, transport would be by water, and he shared Anson's faith in amphibious warfare, using the mobility offered by command of the sea to surprise the enemy by landing troops where they were not expected.

It was these three men – Pitt, Anson and Ligonier – who became the architects of the very first world war. It was they who now picked the most imaginative and vigorous naval and military officers to lead the main offensive in the campaign they would have to fight in North America. The senior naval commander, responsible for shipping expeditionary forces across the Atlantic and maintaining their supplies of weapons, ammunition and reinforcements, for destroying enemy naval forces and for conducting amphibious operations, was to be Admiral Boscawen, who was as much a man of intellect as of action.

The aim, decided upon in 1757, was to eliminate New France by three co-ordinated but widely separated attacks. Two would be expeditions aimed at the capital and heartland, Quebec. One of these, commanded by Boscawen himself, would first take Louisbourg, which commanded the mouth of the St Lawrence, then move upriver to attack the great fortified city itself. The other would move north from New York to Albany, where a strong force was already in place, then continue up the two long lakes, the 30 miles of St Sacrement (as it was called by the French, or Lake George by the British) and Lake Champlain, running more than 100 miles towards the St Lawrence, Montreal and Quebec; this would involve an attack on the French fort of Carillon, otherwise known by its Indian name of Ticonderoga, at the junction of the two lakes. The third and lesser offensive would be by a smaller expedition to Fort Duquesne, aimed both at expunging the disgrace of Braddock's defeat and at breaking the inland chain of French forts with a breach through which a move westward towards the Great Lakes and the Great Plains could eventually be made.

The command and composition of the Fort Duquesne operation was straightforward. It would consist of some 5,000 men – a Highland regiment, a battalion of the Royal Americans (the 60th Rifles) and 4,000 provincial troops – and be led by Brigadier John Forbes of the Scots Greys, who, although past sixty, had shown a flair for bush fighting, encouraged his light infantry to dress like Indians and remembered the lessons taught to the late General Braddock. This would proceed at its own speed, independently of the other two, which would be unaffected should it fail.

The two-pronged offensive against Quebec would be on the grand scale. Early in January, 1758, Pitt, Anson and Ligonier, meeting under the high, coffered ceiling of the committee room overlooking Horse Guards Parade in London, issued their first orders. Sixteen sail of the line would be made ready to sail with Boscawen for Canadian waters, where they would be joined by another seven from Halifax. To these 23 ships, appropriate numbers of frigates would be added, together with sufficient transports to carry 12,000 troops across the Atlantic, or from the American colonies.

The military commander would be General Jeffrey Amherst, who had been recalled from Germany to replace the ineffectual Lord Loudoun as Commander-in-Chief in North America. A tough and experienced soldier of forty, Amherst had made his name as an administrator and as a sound, if unadventurous, commander. His craggy, humorous face and easy manner seemed to ensure that he would remain not only on good terms with his fellow-commanders – and Boscawen was also known as a difficult, opinionated man – but with the touchy, sometimes resentful colonists. The dash necessary for storming fortified cities would be provided by his brigadiers, notably James Wolfe, a tall, thin oddity of thirty-one, whose record belied his curious looks.

The other wing of the advance on Quebec, via the two lakes, would involve a force of about 15,000 men, some 6,000 of these regular infantry and artillery, the rest, provincials and locally recruited rangers for scouting and forest-fighting. Their commander would be Major-General James Abercromby, also known as an efficient administrator but a slow and uninspiring commander, described by Brigadier Wolfe as seeming to be an old gentleman, infirm in body and mind. Aged fifty-two, he was described by Rufus Putnam, one of the young American soldiers he would command, as 'an old man and frequently called granny';[2] another nickname was 'Aunt Nambycromby'. But an administrator would be needed to move such an army by an armada of boats up the lengths of the two lakes; the fighting could be left to the most promising young British officer in North America, Brigadier (now to be acting Major-General) George Augustus, Viscount Howe.

The eldest, at thirty-three, of three able brothers – Richard was a captain in the Navy and had commanded a ship in Canadian waters, and William was to lead his regiment in the Louisbourg expedition – George Howe did not cut the haughty, aristocratic figure that was expected of his title and rank. He had a rounded, countryman's face, a humorous mouth, alert, candid eyes and originality of mind. He had served in Flanders but had made his name in America, where, when commanding a battalion of the Royal Americans, he had taken to bush warfare with enthusiasm. He had been on patrol with the rangers raised by Major Robert Rogers, the New Hampshire frontiersman, to learn, and then teach, the skills of camouflage, tracking and forest tactics with which to fight Indians.

He quickly saw how ill-fitted in training and dress for forest warfare were the British regulars. Tactics were still based on tight drill in the lines, columns or squares of European battlefields, designed to bring concentrated musket-fire to bear on similar enemy formations. The principal weapon was the 'Brown Bess' musket, which could be loaded and fired three times a minute but was inaccurate beyond 50 yards (46 metres) and cumbersome, with a barrel 4 feet (1.2 metres) long. The dress was for show, as a Sergeant Anton said on arrival in North America:

> Our uniform was made so tight that we almost stood like automata of wood, mechanically arranged for exhibition on a large scale. To stoop was more than our small clothes were worth, buttons flying, knees bursting, back parts rending and the long, heavy groan when we stood up, just like an old, gouty, corpulent man after stooping to pick up his fallen crutch.[3]

So Howe ordered his British infantry to discard wigs and crop their hair, cut their coats short and discard unnecessary equipment, wear green, or brown, jackets as camouflage and thick leggings as protection against brambles. 'You would laugh to see the droll figure we all make', one officer wrote home.

> Regulars as well as provincials have cut their coats so as scarcely to reach their waists. No officer or private is allowed to carry more than one blanket and a bearskin. A small portmanteau is allowed each officer. No women follow the camp to wash our linen. Lord Howe has already shown an example by going to the brook and washing his own.[4]

Gradually, Howe lessened the fear of the beautiful, desolate country where they had come to wage war; the fear of the dead silence of the forest that might be broken by the cry of a bird that might, in truth, be an Indian. When it was, the braves flitted through the forest with shrill whoops and yells, their hard, almost naked bodies smeared with paint and feathers in their plaited hair. They, and not the French, were the feared enemy. Those who had escaped massacre before Fort Duquesne told nightmare stories of the torture that captives could expect. Now, this aristocrat from England was teaching the fearful young soldiers how to fight the Indian with his own tactics, confidence grew and the fear began to ease.

Howe was an attractive man with lively good looks and an easy manner. As significantly as his adoption of unconventional tactics, he used his charm and social rank to break down the British regulars' prejudice against American provincials by making friends with them himself. William Pitt had described him as 'a character of ancient times: a complete model of military virtue', while Wolfe, who came second to Howe in the esteem of those who understood modern warfare, declared that he was 'the noblest Englishman that has appeared in my time and the best soldier in the Army'.[5]

At the beginning of February, Boscawen was ready to sail from Portsmouth and, on the 12th, an unexpected visitor arrived from London. Post-haste, down the road taken by Augustus Hervey a year before, came an Admiralty official accompanying a sea-captain from America, the master of a merchantman trading between North American ports and in the St Lawrence. Such was this man's knowledge of those coasts and, particularly, of Quebec itself and Louisbourg, that, when his ship had been taken by the French, he had not been exchanged for a French captain but detained on the direct orders of Montcalm. Three years later, he had been put aboard a ship bound for France, to be held there until the end of the war. During the Atlantic passage, he, the only foreigner on board, had been admitted to the officers' cabin for meals, and in the relaxed atmosphere of a long voyage, had been present when the captain had packed a waterproof bundle of despatches into a weighted canvas bag, explaining that if the ship was in danger of being captured by the British it was to be thrown overboard.

Nearing France, the ship had put into Vigo Bay, anchoring close to British ships trading with the neutral port, to provision and for her captain to ask the Spanish authorities about the whereabouts of British naval patrols. There,

One night, seizing the opportunity of all, except the watch on deck, being sound asleep, he took the packet out of the bag; and, having fixed it in his mouth, he silently let himself down into the bay and, to prevent noise by swimming, floated on his back into the wake of the British ships; where, laying hold of the hauser, he called for assistance, and was immediately taken on board.

The British captain had read the contents of the package and, realising it to be of 'the greatest importance in regard to our success in North America', had sent him overland to Lisbon where he was put on board a sloop of the Royal Navy. On arrival at Falmouth, he had been sent to London, where he was questioned at the Admiralty and rewarded. Then he was sent to Portsmouth and 'immediately introduced to Admiral Boscawen',[6] who added him to his staff and took him back to North America.

Boscawen sailed on 19 February, 1758, with ten ships of the line. As one fine 'seventy-four', the *Invincible*, got under way from St Helen's roads off the Isle of Wight, she snagged her anchor, her rudder jammed and the strong wind blew her onto Dean Sands; for three days she was stuck fast and, although her ship's company were taken off, she finally capsized and became a total loss.[*] A replacement was found, but the admiral also had to provide escorts for four troop convoys from Portsmouth and Cork and ordnance convoys bound for New York and Halifax. Boscawen's squadron brought up the rear of this procession, but bad weather so delayed them that a passage that should have lasted a month took nearly three. 'From Christopher Columbus's time to our own days, there perhaps has never been a more extraordinary voyage', wrote Brigadier Wolfe, who was a passenger in the flagship. 'The continual opposition of contrary winds, calms or currents, baffled all our skill and wore out all our patience. A fleet of men-of-war, well-manned, unencumbered with transports, commanded by an officer of the first reputation, has been 11 weeks in its passage.'[7] On 9 May, Boscawen finally anchored off Halifax.

Meanwhile, Abercromby's force, destined for the inland advance up the Hudson and the line of the lakes, was already in North America. With his headquarters at Albany, he drew his 6,367 regulars from New York and the other garrisons and 9,024 provincials from Massachusetts, Connecticut, New Jersey and New York. The regulars were seasoned, and the provincials acclimatised troops, accustomed to the heat, mosquitoes, blackflies and rattlesnakes of the American summer; they had heard of the terrors of Indian warfare, the arrow and the scalping-knife. Amongst them were veterans of the spasmodic fighting of the past decade, including some who had fought before Fort Duquesne.

One of the latter was the cantankerous Captain Charles Lee of the 44th Foot,[11] aged twenty-six, a survivor of Braddock's expedition, whose lean body, lined face and down-turned mouth marked him as a cynical veteran of wilderness warfare. After the disaster of 1755, he had been posted to the Mohawk Valley, where he had, apparently, married a chief's daughter and been accorded the Indian name *Ounewaterika*, or 'Boiling Water', because of his temper. Lee despised the staff officers and aides-de-camp who surrounded

General Abercromby as much as he admired Lord Howe, thanks 'to whose Vigilance and Caution the Indians with all their Ingenuity, Finesses and Perseverance had not been able in the space of several months to steal off a single sentinel, by which means (for the first time) the French were totally debarr'd from Intelligence'.[8]

By early June, Abercromby's army had assembled at the southern end of Lake George around Fort William Henry. Only three years old, and built on the site of a military encampment pitched there a decade before, the little fort was already ruined and bloodstained. The year before, the Marquis de Montcalm had led a strong force of French regulars and Indians down the lake from Ticonderoga at the northern end and attacked it. After three days, the garrison of some 600 provincials from New York had surrendered and marched out to be disarmed with courteous formality by the French. But their Indian allies had broken open the fort's store of alcohol and the prisoners had rashly tried to ingratiate themselves by offering them rum from their canteens. An Indian had whooped a war-cry and the helpless prisoners, their wives and their children had been butchered with tomahawk and scalping-knife. Montcalm had tried to intervene, baring his own chest and shouting to the berserk Indians, 'Since you are rebellious children, who break the promise you have given to your father, kill him first.'[9] They had not listened, or heard. When 200 had been killed and mutilated, the survivors had been herded towards Montreal, where they were ransomed for two kegs of brandy a man, but only after one had been killed, cooked and forcibly fed to his fellows.

Now a new and powerful British army had assembled. Lord Howe, acting on the advice of Major Rogers, the commander of the rangers, drew up further rulings on dress, weapons and tactics. Regimental colours were to be left behind and officers were to discard their distinguishing sashes. Shiny musket-barrels were to be smeared with mud and red ribbons tied round the muzzles of the friendly Indians' muskets for quick identification in the forest. Rations of salt pork, dried peas, flour and butter were to be on the same scale for all ranks and every man was to carry 30 pounds of meal as 'iron rations' in his pack.

While waiting at the lakeside, strict discipline was imposed, and any man caught gambling was liable to a mandatory punishment of 300 lashes. Meanwhile, the infantry held target-practice, particularly with the new rifles of American design, ten of which had been issued to each regiment.

While the army waited and when all was ready, Lord Howe invited some officers to dine in his tent. On arrival, the guests, expecting the etiquette of a formal dinner party, were surprised to find logs instead of chairs and bearskins instead of a carpet. A servant brought in a large dish of pork and peas and Howe produced from his pocket a small leather sheath, from which he drew a knife and fork, remarking, 'Is it possible, gentlemen, that you have come on this campaign without providing yourselves with what is necessary?'[10] He thereupon presented each of them with a similar knife and fork.

By the beginning of July, Abercromby had assembled a fleet of 900 rowing *bateaux*, and 135 whaleboats bought at Cape Cod, Martha's Vineyard and Nantucket the previous year, rowed up the Hudson and then hauled over the portage to Lake George. There were numbers of heavy flatboats for carrying artillery, three floating batteries, and a big sailing raft, named the *Invincible*, which would mount nine 12-pounder guns and serve as the general's flagship; there was also an extraordinary roofed gunboat 52 feet (15.8 metres) long called the *Land Tortoise*, which was powered by both oars and sails. The only warship recognisable as such was the sloop *Halifax*, which had been sunk during the siege, a year before, and salvaged; she was to bring up the rear of the armada. Some of the craft proved leaky, one boat sank when loaded with 100 barrels of gunpowder, and a raft foundered beneath the weight of two 10-inch mortars.

Finally, all was ready and, on 4 July, the Reverend John Cleaveland, chaplain to the 3rd Massachusetts Regiment, held a service by the lakeside and noted in his diary: 'After another psalm, I gave a word of exhortation and dismissed them with a Blessing. This day we have orders to be in readiness to strike our tents at daybreak and to be on board the battoes by five in the morning.'[11] Next morning, the army paraded in brilliant sunshine, and to the sound of drums and trumpets and the squeal of bagpipes, marched past General Abercromby and down to the beach where the boats awaited and clambered aboard for the voyage of 30 miles up the lake. The spectacle of a seemingly invincible army embarking on a fine summer's day for a voyage down the length of a lake amongst wooded hills towards a battle which they would surely win – they had been told that they would outnumber the enemy by four to one – was inspiring.

But there was one officer, Major Duncan Campbell of Inverawe, second-in-command of the kilted Scottish regiment, the 42nd Foot who was looking strained and apprehensive. The reason for this was well known amongst his brother-officers, who were doing what they could to cheer him. Major Campbell's story was a strange one. As laird of Inverawe in the Western Highlands, he had, many years before, been alone in his small and lonely castle one night when there had come an urgent knocking on the door. He had opened it to a panting, bloodstained man who begged for shelter, saying that he had killed a man in a fight and was being pursued and in danger of his life. Such were the Highland customs of hospitality that Campbell had admitted him and agreed to hide him. Even then, the fugitive made him swear on his dirk that he would not betray him when his pursuers arrived as they doubtless would. No sooner had he done so, when there was another knocking on the door and Campbell opened it to two armed men, who had told him that his own cousin, Donald, had been killed and they were hunting his murderer. Mindful of his oath, he had denied knowledge of any fugitive, sent them away and gone to bed. That night, his dead cousin had appeared in a dream and proclaimed, 'Inverawe! Inverawe! Blood has been shed. Shield not the murderer!'

Campbell had told the fugitive that he could no longer remain in the castle but, being bound by his oath, had shown him a cave in the mountainside where he could hide. The following night the phantom had again appeared in a dream and repeated its command. Campbell had returned to the cave to find the fugitive had gone. On the third night, the ghost had returned again and this time declared, 'Inverawe, Inverawe! Farewell till we meet at Ticonderoga!'[12] The name had meant nothing to Campbell at the time but, years later, long after he had been commissioned and promoted to major, drafted to America, then been sent from New York to Albany and finally to Fort William Henry, he had found out what it meant.

The great fleet of boats six miles long began its progress up the lake, seeming to cover the two miles of its width. The day was perfect, with the sun shining from a blue sky reflected in the glassy lake and the billowing tops of oak, ash, maple, hickory, elm, birch, dogwood and fir rising on the foothills of the Adirondacks to the west and spreading east to the Green Hills of Vermont. The armada moved slowly forward in seven divisions, each of 16 columns. It was led by a large flatboat followed by 40 smaller boats all manned by Gage's Regiment, looking almost like Indians in brown buckskin. Then came Abercromby's flagship, the *Invincible*, followed by 12 rafts, mounting cannon, and the *Land Tortoise*. Immediately astern of these followed a double column of boats loaded with the artillery, ammunition, engineers, provisions, a field hospital, sutlers and a raft loaded with horses, and the sloop *Halifax* bringing up the rear. A double column of boats in six divisions each transported an infantry regiment – the 17th, the 55th (Montgomery's Highlanders), the 42nd (the Royal Highlanders, or the Black Watch), the 27th (the Iniskillings) and the 1st Royal Americans. To the right of them was another double column in five divisions carrying the rangers, the grenadiers and the rest of the infantry. On the left flank of the fleet moved another five divisions with the bulk of the provincial infantry embarked. Every division flew its flag from the bow of the commanding officer's boat, while the sun lit the red coats and white cross-belts of the English, the embroidered, mitre-shaped caps of the grenadiers, the plaids of the Highlanders and the blue of the provincials' uniforms; their bands played, the wail of the pipes carrying across the water to the hills, evoking memories of the Highlands and a melancholy at odds with the martial splendour. Even the unorthodox ranger Major Rogers found it 'a splendid military show',[13] and another declared, 'I never beheld so delightful a prospect.'[14]

The gentle voyage lasted until five in the afternoon, when, at a signal, the leading craft drew in to beach in the lee of Sabbath Day Point, two-thirds of the way up the lake. The entire army disembarked for a meal, then re-embarked and, by n at night, resumed the voyage by moonlight and, in silence. Before re-embarking, camp fires had been lit to give the impression that the army had remained ashore, but the French knew that the British were on their way. At two o'clock on the fifth day of the month, the first news had reached Montcalm at Fort Carillon that the force had set out from Fort William Henry, and he had begun to organise his defence. In and around the fort were 3,500 regular French troops, too many to be contained within the fort and too few to meet Abercromby's army on an open battlefield. However, Montcalm decided to make his stand in the woods west of Ticonderoga, where the outlet from Lake Champlain ran into Lake George. This linking river was impassable to boats, curving through the forest for more than a mile and tumbling down a series of rapids. Fort Carillon would be the final defence and, if that fell, Montcalm could retreat 17 miles up Lake Champlain to another stone fortress at Crown Point on the west bank.

The British army was to land on a sandy beach just out of sight from Fort Carillon and, led by rangers, advance through the forest, then either cross the bridge over the river by a sawmill, or strike inland to cross a narrower stream and so outflank the probable enemy position. All seemed to have gone well and Parson Cleaveland wrote in his diary:

> My heart was much inclined to pour out Desires to the God of Heaven that he would appear for us and intimidate the Enemy and it is wonderful how God appeared for us, for though the Enemy had four battalions in the advanced guard and several cannon, yet by nine o'clock in the morning we were all safely landed: the French only fired a few Small Arms, which did no harm, and then run off.[15]

It would be too dangerous to go ashore by the mouth of the channel linking the two lakes, and at the foot of the portage path. This cut across a loop in its course and crossed it again by a bridge at a sawmill below a waterfall; it was certain to be strongly defended. So the flatboats were beached on the western shore of the lake where they could not be seen from the ramparts of Fort Carillon. As soon as their bows touched the beach, Rogers's rangers leapt ashore, sent a French infantry picket running into the woods and raced after them through the trees. Colonel Gage's light infantry and 500 'battoe men', commanded by Colonel John Bradstreet, followed, forming into four columns along the same line of advance. Howe then chose the inland option of cutting through the forest on the west bank of the channel, crossing a small tributary called the Trout Brook to take the French he assumed would be defending the bridge in the rear. The rest of the army would be on shore by midday and could then follow the portage, cross the bridge and fight the French at Ticonderoga itself.

After pushing for about a mile through the undergrowth and fallen trees that choked the woods, the rangers, led by Rogers, took the lead. Following, but out of sight, came 200 more rangers with Lord Howe and Major Israel Putnam at their head. They had lost contact with all other formations but heard the sound of running water and rightly assumed it was the Trout Brook that they planned to cross. Ahead of them and also out of sight in the trees, some 500 French commanded by a Captain Trepezec had taken up positions on either bank of the stream to guard the head of the portage to the sawmill bridge. Finding themselves outflanked by the wide arc of the British advance, the 350 on the east bank retreated to the bridge, while those on the west took to the woods and were as blinded by undergrowth as their opponents. As both sides groped through the forest, they met. *'Qui vive?'* called a Frenchman. *'Français!'* came the reply, in an English accent that did not deceive. Howe led his men forward and, as Rogers reported, 'broke the enemy and hemmed them in on every side ... advancing with great intrepidity and eagerness upon them'.[16] There were volleys and rifle-shots and David Perry, a sixteen-year-old militiaman from Massachusetts, said later that 'whistling of balls and the roar of musquetry terrified me not a little'.[17] A British officer staggered and fell, a bullet through his heart. It was Lord Howe.

The first and most crucial death was only seen by a few. Cleaveland, with his provincials, just jotted in his diary: 'There was a smart engagement for about an hour, my Lord Howe was killed and about four men missing.'[18] For the rest, the light infantry faltered and took cover behind trees, while the rangers put their training to use, surrounded the French and almost annihilated them. As Howe's body was carried down to the waterside, his aide-de-camp, Captain Alexander Monypenny, saw that 'scarce an eye was free from tears'.[19]

A report of the action was sent back to General Abercromby at the beachhead and the news that Lord Howe had been killed spread quickly through the columns with shocking effect. 'The fall of this noble and brave officer', said Major Rogers, 'seemed to produce an almost general languour and consternation through the whole army.'[20] Major Thomas Mante, an engineer, was to conclude: 'In Lord Howe, the soul of General Abercromby's army seemed to expire. His enterprising spirit infused a noble ardour into every rank ... From the unhappy moment the General was deprived of his advice, neither order nor discipline was observed and a strange kind of infatuation usurped the place of resolution.'[21]

While the British army stood paralysed by the news, Montcalm was only aware of his own initial defeat. Of his infantry trapped by the rangers, nearly 150 had been killed, or drowned trying to swim the channel to safety, about the same number taken prisoner and some 50 had struggled back to Ticonderoga. Expecting more such blows, he ordered that the bridge by the sawmill be destroyed and his whole force concentrated around the grey stone walls of Fort Carillon. This stood at the point of a peninsula with Lake Champlain on one side and the channel from Lake George on the other, its guns commanding the shores of both. The fort itself being too small a defensive work, an officer named Hugues had, a few weeks earlier, suggested that a strong defensive position could be constructed about half a mile from the fort on a high ridge, which fell away steeply to the Lake George outfall on one side and to low ground on the other. Two French engineers, Pontleroy and Desandrouin, had already made rough plans for defences to span this ridge and a battalion of infantry had been put to work digging a rough trench across it. Now Montcalm saw that it was not only a strong position but the only one that offered any hope of success against such odds and, at dawn on the morning of 7 July, ordered his entire force to work on building it with the utmost urgency.

Had Lord Howe been alive, the British would doubtless have rushed the bridge and caught the French with arms piled and spades and axes in hand. As it was, his death had not only brought immediate apathy but confusion and demoralisation compounded, as Captain Lee put it, 'thro' ignorance of the Wood'. He continued: 'An Indian War-Cry was heard on our Flanks; the consequence of it was that some provincials and rangers fired upon each other in confusion.'[22] Abercromby, as stunned as the rest by Howe's loss, had kept his whole army under arms all night and at dawn withdrawn it to the beachhead. There they re-embarked and were landed on the far bank of the channel near the head of the portage. Having left most of his 40 cannon in the boats, a strong British force -- Lee's 44th Foot, six companies of the Royal Americans and 4,000 provincials with two field-guns – captured the sawmill, where the retreating French had destroyed the bridge, within a mile of Fort Carillon. They rebuilt the bridge, crossed and on the afternoon of the 7th camped nearby on the low ground below and to the north-west of the heights of Ticonderoga. That evening the British were joined by the brave and eccentric Sir William Johnson, of New York, the commissioner for Indian affairs, who had recruited more than 400 warriors as guides and scouts. As darkness fell, Cleaveland prudently 'lodged in a Batto and lay very hard upon the barrels'.[23]

Above them on the ridge, the French worked through the night. Seven of Montcalm's eight regular regiments were given a sector of the defences to build, planted their colours, stripped to the waist and, officers labouring beside their men, dug earthworks and felled trees. There would be no time to construct formal defences, so all would depend upon building a great wall of logs. This was sited in a zig-zag line for enfilading musket and grapeshot fire and was open at the rear to the road from Fort Carillon. Massive tree-trunks, some 3 feet (0.9 metres) thick, were piled in a revetted wall 9 feet high, pierced with loopholes and surmounted by sods of earth and sandbags. 'They took care to cut down monstrous oak trees, which covered all the ground from the front of their breastwork about the distance of a cannon shot every way in their front'[24], Scottish officer noted. In the words of an officer from Massachusetts, the forest looked as if it had been blown flat by a hurricane. The lopped branches were dragged around to face an oncoming enemy and sharpened stakes driven into the ground amongst them, to be described as looking like the bristling quills of a porcupine. Infantry assaulting the position would have to mount the steep, wooded slopes, cross open ground under fire and clamber through the spiky thickets of outward-facing branches and stakes before attempting to scale the sheer wall of logs.

The British were silent with grief and depression at the death of Howe, but some Scottish officers tried to cheer Major Campbell, who was further sunk in gloom by the apparent realisation of the prophecy in his dream. They assured him that the place they had reached was not named Ticonderoga, but Fort George. It was to no avail, and next morning a haggard Campbell of Inverawe came into the mess tent and told them, 'I have seen him! You have deceived me! He came into my tent last night. This is Ticonderoga! I shall die today.'[25]

Early on the morning of 8 July, General Abercromby held a meeting of his staff and regimental commanders. There were several options. One that Howe would probably have advocated was a daring move through the woods around both the enemy's flanks to strike through the lightly held ground between the log wall and Fort Carillon. Another would be to contain the French with a covering force and march past Fort Carillon to Crown Point, the fort covering narrows farther up Lake Champlain, and from there blockade Montcalm until his food stocks were exhausted. A third would be to open a long-range bombardment from some high ground, commanding a stretch of the French defences. For a quicker decision, he could drag his guns forward over the next couple of days and blow the log wall to splinters before mounting an infantry assault.

But Abercromby was worried. French prisoners had told him that Montcalm's force numbered 6,000 and that 3,000 regular reinforcements were about to arrive from the north. This estimate of the garrison was almost double its actual strength of seven regiments behind the new breastwork and an eighth on their right flank; some reinforcements were on their way and the first 100 of them reached the French lines that day. But Abercromby had lost confidence and wanted an immediate decision. He had sent an engineer officer forward to study the French defences; this was, in fact, a commissioned 'sub-engineer', Lieutenant Matthew Clark, who had only six months' service and was taking the place of Colonel James Montresor, the chief engineer, who was ill and another experienced engineer officer with whom Abercromby had had an argument. He had reported that the defences looked flimsy and could not only be taken by infantry assault without artillery preparation but could probably be pushed over by the soldiers' shoulders. Several experienced officers, Lee amongst them, urged that guns should be dragged up a nob of high ground named Rattlesnake Hill, from which they should be able to batter a breach in the log wall. Abercromby ignored them but, on reflection, allowed two field-guns to be sited there.

On the morning of 8 July, 1758 – three years less a day since Braddock's little army had been cut to pieces in the woods before Fort Duquesne – the powerful British and American army before Ticonderoga waited in the mounting heat of the summer sun, bemused and virtually leaderless, for their commanding general to make his decision. Finally, he did so. There was to be a frontal assault by infantry without waiting for artillery support; it was to be made with bayonet and sword and 'the troops ... received strict orders that no one should presume to fire till he was within the breastwork'.[26] The whole army excepting the artillery, which remained on the beach, paraded by regiments and divisions and marched to the tap of drums towards the foot of the wooded heights. As usual, the rangers and light infantry led the way, followed by the provincials and, last, the regulars. Then Abercromby decided that the assault would be made by his regular infantry and that they should move forward between the provincial battalions for the attack. Despite the loss of Howe, an undefined over-confidence now prevailed and, as one officer put it, 'We were one and all infatuated by the notion of carrying every obstacle by a mere *coup de* mousqueterie'[27] – but that could only be delivered after the log wall had been scaled.

'What a glorious situation was this!' was Captain Lee's reaction.

In short, everything had so charming an aspect that without being much elated I should have looked upon any Man as a desponding Dastard, who could entertain any doubt of our Success. Little did we dream that it was still in the power of One Blunderer to render all these favourable, promising Circumstances abortive ... Fortune and the pusillanimity of the French had cram'd Victory into his mouth but he contrived to spit it out again.[28]

Lee described how an engineer officer and an aide-de-camp had been sent on reconnaissance. 'What their report was I cannot tell but the regulars were immediately order'd to march through the intervals of the provincials and, with bayonets fixed, attack the Enemy's Lines, which were thrown up before the fort and under their Cannon. The Attack was accordingly made with the most perfect Regularity, Coolness and Resolution.' The two guns had been hauled up Rattlesnake Hill but the order to fire was not given, which, remarked Lee, 'one would imagine must have occur'd to any Blockhead, who was not so far sunk in Idiotism as to be oblig'd to wear a Bib and Bells'.[29] Even the unmilitary Cleaveland was amazed: 'The conduct is thought to be marvellously strange to order the entrenchment to be forced with Small Arms when they had cannon not far off and numbers sufficient to keep the enemy off till we had entrenched and placed our cannon and bomb mortars to play upon the Enemy.'[30]

The attack began with the light infantry driving in the French pickets and then, soon after midday, the firing died away and there was silence suddenly broken by the beat of side-drums for the main assault. First, the whole force marched uphill, led by the light infantry, 'Battoe Men' and rangers; the Boston regiments followed in extended order; next the regular regiments in six solid columns; and finally, a rearguard of the Connecticut and New Jersey regiments. Then, led by grenadiers, the first and second waves halted and the red-coated regulars and the kilted Highlanders tramped up the steep slope in their columns, through the sundappled woods to where the forest had been felled by the French.

As Major Mante recorded, 'The regulars advanced with the greatest intrepidity to storm the breastwork, which they now, when it was too late to retreat, found well-covered with felled trees, extending one hundred yards in front with the branches pointing outwards and strengthened with logs, stumps of trees and every other kind of rubbish.' Suddenly, just when the spiked barrier of branches began to break their ranks, the length of the log wall broke into flame and smoke as the French fired. With a cheer, the British surged forward towards the breastwork, men dropping, or being hit, spinning and falling to hang in the branches, 'but, such was their ardour that many of the officers got to the breastwork itself and were killed in attempting to scale it'.[31]

Charles Lee, leading a company, remembered: 'The unevenness and ruggedness of the ground (which was almost made impassable by great fallen trees) and the height of the Breastworks that was at least eight feet, rendered it an absolute impossibility. The fire was prodigiously hot, the Slaughter of the officers very great; almost all wounded; the men still rushing furiously forwards, almost without any leaders.' A provincial from Connecticut remembered one column of regulars, ten deep, reaching the log wall, when they 'fell like pigeons', while another, Private David Perry, saw that 'the ground was strewed with dead and dying' and 'could hear the men screaming and see them dying all around me'.[32] There was no enemy to be seen except when, as one provincial said, 'they raised their hats above the breastwork, which our people fired at; they, having loopholes to fire through … we did them little damage, except shooting their hats to pieces'.[33] At one point a French officer, Captain de Bassignac, waved a red flag above the parapet and the British took it as a sign of surrender and moved forward to accept it, while the French, imagining it was the British who were surrendering, allowed them to approach. Unaware of this confusion, another French officer, Captain Pierre Buchot, ordered a volley and it 'laid two, or three hundred upon the ground'.[34]

Seeing the English regiments snared in the entanglements, 'the Scots Highlanders, impatient for orders … rushed fowards', drawing their claymores to slash at the branches, seeming to an officer of the 55th 'like lions breaking from their chains. Their intrepidity was rather animated than damped by seeing their comrades fall on every side.' But the felled trees 'not only broke our ranks and made it impossible for us to keep an order but put it entirely out of our power to advance until we cut our way through', recalled an officer of the 42nd, 'even those that were mortally wounded cried out aloud to their companions not to mind, or lose a thought upon them, but to follow their officers and to mind the honour of their country'.[35] A piper, mortally hit, propped himself against the stump of a tree and continued to play them forward until he died. Some reached the foot of the log wall and hacked footholds in the tree-trunks. A few climbed to the top and leapt down the far side, led by Captain John Campbell, and were instantly bayoneted.

Falling back, the infantry left the killing-ground before the breastwork strewn with their dead and wounded. Some had sheltered behind tree-stumps, or even beneath the log wall itself, until shot from a loophole. When the survivors of the first assault straggled back into the trees and word was sent to Abercromby at his headquarters by the sawmill that it had failed, he ordered them to try again. That attack failed, too, and they were ordered to try yet again. At five o'clock another assault was launched by English infantry in the centre and, half an hour later, the 42nd Highlanders made another furious assault on the right.

French-Canadian snipers had climbed trees behind the log wall and shot down into the charging Scots, and it was then that Major Duncan Campbell was, as he had expected, mortally wounded.[*] There had been no need to urge the Highlanders forward but now it was difficult to control them, Lieutenant Grant declaring that 'their ardour was such that it was difficult to bring them off'.[36]

The last assault faltered and the survivors stumbled back across the shambles at six o'clock. No more orders came from Abercromby. 'Five hours they persisted in this Diabolical Attempt', wrote Lee, who had himself been badly wounded,

> and at length were obliged to retire, which they did in pretty good order notwithstanding that they were their own Generals. There still remained in our Camp 1,300 Men fit for duty for the kill'd and wounded at the Attack of the Lines amounted to not more than 2,000. All the eminences that commanded the fort were still in our possession, the communicating Lake George was behind us and would not be interrupted. The troops not in the least dispirited but rather seem'd desirous and eager to be again employ'd. No man dream'd of retiring. Nothing was easier than to have erected Batteries that same night for the fort was in reality invested.
>
> But what did the General do? He most shamefully abandon'd these advantageous Posts and retreated to his battoes with so much hurry, precipitation and confusion as to give it entirely the air of a Flight … He threw himself into one of the first boats, row'd off and was almost the earliest Messenger of the Public Loss and his own Infamy. In this manner did 13,000 men, who were not in the last fright, run away from 3,000, who were in the greatest.[37]

General Abercromby had decided that, after nearly six hours fighting at Ticonderoga, his army had 'sustained so considerable a loss, without any prospect of better Success that it was no longer prudent to remain before it'.[38]

It was not failure on the battlefield that finally demoralised the British army but their general's precipitate retreat. The battlefield itself was evacuated,

Lieutenant Grant proudly reporting that 'the remains of the regiment had the honour to cover the retreat of the army ... When shall we have so fine a regiment again?'[39]

But elsewhere morale and discipline collapsed. Private Perry remembered: 'We lay there till near sunset and, not receiving orders from any officer, the men crept off, leaving all the dead and most of the wounded ... We started back to our boats without any orders and pushed out on the Lake for the night.'[40] Others slept on the edge of the battlefield and woke next morning to find 'that the army was chiefly gone', then made their way to the beach down paths littered with dead and wounded so that they 'could hardly walk without treading on them'.[41] Perry's regiment evacuated their own wounded 'but left a great many crying for help, which we were unable to afford them. None of those that we left behind were ever heard of afterwards.'[42] One militiaman from Massachusetts who had been left on the battlefield, covered with leafy branches, was found alive four days later by the French, but they also came across 'a great number of corpses on litters', who had been abandoned.[43] Along the shore, the boats that had carried them up the lake in such splendour were waiting offshore, 15 deep, and guarded by the American Colonel Bradstreet and his 'bateauxmen' to prevent a panicky scramble aboard.

The 9 July was a Sunday but Parson Cleaveland was unable to hold his customary church parade, writing in his diary:

This morning to the General Surprise of the whole of the Army, we were ordered to row back the Battoes, to leave the ground we had possessed and return to Fort William Henry.

We left the ground about 9 o'clock in the morning and arrived at Fort William Henry, a full forty miles, before sun-set; all disgusted, partly on account of our being without much Food for three Days. This evening, Lt. Burnham (hit in the stomach) was buried, having died upon the water of his wound. I understand he enquired for me, hoping to see me before he died, but I was in another Batto and could not be found, the lake being full of them.

On that long day, the men in the boats drank water from the lake, as a result of which Cleaveland noted soon afterwards, 'I began to feel some working in my Bowels and fear I am going to have the Camp Disorder.'

On arrival, all speculated on the fiasco at Ticonderoga, laying the blame on

Abercromby and his reliance on the opinion of the young engineer officer, Lieutenant Clark, who could not defend his disastrous over-optimism because he was among those lying dead before the log wall he had thought so flimsy. Cleaveland noted: 'Lieut. Elver of the 44th told in my hearing this day his solid opinion that the reason why the General ordered the retreat from Ticonderoga was his hearkening to Boys who never saw a fight and that it was felt that he never did ask counsel of any one experienced officer in the Army.'[44] In characteristically abrasive style, Captain Lee wrote of Abercromby:

> what he is employ'd in, heaven only can guess. Captain Cunningham, one of his aides-de-camp and his favourite oracle, was immediately despatched [to New York] with an Account of this Affair. It must be a curious Piece; I would give the World to see it, but am afraid it would require more genius that even he is Master of to trump up a Story which can palliate and soften Blunders so glaring and Conduct so infamous.[45]

When the cost was assessed, the British had suffered more than 1,300 killed, about the same number of wounded (many of whom would die) and some 40 missing. The heaviest casualties in one regiment were in the 42nd Highlanders, who had lost more than 300 killed and about the same number wounded. The French, on the other hand, had lost only 350 killed or wounded, a tenth of their total strength. Understandably, the Marquis de Montcalm wrote home, 'What a day for France!'[46]

As General Abercromby pondered his defeat, more than 600 miles to the north-east Admiral Boscawen was conducting an amphibious operation on a similar scale – albeit from salt water – at Louisbourg. It was reaching its climax. Both attackers and defenders could muster forces roughly similar in strength to those engaged in Ticonderoga: 12,000 British regulars together with sailors and marines against 4,000 or 5,000 French supported by several companies of French-Canadian militia and some Indians. Here, too, the British arrived by water and launched their initial attack from boats. However, where the water of Lake George had at least been placid, the sea off Louisbourg was tossed by Atlantic gales. Indeed, since he had left Portsmouth early in the year, Boscawen had faced one problem after another with the wind and weather.

In planning the co-ordinated attacks in North America, Pitt had hoped the assault on Louisbourg could begin in April. But Boscawen did not reach Halifax with his fleet and troop convoy until 9 May and General Amherst arrived three weeks later. The fleet of 157 sail, with 12,000 troops embarked, finally appeared off the rocky shores of Cape Breton on 2 June.

Seen through unseasonal, drifting fog, Louisbourg itself, on the tip of a low, rocky peninsula, looked as bleak and exposed to the rigours of the Atlantic as it was. Since the beginning of the year, it had been blockaded by a squadron under Rear-Admiral Sir Charles Hardy, but persistent bad weather had continually driven him off-station. A French convoy from Brest had been able to evade him and leave six sail of the line and some frigates in the harbour at Louisbourg, while the transports sailed up the St Lawrence to Quebec.

Boscawen's fleet entered the wide mouth of Garabus Bay – spelled 'Garaboose' by the British – which offered some shelter from north, west and south but none from the easterly gales howling in from the Atlantic. From the heaving deck of his flagship, the 90-gun *Namur* – once a French prize – Boscawen could see his destination. With its grey stone church, barracks and houses huddled behind its fortifications, Louisbourg looked like a Breton town sheltering from ocean storms. Beyond the town, he could see the masts and yards of the ships of the line sheltering in the almost landlocked natural harbour. Beyond that began the endless forests. Then, in Garabus Bay to the west of the town opened a series of three sandy coves between rocky headlands and a fourth to the east; it was there that the army would have to go ashore. However, the gales still thundered out of the Atlantic and heavy seas burst against the rocks and sent surf surging up the beaches: clearly no boat could survive in such conditions, let alone put soldiers ashore on a beach. For five days, rough seas and sometimes 'fog, thick and wet'[47] put any thought of landing out of the question, while it was obvious that, having seen the invasion fleet, the French could make full use of the time to prepare defences.

Boscawen and Amherst could at least plan their attack. All four beaches would be threatened but three would be feints and the real attack would go ashore in Freshwater Cove. The feints would be made by two brigades commanded by Brigadiers Edward Whitmore and Charles Lawrence, while the assault itself would be made by a third led by Brigadier James Wolfe. Once a beachhead had been established ashore, artillery could be landed and a formal siege of the fortress begun. Wolfe had doubts about the plan, which he said was exactly what the enemy would be expecting; he advocated a more elaborate operation, making use of Boscawen's amphibious flexibility to land himself with a strong force of light infantry miles to the west of Louisbourg and march overland to take the Garabus Bay defences in the rear. General Amherst, like Abercromby, had no liking for such subtleties and ordered a frontal assault on the beaches.

Brigadier Wolfe was to Amherst's army what Howe had been to Abercromby's. Gawkily tall and thin with pale blue eyes, red hair and a sharply receding chin, he did not immediately inspire confidence as an officer. But his conversation reflected a keen intellect and his record a ruthless efficiency. He loved soldiering – 'I had much rather listen to the drum and trumpet than any softer sound whatever', he once said – but did not warm to his soldiers – 'terrible dogs to look at'[48] – and they did not love him as they had loved Lord Howe. The son of a general, he had been appointed a lieutenant of marines at the age of fourteen and at sixteen had become the adjutant of his battalion on active service in Flanders. In 1743 he had fought at Dettingen, where his ability had caught the eye of the Duke of Cumberland, and within a year he was a brigade major. Brought home two years later by the crisis of the Scottish rebellion under Prince Charles Edward, he had been present at its final defeat on Culloden Moor. When it was over and the wounded Highlanders on the battlefield were being bayoneted, it was said that Cumberland had asked a wounded officer to which side he belonged and had been told, 'To the Prince'. At this the Duke had turned and ordered, 'Wolfe, shoot me that insolent Highland scoundrel, who dares look on us with such contempt.' Wolfe had refused and was said to have replied, 'My commission is at your Royal Highness's disposal, but I can never consent to becoming an executioner.'[49] Other officers had also refused and the Highlander, Charles Lovat, the commander of Fraser's regiment, was killed by a private soldier.

Then, and afterwards, he had been aide-de-camp to Lieutenant-General Henry Hawley, known as 'Hangman Hawley' for his savage repression of the clans. Wolfe may not have been brutal himself but he had shown the ruthlessness that counter-insurgency engenders: burning crofts, confiscating cattle and taking hostages. Once, when hunting for a particular chief, he had deliberately sent out a weak patrol, explaining: 'I gave the sergeant orders in case he should succeed and was attacked by the clan with a view to rescue their chief, to kill him instantly, which I concluded would draw on the destruction of the detachment and furnish me with sufficient pretext ... to march into their country, where I would have laid about me without compunction.'[50]

This pragmatic cynicism in his thinking again became apparent when he advocated the raising of infantry regiments from the defeated clans, of whom he had once said, 'As few Highlanders were made prisoners as possible.' He now wrote while stationed at Banff:

I shou'd imagine that ... independent Highland companies might be of use, they are hardy, intrepid, accustom'd to a rough Country, and no great mischief if they fall. How can you better employ a secret enemy than by making his end conducive to the common good? If this sentiment should take wind, what an execrable and bloody being shou'd I be considered.'[51]

He was short-tempered, too, confessing:

My temper .s much too warm and sudden resentment forces out expressions and even actions that are neither justifiable nor excusable ... It is my misfortune to catch fire on a sudden, to answer letters the moment I receive them ... every ill turn through my whole life has had this haste and the first impulse of resentment for its true cause and it proceeds from pride.[52]

He accepted the custom by which a besieged city that refused to surrender after a breach had been blown in its walls and had had to be taken by storm could be sacked and its women raped.

Yet this was the young man who had recently been courting, so it was said, a refined young lady, Katherine Lowther, whom he had met at a ball in Bath. One brother-officer said of him, 'He neither drinks, curses, gambles nor runs after women',[53] and he himself wrote to his mother, 'I am often surprised at the little sensibility I feel in myself at the sight of the fairest and finest females.'[54] Yet he recognised that marriage was a suitable adjunct to a successful military career and a protection against any insinuations of sublimated homosexuality, which may well have been present.[*]

This fierce oddity was considered by the calm and efficient Amherst as the right officer to lead an opposed landing on a rugged coast in bad weather and in the face of a determined enemy. He had had experience of amphibious operations for, in 1757, he had taken part in the botched attack on Rochefort, inland of the Basque Roads, the naval anchorage on the Atlantic coast of

France. He had then been on the staff and aware of, but unable to prevent, the bungling and timidity that led to failure, telling his father in a letter that, 'We lost the lucky moment in war and are not able to recover it.'[55] He understood the importance of taking the initiative and this Amherst recognised.

Several times, Boscawen ordered the troops to embark in boats tossing alongside their transports, but each time the sea was so rough that they had to scramble back again. Finally, on 7 June, the sea had moderated, although surf was still bursting on the rocks and running up into the coves. At two o'clock next morning, the troops embarked again and, at first light, as frigates closed the shore and began to bombard, pulled for the beaches. Lieutenant Adam Williamson described the plan:

> The first landing was divided into three divisions; the right commanded by Brigadier Whitmore for a feint; in the centre, by Brigadier Lawrence and the left by Brigadier Wolfe. The left was composed of 500 Rangers, as many Light Infantry and the Grenadiers (13 companies) ... The whole shore was difficult to land on and only two or three boats could land at a time safely.[56]

Wolfe was determined but worried about both the landing itself and the artillery support they could expect once ashore, complaining: 'General Abercromby has witheld the haut-vitzers [howitzers] that were at New York amongst the stores intended for the siege of Louisbourg ... We ought to have ... half a dozen of the largest sort for this business.'[57]

The French guns were silent until the first boats came within 400 yards (366 metres) of the surf, then they fired, lashing the sea with grapeshot. It was too lethal to withstand and Wolfe stood up in his boat and waved a hand to signal the coxwains to steer away. But on one flank the three leading boats commanded by Lieutenants Hopkins and Brown and Ensign Grant had escaped the fire and, seeing a stretch of beach which seemed to be masked from the guns by rocks, steered towards it and burst through the surf to the sand. Wolfe saw the boats run ashore and signalled the others to follow in their wake.

'The surf was extremely violent,' recalled Lieutenant David Gordon of a Highland regiment, 'most of our boats being stav'd and the Rocks coming out so far that the greatest part of the Army landed to their middle in water. Many were much hurt, others crush'd to pieces, being carried away by the surge and the boats driving over them with the return on it.' But they did get ashore and there met defences such as those at Ticonderoga: The obstacles the troops had to surmount on landing was ... entrenchments being 15 feet above the high mark, the approaches to which was render'd impracticable by large trees being lay'd very thick together upon the Beach all round the Cove, their branches laying towards the sea.'[58]

Some 1,500 French troops – nearly half the garrison – were defending the beach but the first wave of infantry was ashore and, as their ammunition was soaked, fixed bayonets and charged, led by Wolfe holding a cane instead of a sword. Expecting to be cut off from the fortress itself by Whitmore's and Lawrence's landings, the French did not stand and fight but fell back on the fortifications, both sides having lost about 100 men. The other two divisions of boats pulled away from their apparent destinations and followed Wolfe's into the sheltered cove, their troops wading ashore and advancing inland. When the infantry occupied the French batteries they found 17 guns, 14 swivel-guns and two mortars abandoned there.

Meanwhile, the surviving boats had pulled back to the ships to collect more men and by dark the entire army was ashore. This was only just in time, for the wind was strengthening again and that night it was blowing a gale and there was no question of further landings until it abated. However, Wolfe and his rangers and light infantry were not only well inland but had crossed the neck of the peninsula, cutting off Louisbourg from its hinterland, so that the British surrounded it by land and sea.

For the first four days, Louisbourg was besieged by infantry alone. Even when the gale abated, huge seas swept westward to burst on the shore, and the number of boats smashed on the rocks reached more than 100. Further landings were impossible but, finally, the sea was calm enough to put the artillery, ammunition and stores ashore and the siege could begin in earnest. Amherst sited his headquarters just beyond the range of the heaviest of the 200 guns that lined the French defences near the principal camp along two miles of the bank of a stream flowing into the harbour. Seen from the land, it was a formidable fortress, encircled by earthworks, ramparts and four bastions, a mile and a half in circumference, with the strongest, the King's Bastion, fronting the citadel and facing inland.

In the harbour, north of the fortress, lay five ships of the line and seven frigates. It could be seen that their decks had been piled with wetted bales of tobacco to reduce the risk of fire from British bombardment from the western shore and Lighthouse Point, commanding the entrance, which had been occupied by Wolfe's brigade. The mouth of the harbour, narrowed by small islands and shoals, was now sealed with blockships, but not before a French frigate, the *Arethuse,* was towed out to sea on the night of 14 July. She set sail, eluded Boscawen's blockade in fog, and reached France with the first news of the plight of Louisbourg.

When the British had first landed, the scenery – low, rocky shores, pinewoods and distant, wooded hills – had seemed reassuringly familiar to the Celts, particularly the Highlanders, seeing it for the first time; indeed, the mainland hereabouts was known as New Scotland, or Nova Scotia. Camping on the edge of the woods, they had been bothered by flies and mosquitoes, but there was also something new and much worse. As Lieutenant Williamson wrote in his diary, 'Some of our people up the end of the Bay carried away by Indians', and, a few days later, added: 'A carter, who had been taken prisoner by the Indians made his escape from them. He says there were about 200 French and Indians 3 miles from the camp, where he ran away from; that a Frenchman, who spoke a little English, advised him to make his escape as the Indians intended roasting him.' [59] Reports ran through the army of what happened to those unable to escape, and the dread of scalping, or torture, was added to the fear of wounds and disease.

In contrast, chivalry was displayed by the opposing generals. The Governor of Louisbourg, the Chevalier Drucour, sent a message to Amherst that he would be happy to send a French surgeon under a flag of truce to attend any wounded British officer. Amherst responded by forwarding messages into the town from captured French soldiers. He sent Madame Drucour a present of pineapples from the West Indies and she sent him bottles of French wine. He also apologised to her for 'the disquiet to which she was exposed', [60] but this was misplaced since she daily swept along the battlements in her hooped skirt to fire three cannon at the British. Another woman, who added a touch of feminine style to the siege, was a prostitute from one of the British ships, of whom an engineer officer, Captain Thomas Townsend, wrote in his diary: 'Yesterday, Nancy Hamilton, a lady of pleasure, went near Louisbourg and was met by some French officers, who behaved very genteely to her and offered to conduct her into the town.'[61] They drank wine together before allowing her to return to the British lines.

It was 11 days after the landing before the British were able to haul their guns and ammunition inland, construct batteries under long-range cannon-fire from the bastions and finally open a bombardment themselves. Gunfire thumped and rumbled for days and the French made a successful sortie, killing an officer, the Earl of Dundonald, and capturing some grenadiers. The British dug trenches and saps ever closer to the outworks of the fortress in preparation for the eventual assault on a breach.

So the siege progressed with slow formality until 21 July, when the besiegers' batteries concentrated on the ships in the harbour. As Townsend recorded, 'A lucky ball from Mr Wolfe by some accident set fire to a parcel of cartridges on board one of the ships, which caused a great explosion and soon after we saw the ship in flames and she set fire to two more so that this accident has burned three of their capital ships.'[62] Watching from another vantage-point, Lieutenant Williamson wrote: 'A red-hot shot from one of our Batteries to the left blew up the Powder Magazine of one of the French 64-gun ships in the harbour and set it on fire. Two more 64s being near, the fire communicated and entirely consumed the three; a fourth was on fire but was put out.'[63]

Two nights later, Boscawen sent a cutting-out expedition of 600 seamen into the anchorage to board and capture the two remaining ships of the line. One ran aground and had to be burned but the other was towed out to sea under fire. By now the British bombardment had smashed the batteries on the landward ramparts so that, as one French officer noted in his diary, 'The fire of the place is so weak that it is more like funeral guns than a defence.'[64] Although Amherst had ordered his gunners to spare the civilians' houses, this had proved impossible, and the diarist continued:

There is not a house in the place that has not felt the effects of this formidable artillery. From yesterday morning till seven o'clock this evening, we reckon that a thousand, or twelve hundred, bombs, great and small, have been thrown into the town, accompanied all the time by the fire of forty pieces of cannon, served with an activity not often seen.

The hospital and the houses around it, which also serve as hospitals, are attacked with cannon and mortar. The surgeon trembles as he amputates a limb amid cries of *Garde la bomb!* and leaves his patient in the midst of the operation, lest he should share his fate. The sick and wounded, stretched on mattresses, utter cries of pain, which do not cease until a shot, or the bursting of a shell, ends them.[65]

By now, the hospitals were crowded with more than 1,300 sick and wounded.

On 26 July, the last gun was silenced and a breach had been blown in the walls. Thereupon Amherst sent an officer under a flag of truce to demand surrender. Governor Drucour refused, sending an officer with that message; then, reflecting on what would happen to the civilians if the fortress were taken by storm, he changed his mind and sent a second man. As a British officer watched the first approach, he saw 'a lieutenant-colonel running out of the garrison, making signs at a distance and bawling as loud as he could, *"We accept! We accept!"*'[66]

What the alternative would have been under the customs of war was illustrated by a letter Brigadier Wolfe wrote home immediately after the surrender:

> Went into Louisbourg this morning to pay my devoirs to the ladies but found them all so pale and thin with long confinement in a casement, that I made my visit very short. The poor women have been heartily frightened, as well they might; but no real harm … has befallen any. A day or two more and they would have been entirely at our disposal.[67]

So Louisbourg fell and the way to the St Lawrence and Quebec was open. It had not been a costly victory, the victors' losses amounting to about 500 killed and wounded. French casualties were never assessed but, since 5,600 soldiers and sailors were taken prisoner and their original strength was thought to have been some 5,000 regular soldiers and militia and more than 2,000 sailors, their losses were estimated as having been higher than the British. Those captured were to be sent to England as prisoners of war.

Drucour's defence had not been wholly unsuccessful for, combined with bad weather, it had so delayed the British that there would not be time to continue up the St Lawrence to attack Quebec before winter set in and the river froze. Boscawen and Amherst imagined that, by now, Abercromby and Howe would have taken both Ticonderoga and Crown Point and might already be laying siege to Montreal on their way to Quebec from the south. For their own part, the grand attack on Quebec would have to wait until 1759; meanwhile, Brigadier Wolfe could be sent ahead to burn French settlements on the lower shores of the St Lawrence. On 31 July, news arrived of the defeat at Ticonderoga.

A month after the fall of Louisbourg the news reached London, to be welcomed by the firing of guns at the Tower, the ringing of church bells and the striking of a suitably heroic commemorative medallion. In New York, there was a celebratory dinner at the Province Arms on Broadway; in Boston a fireworks display with 'a stately bonfire like a pyramid ... on the top of Fort Hill, which made a lofty and prodigious blaze'; and at Newport, Rhode Island, more fireworks and a sermon declaring that Christians would take note of 'so signal a favor of Divine Providence'.[68]

At the same time as the news arrived in London, it reached the camp at Fort William Henry on Lake George, where most of Abercromby's defeated army was still encamped. He had given nearly 3,000 men to Lieutenant-Colonel John Bradstreet, the efficient American who had commanded the boats on Lake George, for an attack on Fort Frontenac at the junction of the St Lawrence and Lake Ontario; this he took at the end of August after a long journey south to Albany and then north-west towards the Great Lakes.

Meanwhile Forbes was on his way to Fort Duquesne, at the junction of the Allegheny and Monongahela rivers, remembering the lessons of the first attempt. He captured the fort in November, finding it abandoned and burned by the French, the Indians having decorated the charred ruins with the heads of captured Highlanders on spikes, festooned with their tartan plaids. Forbes renamed it Fort Pitt, or Pittsburgh, in honour of the principal strategist of the war, and, on the long march back to Philadelphia, paused at the scene of Braddock's defeat to bury the bones that had been lying scattered there for three years.

Abercromby had been talking of another attack on Ticonderoga, but he decided to await the reinforcements that he had heard Amherst was sending, or bringing, from Louisbourg. So there was time to celebrate the news and Parson Cleaveland presided over the singing of hymns of thanksgiving, writing in his diary: 'The General put out orders that the breastwork should be lined with troops and to fire three rounds for joy and give thanks to God in a religious way' and to wave their hats and give 'three Huzzas'.[69] Amherst was indeed on his way with six battalions and reached New York in December. He had been ordered to take over command of the army in North America, so Abercromby never returned to Ticonderoga but, on 24 January, 1759, sailed for England in a frigate.

A new self-confidence began to grow, reflected in the extravagantly patriotic, mock-classical recitations popular in London at the beginning of 1759:

Now Mars his bloody banners hangs in air,
And bids Britannia's sons for war prepare;
Let each lov'd maid, each mother bring the shield,
And arm their country's champions for the field.
Arm'd and inflam'd, each British breast shall burn,
No youth unlaurel'd shall to you return.[70]

The taking of Louisbourg had wiped out the shame of Ticonderoga and Fort Duquesne with the realisation that the British could prevail in the North American wilderness of trees, rock and water.

'The spirit of a duel'

At the beginning of 1758, three ships of the line and two small frigates dropped down the Hooghly from Calcutta. Since the squadron's most powerful ship, the *Kent*, had been so shattered off Chandernagore, she had been abandoned in the river and Vice-Admiral George Pocock, whose promotion had just been gazetted, flew his flag in the *Yarmouth* of 64 guns. They were sailing for the Coromandel coast to meet the threat of a large French naval and military force that was reported to be on its way to their base at Pondicherry, south of Madras, or even to have arrived there. These reports had been arriving at Calcutta since September, when two British frigates, which had been watching Pondicherry, were surprised by a strong French squadron and had had to run under all sail for safety. This had been the first of the French reinforcements. But the British still gave the highest priority to the security of the newly conquered Bengal, and it was only now that it was decided to seek out the enemy at sea.

It was not only the ghost of Byng that was about but the memory of the Comte de la Bourdonnais, the French naval commander, who, a decade before, had swept the British from the Indian Ocean and captured Madras. The city had been returned under the peace agreement but the memory of the humiliation remained. Pocock's instructions from the Admiralty had been to protect both Madras and Calcutta, but, although his squadron combined ships of the Royal Navy and the East India Company, it was too small to be divided. He had therefore to assess his enemy's intentions, though even if he were successful in this, he could never bring overwhelming force to bear. At best, it would be a fight between evenly balanced opponents.

When he sailed down the Hooghly on 20 January, 1758, Pocock had been absent from southern waters for 17 months, engaged in the operations upriver from Calcutta. He cannot have been sorry to leave the city. Although the rainy season of 1757 had been less sickly than usual and only about 40 British soldiers had died there and at Chandernagore, drunkenness, which had become endemic after the distribution of prize-money following the victory at Plassey, had so weakened resistance to disease that by the end of October, two-thirds of the troops there were in hospital together with several hundred seamen.

Symptomatic of the problems of morale, health and organisation was that of desertion by sailors and soldiers. It being difficult to hide amongst the Indian population, deserters tried to join the other service, albeit temporarily. Clive wrote indignantly to Pocock:

> I am much concern'd at the Sickness and slow Recovery of the Seamen and much more so that you should think I connive at the enlisting of any of His Majesty's Seamen. It is very possible there may be many in Camp without my knowing anything of the matter ... If there be any, they must have been receiv'd at Calcutta and in all probability must have receiv'd the enlisting money ... You are very sensible, Sir, many of our Military were receiv'd on board the squadron without either your, or Mr Watson's, knowledge, or even the knowledge of the Captains – the like may very easily happen on shore.[1]

On enquiry, Clive discovered ten seamen pretending to be soldiers, and two more who had originally been soldiers but had deserted to the Royal Navy before drifting back without admitting their former occupation.

However, Colonel Clive had decided that Calcutta must now be able to defend itself and had begun the planning of a vast star-shaped fortress – a new Fort William – to be built just outside and downstream of the city. During Pocock's and Clive's absence, the Coromandel coast, the Carnatic and the territories between Madras and Calcutta, known as the Northern Sirkars, had been sparsely defended. At the same time as the British had taken Chandernagore, the French had seized Vizagapatam, despite the soldiers landed there by Pocock. Now that huge reinforcements were reported to have left France for Pondicherry, the balance seemed likely to be loaded further in their favour. To Pocock, as to Watson, the strategic key to India was naval power: whoever commanded the sea controlled the flow of troops and traders and trade itself. To the European rivals it was trade and not territory that mattered, except to Colonel Clive, who was already dreaming of ruling an Indian empire for King George.

If these dreams were not shared by the politicians at home, news was arriving in India that he had been hailed as a hero at Westminster. When news of the recapture of Calcutta and the taking of Chandernagore had reached London in October, it had followed news of failure elsewhere. In the House of Commons, William Pitt, the Foreign Secretary and Secretary of State for War, declared in terms that would have irritated Admiral Watson:

> We have lost our glory, honour and reputation everywhere but in India.

There the country had a heaven-born general, who has never learned the art of war, nor is his name enrolled among the great officers, who have for many years received their country's pay. Yet he was not afraid to attack a numerous army with a handful of men and overcome them.

'Name him!' shouted Members of Parliament. 'Everyone knows I mean Colonel Clive,' Pitt declared.[2]

As Pocock sailed south for Madras, the ghost of his cousin hovered over the sea, a sad wraith in contrast to the glittering image of Clive. It was two years since Byng, like Pocock, had been sent to protect British possessions with an inadequate fleet. Until this moment, both British and French squadrons in the Indian Ocean had been of a strength to maintain the balance but not to wrest the control of the other's trade and communications. Pocock knew that he would soon face an enemy line of battle perhaps double the strength of his own, and even when the reinforcements promised by the Admiralty finally arrived, he would still be outnumbered.

These were to include four small ships of the line commanded by Commodore Charles Steevens, whose voyage was more dangerous than he can have realised. The Comte d'Aché had sailed with a squadron drawn from Brest and Lorient, reaching Mauritius in December, 1757, and there he had joined the small squadron already on station to make a force of 11 ships, which lay between Steevens's ships and Pocock's. By luck, Steevens avoided the French and, on 24 March, sighted Pocock's ships at anchor in Madras road. The British squadron now consisted of seven small ships of the line and one frigate. On 17 April, Pocock sailed for Fort St David south of Pondicherry, which he knew would be the British settlement most at risk.

The French – ten ships of the line and a big frigate – were approaching from the south. The Comte d'Aché, ten years younger than Pocock, was a brave but unaggressive commander, seeing his principal task as the safe delivery of the new Governor of French settlements in India, the Comte de Lally, to Pondicherry together with 3,500 regular French troops for the defence of French settlements. Passing between Ceylon and the southern cape of India, he ran into headwinds as he sailed up the east coast, finally reaching Fort St David on 28 April. His arrival took the British by surprise and two frigates, the *Bridgewater* and the *Triton*, lying at anchor in the road, had no time to make sail and escape but had to be run ashore and burned while their crews took refuge in the fort. On the same day, the 74-gun *Comte de*

Provence, with Lally, on board, sailed for Pondicherry, accompanied by a frigate.

Next morning, Pocock's sails came over the horizon. For ten days he had been working his squadron into a commanding position to windward of the enemy's probable track. This had taken him as far south as the northern cape of Ceylon; he had arrived off the Indian coast on the 28th and followed it northward until sighting d'Aché's ships at anchor off Fort St David. Pocock's tactical options were limited by the Admiralty's *Fighting Instructions*, which insisted on rigid adherence to the line of battle as the fighting formation and that each ship must be placed opposite her exact opponent in the enemy line. This had imposed an inflexibility on naval tactics that had been partly responsible for Byng's poor showing off Minorca. But Pocock was aware of one daring, relatively new and liberating option that had been used to effect in action off Cape Finisterre a decade before: the general chase. Once ordered by signal, every captain would crowd all possible sail and make straight for the enemy; then, if necessary and possible, they could put over their helms and form a line of battle. If not, a mêlée would ensue and superior British gun drill and rate of fire might prevail.

So Pocock hoisted the signal for 'general chase' and, under full press of canvas, his seven ships of the line and single frigate steered for the enemy's line, now reduced to nine sail of the line but including one 'seventy-four', the flagship *Zodiaque*. D'Aché stood out to sea, steering north-east under a south-easterly breeze, then made the signal for line of battle and, off Allempawee, waited for the British under easy sail. At half-past twelve, Pocock, too, made a signal for line ahead with 100 yards (91 metres) between each ship. Two of his ships, the *Cumberland* and the *Tyger*, were, however, undermanned and sailing badly, so more men had to be sent to them by boat; but they had lagged astern and it was a quarter-past two before the line could be formed. Pocock in the *Yarmouth* lay at the centre of the British line and d'Aché in the *Zodiaque* at the centre of the French, and the former steered his ship straight for the latter. As the British came within range, the first French broadside flashed and thundered along their line.

Pocock held his fire. Looking ahead, he was gratified to see that Captain Latham had been able to lead the line with the *Tyger*, followed by the *Salisbury* and Commodore Steevens in the *Elizabeth* ahead of his flagship. But, astern of the *Yarmouth*, the line seemed to have disintegrated. The next ship, the unlucky *Cumberland*, commanded by Captain Brereton, was sailing so slowly that, while the four leading ships were under heavy fire, she was not yet within range. Astern of her, Captain Legge of the *Newcastle* and Captain Vincent of the *Weymouth* seemed to be making no attempt to get their ships into action. Then, at five minutes to four, the *Yarmouth* was within point-blank range of the *Zodiaque*, and Pocock gave the order to fire.

Still the British line straggled. A repetition of Byng's action off Minorca seemed to be unfolding when the *Cumberland*, belatedly struggling into action, ran foul of the *Yarmouth*. To make space to manoeuvre, the flagship had to be slowed by backing her topsails; this was imitated by the *Newcastle* and the *Weymouth* so that they fell astern of the rear of the enemy line and so remained outside the action. So four of seven British ships bore the full force of enemy broadsides, which might have meant disaster had not the French line been equally bedevilled. One French captain took his ship behind d'Aché's line and fired between his ships when he could; another, the frigate, was too weak to stand in the line and turned away after the first British broadsides; a third lost her rudder and also fell away.

The van and centre of both lines fought furiously as 'Pocock and d'Aché, as with the spirit of a duel, kept close and directed their fire entirely against each other'.[3] Both admirals angrily signalled their reluctant captains to join the action and, eventually, all the British ships, except the *Newcastle*, joined the line. None of the French did so, although the ship of the line and the frigate which had taken Lally into Pondicherry could now be seen returning. This advantage was lost when explosions of gunpowder on board two French ships – one of them the flagship – threw them into confusion. Finally, at half-past four, the French line concentrated their fire on the *Yarmouth*, sailing past her in succession, then put their helms over and ran before the wind. Pocock at once hoisted the signal for general chase and the effects of British and French gunnery became apparent. As was their custom, the British had fired roundshot into the enemy's hulls, inflicting heavy casualties and damage to their guns. The French, however, as was *their* custom, had fired at the masts, yards and rigging of their opponents, using ammunition – such as double-headed chain-shot and bar-shot – designed for the purpose. So while the shattered French were able to run easily before the wind, the British, their sails and spars torn and splintered, could manage only a third of their speed.

Seeing, at six o'clock, that d'Aché had come up with the returning *Comte de Provence* and was continuing towards Pondicherry, Pocock sent the frigate *Queenborough* to shadow them while he followed at his best speed through the night. The French had suffered heavy casualties: 162 killed and 360 wounded, many of whom would die. The *Zodiaque* herself had suffered 236 casualties, 11 of them officers. Such losses were partly due to so many soldiers being on board, since there had been no time to land them at Pondicherry. This had brought the squadron's manpower to some 5,000 against 3,200 British seamen and marines. Among the French casualties were musicians on passage from France, who had been expected to amuse the new Governor on the long, hot evenings, d'Aché complaining that he had lost all his fiddlers. The British, on the other hand, had lost only 29 men killed and 89 wounded.

A strengthening wind had raised a heavy swell and both squadrons anchored for the night off the coast, 15 miles apart. One French ship, the *Bien-Aimé*, had been so badly damaged that she drove ashore and had to be abandoned. Next morning, the French were in no state to give battle and made their way slowly to Pondicherry, where they landed 1,200 wounded and sick. Watching them through his telescope, Pocock noted: 'Monsieur d'Aché keeps with his Squadron close in with the surf under the guns of Pondicherry.'[4]

With hindsight, Captain Richard Kempenfelt, Steevens's flag-captain in the *Elizabeth*, thought that an annihilating victory might have been achieved. While he admired Pocock's 'great gallantry' and his 'close and smart' tactics, he criticised his decision to chase the French relentlessly for as long as his damaged ships could maintain the pursuit. Instead, he thought, the admiral should have made straight for Pondicherry and anchored there, keeping to windward of d'Aché, which would have

> laid them under a necessity of either quitting the coast or risquing another Action, which last as our Men were flushed with the success they already had … would have been running a great hazard, and if they had left the Coast, their whole expedition would have been abortive, as their Troops were not landed and they would have been drove to the umost distress for provisions and Water. But this oversight of ours saved them.[5]

But Pocock's eagerness to continue the closest possible pursuit may have had reasons of which Kempenfelt was unaware: the memory of what had happened to his cousin for not having been seen to 'do his utmost' to defeat the enemy.

Pocock put his helm over and steered for Madras, where he repaired his ships and received a draft of a 120 more seamen from the hospital and 80 Lascar seamen to replace casualties. He then set out in pursuit of the French. Again he had to sail far south to get to windward of the coast, where he thought they must be, and it was not until 30 May that he sighted them off Pondicherry and prepared for action.

D'Aché was not his own master when within sight of the supreme commander. Thomas-Arthur, Comte de Lally, the son of an Irish Jacobite, had served in the Irish Brigade of the French army and had fought for Prince Charles Edward, 'The Young Pretender', in Scotland and England in 1745. Now aged fifty-eight, he was an imperious, short-tempered man with a reputation for bullying subordinates and alienating allies. Although his admiral had no wish to renew the fighting, the Governor sent him 400 Lascars to help man his ships and ordered him to sea and to fight.

Lally himself was on the point of marching south to besiege Fort St David, and as soon as he was gone, his deputy and the city council recalled d'Aché to protect the town. This, Pocock believed, saved three valuable East Indiamen bound for Madras, which might otherwise have been captured had the French been at sea. During the French squadron's brief venture beyond the range of the shore batteries, Pocock tried to intercept them, but contrary winds and the *Cumberland*'s bad sailing prevented him.

However the battle, indecisive as it might have seemed, had demoralised the French. Their arrival on the Coromandel coast to attack Fort St David and the burning of the two British frigates had given them a taste of victory that would be the talk of Versailles. But it had turned to ashes under the pounding of Pocock's guns. Bitterly seeking excuses, they first blamed the detaching of a ship of the line and a frigate to take Lally into Pondicherry when a launch could have performed the duty without weakening the squadron.

One angry French officer, who had sketched the action, sent his drawings to France with an accompanying account of the action. 'Our operations seeming at last to have succeeded', he wrote, 'when a set of circumstances prevented us from scattering an enemy squadron inferior in ships and men; one saw how Mr Pokop [Pocock] by his good luck and courage saved the English Company from ruin, which could change the face of commerce on the coast of Coromandel.'[6]

Now that Fort St David was besieged, Pocock heard of a threat to match the disaster at Calcutta two years before. Madras itself was likely to be attacked and he realised that he might be deprived of any port for victualling and watering his ships. So he sailed for Madras, arriving there on 6 June, and while anchored off Fort St George, he brought the three reluctant captains, Legge, Vincent and Brereton, to trial, charging them with 'keeping back in time of action'.[7] As the admiral put it, 'Their manner of acting in the Engagement appeared so faulty that, on my return here, I ordered a Court Martial to assemble and enquire into their conduct … Sorry I am beyond Expression that any officer under my command should have failed in the most material part of the Duty they owe to His Majesty and their Country.'[8]

The courts-martial sat during June and July with Steevens as President and four captains, including Kempenfelt, composing the court. The three accused captains put forward a variety of excuses, including battle-damage aloft hampering the handling of their ships and failure to see signals 'for the smoke of our Fleet'.[9] There were no mitigating circumstances in the case of Legge and he was dismissed the service, while Brereton only lost one year's seniority on the captain's list. Vincent protested his innocence but was sentenced to be dismissed his ship.

If Pocock was driven by the example of Byng, his sympathy was aroused by it. He had called the courts-martial so as to be seen to be doing his utmost in battle and to be demanding this of his captains. However, on reading the proceedings of Vincent's trial he came upon the prisoner's defence that 'When I consider that a misfortune of this kind is so common now after every Sea Engagement, that the most exact conduct cannot secure any man from the danger of it'. The relevance was obvious. During the two subsequent trials fresh evidence supportive of Vincent was submitted and the court unanimously recommended that his sentenced be 'softened',[10] to which the admiral agreed, although Vincent was still relieved of his command.

When news of the action and subsequent courts-martial reached London, there was no question of any failure on the part of the admiral. Indeed, the *London Chronicle* concluded: 'Had Mr Pocock been properly supported, he would most probably have gained a complete and glorious victory.'[11] Despite the three captains, the action had been a success: the French had lost one ship as a direct result and a large number of trained men who could not be replaced. It had also to be regarded as the opening shots of a duel between Pocock and d'Aché for control of the Indian seas.

Ashore, the war was going badly for the British in the face of the largest European army yet seen in India. In mid-May, the Comte de Lally's army of

5,000 – half French, half Indian – had besieged Fort St David, which was defended by 400 European troops, half of them sailors, often befuddled with arrack. On 2 June they had surrendered and Lally, with the ruthlessness that he was introducing to warfare, had ordered that not only should the fortress be razed to the ground but also the houses of the Company's merchants and of the Indians who happened to live there. There was none of Clive's mixture of flattery and threat in Lally's attitude to the Indian rulers, and, when financial demands on the neighbouring Rajah of Tanjore were not met, he marched his army against the capital to take what he wanted by force. The Tanjoreans put up a spirited resistance and the French troops, as yet unacclimatised, became so debilitated by fatigue, heat and sickness that he had to raise the siege and retreat to the small French coastal settlement of Carical.

It was then that Lally was further infuriated to hear that, in his absence, the Comte d'Aché had told the authorities at Pondicherry that he proposed to withdraw his squadron to Mauritius for the autumn and winter monsoon season. This would leave the command of the sea to the British, thereby undermining the Governor-General's success on land and putting at risk his proposed attack on Madras itself. So he sent the Comte d'Estaing to Pondicherry to forbid any withdrawal and urge d'Aché to put to sea and fight.

Meanwhile, Pocock had refitted his ships at Madras and, on 25 July, led seven ships of the line and a frigate south along the coast, searching for the enemy. Two days later, just before sunset, they sighted d'Aché's ships still at anchor off Pondicherry and waited for them throughout the night. He was aware not only that d'Aché had one more ship of the line than himself but that the French ships were heavier, two of them 'seventy-fours' and two 'sixty-fours', whereas his heaviest ships were the *Yarmouth* and *Elizabeth*, both mounting 64 guns.

At ten next morning, the French ships weighed anchor and made sail, steering south along the coast and in the direction of Mauritius and safety. Pocock signalled for a general chase but contrary winds held him back, leaving the French free to anchor offshore again that night and the next. Finally, on the morning of 1 August[*] he sighted eight French ships of the line and a frigate at anchor off Tranquebar. On seeing the British, d'Aché made sail and stood out to sea. But this time he did not try to avoid action, first forming a line of battle and then turning into line abreast and bearing down upon Pocock. When two miles distant, d'Aché held off, sailing south-east with Pocock following. Keeping his line until midnight, when he judged the French must have tacked away, Pocock then put his own helms over and steered west. Next day, he saw only an empty sea.

That evening, however, four sails were sighted inshore and, at five next morning, the bright early-morning sun lit the whole enemy squadron sailing in line of battle off Negapatam. Pocock, too, formed line of battle and bore down on the enemy, but then the wind dropped and his ships slowed and lay becalmed on the glassy sea. At 11, a light breeze off the land filled the French sails and they were able to sail out to sea, passing the rear of the stationary British line at right angles. But by noon a full breeze was blowing, giving Pocock the advantage of the wind, both squadrons formed line of battle and Pocock made the signal to engage.

The two lines closed, their leading ships, the *Elizabeth* and the more powerful *Comte de Provence* opening the engagement with simultaneous broadsides and the latter's mizzen mast catching fire. Quickly, both lines were engulfed in the stabbing flashes and billowing gunsmoke. Several French ships suffered heavy damage, one caught fire when a gun burst, and, as they fell out of the line or crashed together, their whole line seemed to disintegrate. D'Aché managed to extricate the *Zodiaque* from the smoke and, soon after two o'clock in the afternoon, put her helm over and ordered the rest by signal to do likewise. As the French sailed away from the muzzle-to-muzzle combat, Pocock again ordered a general chase. The result was as before: his ships were too shattered aloft to keep up with the French, whose hulls were shot through and through but whose masts, yards, rigging and sails still stood and carried them away. An hour later, after the French had cut free the ships' boats they had been towing astern to keep their decks clear for fighting, the wind bore them out of range. Pocock pursued until dark and then, at eight o'clock, anchored off Carical, while his quarry headed back to Pondicherry.

It had been another day of bloody fighting without a final decision. Although their soldiers, who had suffered so much in the first battle, were now ashore, the French had lost 250 killed and 602 wounded, more than 180 of them in the flagship *Zodiaque*. In the British ships, only 31 had been killed and 162 wounded; both admirals had been cut by splinters. Surveying the devastation, the British realised that, had the weather not been so calm, they would have lost their damaged masts overboard; the French, shaken by several fires that had almost cost them two ships, accused the British of using unethical inflammables but were unable to prove it. So fearful of fire had d'Aché become that, safely anchored off Pondicherry, he imagined that Pocock might send fireships among his ships in the night and moved them as close as possible under the shore batteries.

Another worry beset him. The stocks of spars, sails and rope kept at Pondicherry had been exhausted by his demands after the first action and the nearest source was in Mauritius. So, for that reason alone, he needed to retire there without more delay, ignoring the orders relayed by the Comte d'Estaing from the Comte de Lally. He still refused when d'Estaing offered to give him as many French troops as he needed to man the guns and to accompany the squadron himself if only he would put to sea and fight the British once again. When Lally returned to Pondicherry at the end of August he, in person, ordered d'Aché to sail but the admiral, supported by all his captains, refused. Finally, d'Aché landed 500 sailors and marines to join the land forces and, on 3 September, sailed for Mauritius.

In the British ships, Pocock thought it too early for the French to avoid the monsoon by retiring to Mauritius, so he followed them to the coast of Ceylon and put into Trincomalee. Keeping his ships near the mouth of the great natural harbour, he sent a Company ship, the *Revenge*, to look for the French and on the morning of 2 September she found them. Pocock at once put to sea in pursuit but could not get within range before sunset and lost them in the night. So he headed for the British dockyard at Bombay, which had all the skills and equipment necessary to repair his ships, and the sea-fighting season was over for the year.

With the prospect of any fighting at sea at end for several months, Lally felt free to exercise his superiority on land to clear the British settlements from the Coromandel coast. The French and British armies in India had once amounted to a few hundred Europeans – with small reinforcements arriving from time to time – and 1,000 or so sepoys, but the French army that marched on Madras in December, 1758, numbered some 3,000 French troops, more than 2,000 sepoys and 500 Indian cavalry. Delayed for weeks by heavy monsoon rains, the French did not arrive before Fort St George until 14 December. The defenders had time for some preparations. Colonel Stringer Lawrence, a tough, portly old soldier with long experience of war in India, was in command under Governor Pigot and immediately ordered his outlying detachments to fall back on the city. This brought his garrison to a little more than 1,700 Europeans and 2,000 sepoys.

Significant reinforcements had been expected from England, sent by the Prime Minister, William Pitt, whose grandfather had been a Governor of Madras, and who was showing more interest in India than his predecessors. Pocock had left 100 marines and, in September, one ship had arrived with a company of about 100 regular infantrymen on board, but the main force of more than 600 had lost 50 men from typhus on the voyage from England and had been delayed at Bombay; they could not be expected until the monsoon ended. This was the 79th Regiment, newly raised at Colchester in England by their commanding officer, Lieutenant-Colonel William Draper, who had already arrived with the advance party.

Now aged thirty-seven, Draper was an unusual soldier to find in India. Scholar and athlete, he had been educated at Eton and at King's College, Cambridge, with the intention of becoming a clergyman. He was good at games, particularly tennis and cricket, in which he had played for his old school in the first three-day match, in which he gained the highest score for the Gentlemen of Eton against the Rest of England in 1751.[*] Instead of the church, he chose the Army and fought at Falkirk during the rebellion in Scotland. He caught the attention of the Duke of Cumberland, who appointed him adjutant of his own regiment, the 1st Foot Guards, and seemed set for the life of a fashionable officer.

He was also strikingly handsome – on a visit to Versailles, Louis XV had called him '*le beau garçon Anglais*'.[12] He had enjoyed many love affairs, including one with the actress Polly Hart, who was to be mistress of Dr Johnson's friend, Henry Thrale; and in 1756 he married Caroline Beauclerk, a granddaugher of King Charles II and Nell Gwynn. Comfortable appointments in London were his for the asking, and he had been aide-de-camp to the Duke of Marlborough and in touch with the centres of power in the capital when he had been asked to raise a regiment for service in India. Perhaps for the excitement of active service in the tropics, or the enticement of the fortunes which had been made there, he readily agreed.

At Madras, Lawrence put up a spirited defence. Hearing that, when Black Town (the Indian quarter outside the walls) had been occupied by the French, their discipline had broken when they had looted liquor stores, he ordered a sortie by 600 of his best troops, led by Colonel Draper. 'The English drummers, most of whom being black boys, began to beat the Grenadiers' march as soon as they entered the street, on which the whole line from one end to the other set up their huzzas.'[13] They advanced down the long main street to a square at the end, where, out of sight, French guns awaited and greeted them with blasts of grapeshot. Street-fighting spread through Black Town and Draper, outnumbered and in danger of being cut off, led his men across waste ground and back through the fortifications by another gate. Both sides had lost upwards of 200 men.

In Bombay, Pocock heard of the attack on Madras, but there seemed to be little he could do. It was not only that a return to the Coromandel coast at the height of the monsoon season was unthinkable, but that he could not abandon Bombay while d'Aché's squadron lay at Mauritius. There was one hope: it was known that, in the tropics, besiegers could suffer as much as the besieged if a quick victory was not achieved; if Madras could hold out until the French began to suffer the usual range of ailments, including the inevitable heat exhaustion and dysentery, a fast convoy might get through to the city to give the garrison the edge in survival. There would probably be French frigates, or other armed ships, off the coast and that risk, together with the weather, would make it dangerous. But an exceptional naval officer might succeed.

The officer Pocock chose to command this forlorn hope was Captain Richard Kempenfelt. The son of a Swedish officer in the British Army, Kempenfelt was a striking man of forty with a strong, big-boned face, an air of command and a questioning intellect that led him to evolve new systems of signals. He had fought under Admiral Vernon at the capture of Porto Bello 20 years before and had joined Pocock as Steevens's flag-captain. So Kempenfelt was given command of a fast convoy to relieve Madras; with an escort of two frigates, the *Queenborough* of the Royal Navy and the Company's *Revenge*, it consisted of four East Indiamen loaded with stores, ammunition and six companies of regular infantry, and the hospital ship *Shaftesbury*. If it could arrive before Fort St George fell, there was a chance that it could prove decisive.

Meanwhile, the siege began in earnest, the French digging trenches, throwing up earthworks, mounting batteries and beginning to sink saps beneath the defences for mining. Bombardment and counter-bombardment caused losses to both sides, the British realising too late that, when planning the fortifications, they had forgotten to build more than one 'Bomb Proof Lodgement', except for one that was used as a hospital. Then, on 30 January, 1759, a sail was sighted from the seaward bastions of Fort St George and spirits rose. As she reached the line of breakers and the surfboats went out to meet her, she was identified as the East Indiaman, *Shaftesbury*, the hospital ship, which had become separated by bad weather from Kempenfelt's convoy. So, to the dismay of the garrison, she disembarked 36 sick soldiers instead of the expected reinforcements, but then, to their relief, she began to discharge a cargo of mortar-bombs and grenades. Even more heartening was the news she brought that Kempenfelt's ships and reinforcements were somewhere in her wake.

The siege was reaching a climax. The morale of the French troops suffered under the rigours of a siege-camp and they grumbled that they had not been paid. Moreover, near Vizagapatam a French force under the Marquis de Conflans had been defeated by a British detachment from Bengal and expected reinforcements had had to be diverted to meet a threat from Clive's energetic little army in the north. So Lally proposed an attack led by himself to reach an abrupt conclusion before reinforcements could reach the British by sea. Then, just after sunset on 16 February, when all was ready for a great, formal assault, sentries on the ramparts of Fort St George sighted the sails of six ships on the horizon.

'As soon as it grew dark', ran a contemporary account,

three lights were hoisted at the Flag Staff as a mark for the Ships to come by. At about Eight o'Clock at Night the Six Ships anchored in the Road and to the great Joy of the Garrison proved to be His Majesty's Ship *Queenborough*, Capt. Kempenfelt, and the Company's Frigate *Revenge* with the *Tilbury*, *Winchelsea*, *Prince of Wales* and *Britannia*, having on board Six Companies of Colonel Draper's Regiment.

Disembarkation of troops began at once,

it being apprehended that, if Mr Lally does intend to make any push, he will do it this night before any Succours can come to our Assistance. All the Garrison, the Company's Servants and the Inhabitants were therefore ordered under Arms and continued so the whole Night at their several Alarm Posts and about two Companies were landed from the Ships in the Night. A Constant fire was kept upon the enemy's trenches, which they sometimes returned and threw a few Shells in the beginning of the night, but none after Eleven o'clock. About Midnight three deserters came in separately ... and report that the French entirely abandoned ... their Posts ... and that the Enemy intend to raise the Siege and march off before daybreak

So it proved. 'At about three in the morning, the enemy set fire to several large piles of wood in the rear of their guard battery and, as soon as the day broke, it appeared that the enemy had abandoned their trenches and batterys and were retreating.'[14] By noon, all 600 troops had been landed from the transports and the French siege-camp lay deserted before the city. Joy and curiosity carried out every one to view and contemplate the works from which they had received so much molestation, for the enemy's fire had continued 42 days,' recorded Orme.[15] Not only were 33 guns – some still serviceable – found abandoned in the batteries, together with ammunition and stores, but 44 sick and wounded Frenchmen were found in the field hospital without medical care but with a letter recommending them to the mercy of Governor Pigot.

The victorious defenders began compiling statistics, noting that the French must have fired some 8,000 shot and shell into the city. For their part, the defenders had used 1,768 barrels of gunpowder to fire 26,554 cannon-balls and 7,502 mortar-shells. They had thrown nearly 2,000 hand-grenades and fired 200,000 cartridges from their muskets. Their casualties had amounted to 13 officers killed, or died of sickness, and 20 wounded and nearly 200 European troops killed and some 350 dead from disease, wounded or missing; losses among Indian troops had been about half this total but 440 had deserted. French casualties were unknown but an intercepted letter from their headquarters suggested that the number of their effective European troops had been reduced by about 1,000.

Meanwhile, Clive remained in Bengal facing two new threats, one familiar, the other unexpected. The first was the customary intrigues amongst Indian rulers and, often, the Europeans. The Mogul Empire, which had dominated India for so long, was in decay, but the heir to the throne was said to be planning to overthrow Mir Jaffir and annex Bengal. The old Nawab, whom Clive had installed, had become overconfident, neglected to pay his army and seemed ripe for deposing. When news reached Calcutta that a Mogul army was actually on the march and had enlisted allies, Clive set out with another of his little armies to teach them a lesson. Although, as usual, greatly outnumbered, he found that no battle was necessary as his potential enemies melted before his advance. So he returned to Calcutta, leaving a peaceful Bengal and with the guarantee of a new and enormous private income from the Nawab.

In August, he wrote to Pocock: 'Whilst you are watching the motions of a vigilant and active enemy and have nothing but hard blows to expect, we are employed in bullying and keeping under the black fellows, the superiority of Our Arms in these parts will easily be preserved so long as the French are prevented from interfering.'[16] But this time it was not to be the French who provided the other threat. It was, surprisingly, the Dutch.

Hitherto, the Dutch had been spectators of the rivalry between the British and the French, and regarded by the former as friends and trustworthy trading partners, if not allies. They had traded peacefully from their settlement at Chinsura, upstream of Calcutta on the Hooghly, but their leadership had grown increasingly resentful of the success of the aggressive British. So, as the French were beaten back by Clive and Pocock, the Dutch, in their turn, began intriguing with Mir Jaffir, who told them he also resented the domineering British. They then reached a secret agreement with the Nawab to bring a Dutch expeditionary force from Batavia (now Jakarta) up the Hooghly to Chinsura to challenge the dominance of the East India Company at Calcutta. Once again, Clive had to prepare to face an invader of what he now regarded as his, or his country's, territory in Bengal.

Meanwhile, on the far side of the sub-continent, both the British and the French had made ready for another fighting season on the Coromandel coast. 'Bombay is now a very commodious Port to refit our ships', wrote Pocock, 'and will be better next year with regard to the Dock, the Superintendent, Mr Hough, being a diligent, active and skilful man in his office, both with respect to the King and the Company's affairs.' As an example, he cited that he had made the troublesome *Cumberland* 'a tight ship by stopping all her leaks'.[17] The dockyard could provision ships and their companies and press seamen from passing merchant ships; before the arrival of reinforcements, the Governor had offered to press men from the merchantmen *Drake* and *True Briton*. In April, 1759, Pocock, his ship's companies made up to strength with impressed merchant seamen, sailed from Bombay, passed Ceylon and, in June, was joined by two more ships of the line, the *Grafton* and the *Sunderland*, and five East Indiamen loaded with stores. At the beginning of August, he was cruising in line of battle past the deserted roadstead off Pondicherry.

At Mauritius, d'Aché was reinforced by three sail of the line and some storeships, but the French base was running so short of provisions that ships had to be sent to Cape Town to buy more. To man his ships, the admiral had to recruit Africans, who were good seamen but untrained in the skills of naval warfare. On sailing for the Coromandel coast, d'Aché called at Madagascar and Ceylon for stores and, at the latter, for any news of Pocock. He now commanded a powerful fleet of 11 sail of the line, including two 'seventy-fours', and two frigates. Against this, Pocock commanded nine sail of the line – the heaviest a 'sixty-eight' – and one frigate, but, outgunned as his squadron was, it had the advantage of well-trained British crews.

For a month Pocock searched without sight or word of the enemy and then had to call at Trincomalee for provisions and water. When he sailed again on 1 September, d'Aché was also victualling on the coast of Ceylon, at Batticaloa, about 60 miles to the south. Next day, the Company's frigate *Revenge*, scouting to the south, returned to the squadron, signalling that she had sighted 15 sail to the south-east and had been chased by a frigate. Pocock yet again made the signal for general chase and soon a frigate's sails came over the horizon, followed by the whole array of the French squadron. But, just as it seemed that a fleet action was inevitable, the wind dropped and, at dusk, the French drew away. Pocock sent the *Revenge* after them and she caught up with them shortly before midnight, making a signal to the admiral with flares in the hot night. But, within an hour, a sudden squall blew out of the stillness and the British had to clew up their sails to save their masts. Yet at first light, the enemy were still in sight and about five miles distant.

Again Pocock ordered a general chase and this lasted all day, the opponents remaining several miles apart. The wind fell again, heat haze blurred the horizon and the enemy was lost again. This was repeated next day with only four enemy ships in sight; another general chase was ordered but again the quarry was lost. Concluding that d'Aché would make for Pondicherry, Pocock did so too, arriving there on 8 September to find the anchorage still empty. But his assumption had been correct and, soon after midday, 13 sail were sighted on the horizon. With an offshore breeze behind him, Pocock stood out to sea. The chase lasted all day and, next morning, he counted 16 sail ahead. Both squadrons formed lines of battle and an action seemed imminent, but again darkness fell before it could be joined.

At six o'clock on the morning of 10 September, the sun lit the French line of battle, nearly ten miles distant on the starboard tack. At ten, the French went about and hauled into a line of battle ahead and, an hour later, the British did the same; it was clear that a third battle was inevitable. As the two ragged lines came within range, Pocock's second-in-command, Commodore Steevens, found his ship, the *Grafton*, which was the third in the line, abreast d'Aché's flagship, the *Zodiaque*, which was the sixth in the French line, and immediately engaged her. Seeing Pocock coming up in the *Yarmouth*, the next astern, Steevens shifted his fire to the next ahead and drove her out of her line and moved on to support the British ships ahead of him. Thereupon the action became general, gun-muzzle to gun-muzzle at point-blank range. As the *Newcastle* closed the enemy, Captain Michie was shot through the head by a musket-ball. In Pocock's flagship, 'One officer was quite cut in two by a double-headed shot as he was standing between the admiral and captain.'[18] The *Salisbury*, the weakest ship in the British line, found herself fighting two French ships and was so shattered that she had to haul out of the line. The *Elizabeth* set fire to the *Actif*, which was silenced for a time, and both the *Comte de Provence* and the *Duc de Bourgogne* were so badly damaged that they, too, fell out of the line.

By four in the afternoon, only six French ships were fighting in line of battle and then two of those fell away. 'It is almost impossible to describe the Massacre that was on board the French Ships', said a survivor, 'the least had one hundred men killed or wounded.'[19] The captain of the French flagship had been killed and d'Aché himself had been hit in the thigh by grapeshot and fainted from loss of blood. The first lieutenant of the *Zodiaque* thereupon took her out of the line and signalled the other French ships to haul away to the south-east out of the battle.

As the sea cleared, the British were once again in no state to pursue, their upper decks and sides swagged and festooned with collapsed sails, loops of rigging and splintered spars. Only two, the 60-gun ships *Sunderland* and *Weymouth*, were in a state to chase the enemy, which they did, the others following as best they could. The little *Revenge* was again ordered to shadow the enemy until dark and did so. At daybreak, the French were sighted some 12 miles distant and, seeing the British following, put about and made sail to the south until their sails could hardly be seen from the maintops of the British squadron. The battle was over and, unable to pursue further with any hope of success, Pocock continued under easy sail to the south-west, three of his ships towing three others.

Pocock had won another victory, although no enemy ships had been destroyed or taken. His immediate success had to be measured in casualties and these had been heavier than ever. The French had lost two captains and nearly 1,500 men killed and wounded and their ships' hulls again shattered. But the British, too, had lost heavily: 118 killed (including the captain of the

Newcastle), 66 dying of wounds and more than 500 wounded. Pocock and Steevens, 'who had been in many engagements', it was reported, 'said this was the severest they ever saw'.[20]

On 12 September, the British were off Negapatam but the enemy were not lying in the road, so Pocock anchored and sent the *Revenge* to Madras with his despatch. Assuming that d'Aché must have made for Pondicherry, which lay between himself and Madras, he determined not to pass it by night, although his ships were in no condition for further fighting. Sure enough, on the 27th, he sighted the French there, lying at anchor, close under the shore batteries. So, slowly, the British squadron sailed past in line of battle, guns run out, almost within range of the heavy guns ashore, challenging d'Aché to come out and fight again. An offshore breeze blew and the French were seen to be weighing anchor and making sail. This time it could only be a fight to the finish.

As the wind drove the British further from the coast, the French put their helms over and, close-hauled, turned south, Pocock in pursuit. By sunset, they were nearly 12 miles to windward off Pondicherry; d'Aché had refused to go ashore, but he had received news of a British reinforcement of four ships of the line due to reach Pocock at any time. Those were odds he could not face and he announced his intention of making straight for Mauritius. In vain, Lally ordered him to remain, hectored and pleaded. Finally, d'Aché called a meeting of all his captains and they unanimously supported his decision to retreat but, as a gesture of compliance, agreed to land 500 sailors and marines to join the garrison. By the end of the month, the squadron had left the Coromandel coast to the British. As the council at Madras put it to Pocock in a letter, when they heard the news, 'Mr d'Aché seems by his Manoeuvre not to be inclined the risque a second Action'.[21]

Pocock returned to Madras to land his wounded and sick and to victual and water his ships. The monsoon season was about to break there so they sailed for Bombay on 16 October, next day meeting the reinforcements from England: Rear-Admiral Samuel Cornish with four sail of the line and three East Indiamen with troops on board bound for Madras. After a stormy passage, the squadron reached Bombay, where Pocock received a gratifying formal welcome from the Governor: 'We behold the Particulars of the Defeat of the French squadron with equal Joy and Admiration considering their great Superiority in Strength and Numbers to His Majesty's Ships under your Command ... Your Success, Sir, deserves to add fresh Lustre to the great

Reputation you have so justly acquired.'[22] There he formally handed over his command to Rear-Admirals Steevens and Cornish and prepared to sail for home. Then, hearing news of more trouble in Bengal, he waited until he heard that, in November, the expected Dutch incursion had taken place but had been dealt with by Clive with characteristic ruthlessness. In half-an-hour's fighting, half their force had been killed, wounded or taken prisoner and the Dutch leadership made ready to agree to any terms Clive dictated. No more would be heard of a Dutch threat to Bengal.

Pocock made his farewells, but by now all his captains were aware that such was the extent of the war that they would probably meet again in another theatre of operations. As Steevens wrote to the admiral in a farewell letter, he hoped for 'an everlasting friendship between us to keep up a constant correspondence from any part of the World the public service may require our attendance in the present war'.[23] On 7 April, 1760, Pocock sailed for home in the much-repaired *Yarmouth,* with Colonel Draper, who had commanded the sortie at Madras, as a passenger. Rounding the Cape of Good Hope, he reached the island of St Helena in June and there met a homeward-bound convoy of 17 East Indiamen – 11 of them from China – which he accompanied. Safely shepherding them up the Channel to the Downs anchorage off Deal, the fleet made its way up the Thames, the richest ever to reach London.

George Pocock was the hero of the hour. Made a Knight Commander of the Order of the Bath at an audience with the King, he received a succession of accolades. The East India Company gave him a fulsome welcome and, declaring that such a rich man could not be in any need of financial recognition, they offered him a choice of having his portrait painted or sculpted; he 'made choice of the marble'.[24][*] A week before Christmas, he was accorded 'an elegant entertainment'[25] at the King's Head tavern in Cornhill.

More news arrived from India. In January, Colonel Eyre Coote had decisively defeated the French at Wandewash and Pondicherry seemed to be at his mercy; soon afterwards, Clive and his family left Calcutta for home leave. The greatest news was the realisation that the balance of power in India had been changed. The French navy had been swept from the Indian Ocean by Pocock.[†]

Without maritime communications, what remained of French military and commercial power would wither. Of their two great settlements, Chandernagore had been lost and would soon be followed by Pondicherry. Not only were the British now supreme in India, but they could think of using their bases there for further conquests beyond the sub-continent. Only Clive might be dreaming of a British empire in India, but already a glittering vision of wealth and power was assuming reality, and only those who had been there could begin to understand what forces they had let loose.

'Come follow the Hero that goes to Quebeck'

Not since Generals Abercromby and Howe had led their armada up the length of Lake George a year before had the waterways of North America presented such a spectacle. The St Lawrence river was not much wider than the lake and, in June, 1759, it was crowded with 22 sail of the line, a dozen frigates, sloops, bomb-ketches and fireships. On board 119 transports were embarked an army of 9,200 men commanded by Major-General James Wolfe, who had led the assault on Louisbourg.

When that campaign had been successfully completed, Wolfe had been among the officers given command of small expeditions ordered to attack French settlements along the coast and near the mouth of the St Lawrence. As in the Scottish Highlands a dozen years earlier, villages and crops were burned and the villagers turned out of their homes. 'We have done a great deal of mischief, Wolfe reported to Amherst, 'spread the terror of his Majesty's arms through the whole gulf but have added nothing to the reputation of them.'[1] Despite his ruthlessness, Wolfe had been appreciative of the remote beauty of his surroundings, writing in his journal: 'The isles of d'Oiseau we saw also … wholly inhabited by Birds, many of whom came into our Ship, some with red heads, others with red and yellow rings round their necks, all extremely small. These islands look oddly with the roosting of so many thousand birds, the eggs of many very good, ships frequently load with them.' There were strange mammals, too, such as 'sea cows … who for horrid ugliness may vie with any other creatures'.[2]

As winter drew in, the expeditions had returned to Louisbourg, where Wolfe had embarked with Boscawen for England. On arrival at Portsmouth, he had rejoined his regiment at Salisbury and on 17 November gone on leave. James Wolfe had become something of a hero for his feats at Louisbourg and was lionised at home in Blackheath and at Bath. There, he again met Katherine Lowther, the self-possessed, cool and elegant sister of the heir to the earldom of Lonsdale, and they became engaged. In December, he was summoned to Whitehall for an interview with Lord Ligonier, who told him that the main attack would be made on Quebec in the following year. Again it would be from two directions: a second, northward, attempt via the lakes, Ticonderoga and Crown Point, to be led by Amherst himself, and a drive south-west, up the St Lawrence, to attack the capital of New France itself.

The command of the attack upriver was offered to James Wolfe.

Suffering from chronic ill health, Wolfe had just complained to a friend: 'I am in a very bad condition, both gravel and rheumatism, but I would much rather die than decline any kind of service that offers.' So he accepted with alacrity, writing to Amherst: 'They have put a heavy task on my shoulders and I find nothing encouraging in the undertaking but the warmest and most earnest desire to discharge so great a trust to your satisfaction as my general and to His Majesty and the Publick.'[3] The King reciprocated his dedication and, when told that Wolfe was regarded as eccentric to the point of imbalance, replied famously, 'Mad is he? Then I wish he would bite some of my other generals.'[4] Wolfe was thereupon promoted to acting major-general at the age of thirty-two.

With Wolfe would be three brigadiers: Monckton, Murray and Townshend. Although described as 'Fat Headed', the Honourable Robert Monckton, the son of Lord Galway, had proved himself an efficient soldier and an amiable man. The Honourable James Murray, the son of Lord Elibank, was a stubborn, forceful Scot with thin, tight lips and a sharp, enquiring nose and, according to a contemporary, 'the very Bellows of sedition; Envious, Ambitious, the very mention of another's merit canker'd him'.[5]

The Honourable George Townshend, the son of Lord Townshend, the Norfolk landowner and agriculturalist, had a restless, sardonic manner and, according to Horace Walpole, was of a 'proud, sullen and contemptuous temper',[6] but he had a ready wit and devastating skill as a caricaturist. He had been to school at Eton, where he had played cricket with William Draper and, like him, had become a soldier. He had fought at Culloden but had quarrelled with the Duke of Cumberland, whom he delighted in caricaturing as a fat dandy. On the outbreak of war, when Hanoverian troops were being used for the defence of England during the fear of French invasion, he had been active in advocating a militia. Before sailing for Canada, he had collaborated with another Norfolk landowner in writing a manual explaining how 'an healthy robust countryman, and a resolute mechanic, may be taught the use of arms and how very attainable that degree of military knowledge is, which will enable a country gentleman to command a platoon'.[7]

This manual showed Townshend to be at the cusp of military thinking, for he was aware that the rigidity of traditional tactics could not survive in the wilds of North America. In his introduction he ranged over military history, noting that the favourite weapon of the Franks had been 'the hatchet, which they use as a missile, throwing it in the same manner as the North American Indians do theirs, which they call tomahawks'.[8] The book described exactly the newly introduced 'Prussian step', or 'goose-step', favoured by the Hanoverians: 'carrying the foot directly forward with a straight knee almost parallel to the ground ... a motion extremely beautiful and graceful when well performed'.[9] But Townshend had added a note that two infantry regiments preferred their own, more relaxed method of marching, which he described as 'an easy, genteel manner of walking in cadence' that lost 'a little of the exactness of the Prussians and ... takes off that appearance of stiffness and dancing, which some have objected to in the Prussian step'.[10]

Townshend was a tall, elegant man, often wearing a sardonic smile, with humour in his sidelong glance. He was talented but difficult, 'subject to very high and low spirits ... the appearance of an excess of good nature, at times of bitterness', wrote one who knew him. 'He has a great deal of humour, well stained with bawdy and may be esteemed an excellent tavern acquaintance.'[11] There was more to him than that: thoughtfulness and enthusiasm among his positive qualities; selfishness and arrogance among the negative.

The naval command was given to Vice-Admiral Charles Saunders, who had sailed round the world with Anson and remained in the First Lord's favour. Now aged forty-five, Saunders had relieved Admiral Hawke in the Mediterranean after Byng's disgrace and his tough, pugilistic looks reflected his reputation as an aggressive commander. On 17 February, 1759, he had sailed from Spithead with eight ships of the line to join the rest of the fleet off Louisbourg in April.

Wolfe was aware that his mission involved more than the defeat of a French army and the occupation of New France. If and when that was achieved, the whole of North America as far south and west as the Spanish settlements in Florida and California would be at the disposal of the inhabitants of the British Isles. 'This will, some time hence, be a vast empire, the seat of Power and Learning', he wrote to his mother. 'They have all the Materials ready, Nature has refus'd them nothing, and there will grow a people out of our little spot that will fill this vast space and divide this great Portion of the Globe with the Spaniards, who are possessed of the other half.'[12]

As the fleet approached the Canadian coast it became obvious that delays were to be expected because it had been one of the hardest winters in memory and the St Lawrence estuary was perilous with 'floating islands of ice'.[13] They knew what could be expected. 'Not a winter passes without the loss of limbs by the benumbing cold', they had been warned. 'When the wind blows from the west, the cold is so piercing that it almost peels the skin off the face ... During this terrible season, which is attended by the purest sky imaginable, the cold is so sharp and intense that even the bears avoid stirring out of their dens.'[14]

As the thaw progressed, the water was calm but the tides rose and fell 20 feet (6 metres) and the currents were strong; there were shoals and all was bedevilled by recurrent fog. When the wind was southerly, the fleet had to tack and this was inherently dangerous in confined waters. Amongst the soldiers watching apprehensively was Brigadier Townshend, who recorded:

> Before 12, the Fog cleared and we stood for the Southern Shore. Continued tacking and standing all the Evening from one shore to the other when, about 8, five of the Capital Ships upon a tack were near running on board each other. The Current being very strong, few would answer the helm at first. Our own Frigate, the *Diana*, remain'd ungovernable for a long while and in the greatest Danger of having the *Royal William* of 90 guns and the *Orford* of 70 on board us.[15]

The French had removed all the buoys marking the channel and, although a couple of French charts had recently been captured, most ships' masters had to navigate by eye and by taking soundings. Some in the expedition had seen the *New and Correct Chart of North America* published by Mount and Page in London four years earlier, but that showed the lower St Lawrence far wider than it was, did not mark Louisbourg and misplaced Quebec.

French pilots had been lured aboard the British ships by the hoisting of false colours but baulked at being ordered to guide the British up the river:

> The man who fell to the *Goodwill's* lot gasconaded at a most extravagant rate and gave us to understand it was much against his inclination that he was to become an English pilot ... He made no doubt that some of the fleet would return to England but that they should have a dismal tale to carry with them; for Canada should be the grave of the whole Army and he expected in a short time to see the walls of Quebec ornamented with English scalps. Had it not been in obedience to the Admiral, who gave

orders that he should not be ill used, he would have been thrown overboard. [16]

So Saunders preferred to rely on his own navigating masters. One of these was James Cook[*], sailing master of the *Pembroke,* who was already proving himself in surveying the river ahead of the fleet. 'I was on board the *Pembroke*', recalled an Army surveyor, 'where the great cabin, dedicated to scientific purpose and mostly taken up with a drawing table, furnished no room for idlers … Mr Cook and myself compiled materials for a chart of the Gulf and River St Lawrence.'[17]

The most testing reach of the river was the Traverse Channel, between the high headland of Cap Tourmente and the Ile d'Orléans, a low, whalebacked island, 21 miles long and up to 5 miles wide, stretching to within sight of Quebec, distant across a wide basin. The French pilot on board the transport *Goodwill* declared that the British would never navigate the dangerous channel without the help he was unwilling to give, saying that the ship 'would be lost, for that no French ship ever presumed to pass there without a pilot'. But the sailing master, named Killick, replied, 'Ay, ay, my dear, but damn me, I'll convince you that an Englishman shall go where a Frenchman dare not show his nose!' So, recorded the French-speaking Captain John Knox of the 43rd Regiment, Killick 'would not let the pilot speak but fixed his mate at the helm, charged him not to take orders from any person but himself and, going forward with his [speaking] trumpet to the forecastle, gave the necessary instructions'.

Knox joined Killick in the bows and remembered that the latter

pointed out the channel to me as we passed; showing me by the ripple and colour of the water where there was any danger, and distinguishing the places where there were ledges of rock (to me invisible) from banks of sand, mud or gravel. He gave his orders with great unconcern, joked with the sounding-boats, who lay off each side with different-coloured flags for our guidance; and when any of them called to him and pointed to the deepest water, he answered, 'Ay, ay, my dear, chalk it down – a damned dangerous navigation, eh? If you don't make a sputter about it, you'll get no credit for it in England.' After we had cleared this remarkable place, where the channel forms a complete zigzag, the master called to his mate to give the helm to somebody else, saying, 'Damn me, if there are not a thousand places in the Thames fifty times more hazardous than this; I am ashamed that an Englishman should make such a rout about it.' The Frenchman asked me if the captain had not been there before. I assured him in the negative; upon which he viewed him with great attention, lifting at the same time his hands and eyes to heaven with astonishment and fervency.[18]

When they could look up from the surface of the river, they saw range beyond range of wooded hills, stretching away into unknown territory. 'In this country are unbounded forests, not planted by the hands of men, and in all appearance as old as the world itself', a traveller wrote, listing varieties of pine, fir, cedar, oak, maple, ash, walnut, beech, poplar, alder, chestnut, blackthorn, pear, cherry, plum and elm that formed 'many magnificent prospects'. But along the St Lawrence, he warned, the country was mostly 'wild and uncultivated ... covered with impenetrable woods, mostly of pine and dwarf spruce, with stupendous rocks and barren mountains, which form a dismal prospect'.[19] This monotony was about to give way to scenery worthy of the great event they all knew lay before them.

Wolfe himself was in the frigate *Richmond*, following in the wake of the *Goodwill* as boats manned by armed sailors took soundings ahead of the slow procession of ships. As they reached the Ile d'Orléans, it could be seen that while there was some cultivation along the western shore, it was otherwise thickly grown with forest. Major Patrick Mackellar, the expedition's chief engineer, had suggested the island as the most promising site for an initial landing and encampment. That night, 26 June, a Lieutenant Meech landed with 40 New England rangers, skirmished with some French Canadians but, next morning, declared that it was safe for the army to disembark. When they did so, they entered a deserted church to find a note from the priest asking the British to respect it and inviting them to enjoy the asparagus in his garden; they also found the scalped and mutilated body of a ranger who had disappeared during the night, and realised that both European courtesies and the horrors of Indian warfare could be expected in the campaign to come.

The southern tip of the island commanded the view that Wolfe had imagined for the past year. Ahead, across four miles of shining river, stood their goal: the bastions, ramparts, towers and spires of Quebec, high on its rocky headland. Protected by the wide, swirling river, cliffs and massive fortifications, and crowned by a citadel, it was a handsome city: 'the only city in the world', it was said, 'of a fresh water harbour capable of containing one hundred men-of-war of the line at one hundred and twenty leagues distant from the sea ... on the most navigable river in the universe'.[20] Along the waterfront, below the cliffs, crowded the merchants' stone houses and tall warehouses; 200 feet (61 metres) above them stood the magnificent buildings of the upper town, the cathedral and episcopal palace, churches, convents, seminaries and fine stone houses reminiscent of prosperous, provincial France.

The city divided the St Lawrence, running south towards Montreal, from the St Charles river; below it, the former river spreading a mile wide between the high, wooded, eastern bank of Pointe Lévis and the opposite shore. There the village of Beauport stood between the St Charles and the great waterfall where the Montmorency river plunged nearly 200 feet (61 metres) into the St Lawrence. 'We are entertained with a most agreeable prospect of a delightful country on every side', wrote Knox in his diary. 'Windmills, watermills, churches, chapels and compact farmhouses, all built with stone ... The weather today is agreeably warm. A light fog sometimes hangs over the highlands but on the river we have fine, clear air. In the curve of the river, while we were under sail, we had a transient view of a stupendous natural curiosity called the waterfall of Montmorenci.'[21] But, until he scanned the panorama through his telescope, Wolfe did not know exactly where Montcalm had concentrated his army, or what his own plan of attack should be.

It was a stirring sight, particularly to those with visions of empire. 'When this capital of New France shall be as flourishing as that of the Old (and Paris was once less than Quebec is now), what a prospect will this afford of towns, castles and villas?' wrote an imaginative contemporary.

Below is a noble bason, filled with vessels from all parts of the world: opposite to it, the Isle of Orléans, and the shores on each side of it, adorned with beautiful meadows, verdant hills and corn fields. On one side, the river St Charles, winding through a charming vale, crowded with villages; the port beneath, adorned with spacious quays and magnificent buildings. When all this happens, you will grant this terrace is admirably situated. Even at present, the view from it is delightful.

But, when Wolfe first saw it, there was the tense stillness about the scene that comes with the imminence of war.[22]

Although the French had long been aware of the British approach, their arrival in the basin below the city came as a surprise. As the first of the British ships came within sight of Quebec, the Marquis de Vaudreuil was astonished for, as he reported to Paris, 'The enemy passed sixty ships of war where we hardly dared risk a vessel of a hundred tons.'[23] In preparation for the attack, the Governor-General had ordered Montcalm to deploy the bulk of his army along the seven miles of low cliffs between the St Charles river and the Montmorency Falls, which he thought most vulnerable to a British landing and from which they could make a direct assault on the city. So there were encamped most of his 15,000 troops – regulars, militia and Indians – and there, at Beauport, he established his own headquarters, while less than 2,000 manned the fortifications of the city.

When, on 27 June, Wolfe himself landed on the Ile d'Orléans, he was accompanied by Lieutenant Adam Williamson, who noted: 'Went on shore with the general at the west end of the Isle d'Orléans. Had a very fine view of Quebec. Saw the Falls of Montmorency, very fine and steep, many encampments between that and the town.' The scene was not as placid as it looked; it darkened, as if in warning, and he continued: 'About 3 o'clock a very violent storm arose and put most of the ships in great distress, many lost all their anchors and boats and several their masts and bowsprits. Storm continued till dark. Isle Orleans extremely beautiful and well cultivated. Most of the troops got on shore.'[24]

The French had more reason for confidence than the British. Although Wolfe now commanded only about 9,000 troops, instead of the quoted strength of 12,000, there were some 13,000 sailors and marines on the river. His was an all-regular army of ten battalions, including one of Highlanders, two of the Royal Americans and the grenadier companies combined in the newly formed Louisbourg Grenadiers. He had to win quickly. He had to take Quebec within three months before the onset of winter, when the fleet would have to leave the St Lawrence before it froze. There probably was not time to starve the city into submission by blockade; it could only be besieged and stormed if he could get his army and its artillery ashore upstream of the city; or he had to lure Montcalm from behind his defences to fight and be defeated on an open battlefield. Well aware of Wolfe's dilemma, Montcalm knew exactly how long he needed to hold out.

But Montcalm was aggressive and, on the night of 28 June, he counter-attacked on the water. Seven merchant ships had been fitted as fire ships, packed with combustibles, explosives and loaded guns which would fire when the flames reached them. These were to be sailed towards the British fleet, set alight and abandoned by their crews to drift down on the ebb tide upon the anchored ships. At 11 o'clock that night, two signal guns were fired and an extraordinary spectacle began. Captain Knox watched

> the grandest fire-works ... that can possibly be conceived, every circumstance having contributed to their awful, yet beautiful, appearance; the night was serene and calm, there was no light but what the stars produced, and this was eclipsed by the blaze of the floating fires ... add to this the solemnity of the sable night, still more obscured by the profuse clouds of smoke, with the firing of cannon, the bursting of the grenado's and the crackling of the other combustibles; all of which reverberated through the air and the adjacent woods.[25]

The British were alert, however, and boats manned by sailors with grappling-irons were rowed out to meet the blazing hulks and tow them ashore. It might have been otherwise and, after a second attempt with several smaller fireships chained together had failed, Wolfe sent a message to Montcalm threatening that, if there was another, the fireships would be made fast to the transports in which French prisoners were held.

Montcalm and Vaudreuil had watched, first with elation and then with disappointment, from the north-west bank of the river near Beauport. By concentrating on that shore, in order to block the obvious approach to Quebec, the French had left the south-east lightly defended. Although narrows half a mile wide separated the high Pointe des Pères from Quebec itself, they felt sure that the city would be beyond the range of British artillery, although the lower town by the wharves at the foot of the headland might be vulnerable. This would have been so had Wolfe not been able to land the heavy guns of the fleet. Therefore his first objective was the high, south-eastern bank of the river, Pointe des Pères and Pointe Lévis.

The night following the fireship attack, Monckton's light infantry crossed from the island and next day cleared the south-east bank of several hundred French Canadians and Indians. On 1 July, Wolfe himself visited Pointe des Pères and criticised the preparations for siting his batteries there, noting in his journal: 'I was amaz'd at the ignorance in the construction of the Redoubts – directed some new works.' Then and next day he could at last see his objective at close quarters, the individual houses of the city and, through his telescope, the faces of its defenders on the ramparts. 'Saw the Town of

Quebeck weak to excess in the lower Town and an appearance of great Want', he noted. 'Easy bombardment of the place from Pt. aux Pères.'[26]

From there, the division between the upper and lower towns was clear. Lieutenant Williamson, who also scanned the opposite shore, noted that the upper town, set back behind fortifications at the top of cliffs rising from between 200 to 300 feet (61–91 metres), was invulnerable to bombardment from ships since the guns would have to be so elevated that 'the Shott must fly over all'. However, he noted,

> The low Town on the east side is a fair object for both Shott and Shells, the buildings are in general high and pretty close. This is by much the richest part of the whole, being taken up with the dwellings, Warehouses and Magazines of the Principal Merchants … This part of the town can be hurt by land batteries only from the hills on the South [south-east] Side of the river and they are distant 1,300 or 1,400 yards.[27]

Both Williamson, and the French, were wrong; once the big naval guns and mortars were landed, they would be able to reach both lower and upper towns.

While British gunners worked on their batteries, they came under fire from the city and ducked at the sentries' warning shout of 'Shot!' as the flash of a gun was seen on the ramparts across the water, or 'Shell!'[28] as a mortar-bomb trailed its smoking fuse in a high arc across the sky. Then the French launched an attack across the river by night, but the landing-parties were separated, mistook each other for the British, fired on each other and were driven off. The first guns began to fire on Quebec three days later and, as more and heavier weapons arrived, it became clear that, whatever else might occur, the handsome city would be demolished before winter brought the campaign to an end.

Although Wolfe now commanded the basin below Quebec, he was no nearer defeating the enemy, or taking the city. There were several options but Wolfe kept his thoughts to himself, not even sharing them with his brigadiers, partly for security and partly because he was feeling ill and uncommunicative. 'Bladder painful', he recorded on the day he observed Quebec at close quarters. 'A good deal racked.'[29] It was not only gravel that bothered him but a recurrent fever and what some were to see as the early stages of tuberculosis. It was not only the seasons that dictated the need for urgency. He had distanced himself from his brigadiers and they, being opinionated, sometimes quarrelsome, men, reacted by complaining and criticising him and what they imagined his strategy might be. Morale at command level began to suffer.

On 9 July, Townshend's brigade had been landed on the undefended north-west shore of the river downstream of the Montmorency river, moving up it to face the flank of the main French defences; these ran along the St Lawrence to the St Charles river and the city beyond. Three days later, on the far side of the basin, where Monckton was well-established, six 32-pounder naval guns and five 13-inch mortars opened fire on Quebec and its demolition began.[*]

A conventional European soldier would now have seen Wolfe's army as dangerously split into three across six miles, divided between camps on the Ile d'Orléans, the Pointe Lévis and at Beaupré on the north-west shore. However, Wolfe and Admiral Saunders saw it differently: instead of being divided by water they were linked by it thanks to their command of the river. An attack had to be made and Wolfe decided that, by making use of his amphibious capability, he could bring overwhelming force to bear on any point he chose. The most direct thrust would be somewhere along the seven miles of the main French defences upstream of the spectacular Montmorency Falls, a thundering rush of white water and spray which poured into the St Lawrence and now marked the front line between the British and the French.

Inland from the waterfall, rangers moved up to the Montmorency river seeking a ford, watched by French-Canadians and Indians on the far bank. Sometimes they met and fought, Townshend noting of one action: 'A number of their Savages rushed suddenly down upon us from the Rocky Wooded Height [and] drove a few Rangers that were there down to my Quarters for refuge, wounded both their officers [and] in an instant scalped 13 or 14 of their men.'[30] It had been found that French-Canadians sometimes disguised themselves as Indians, accompanied their war-parties and scalped prisoners, 'a barbarity which seems so natural to a native of America, whether of Indian, or European extraction', as a Scottish colonel remarked.[31] The practice was being emulated by rangers and British irregulars to an extent that Wolfe had to forbid 'the inhuman practice of scalping, except when the enemy are Indians, or Canadians dressed as Indians'.[32]

The assault on the main French defences at Beauport was to be launched both by Townshend's brigade, which had been joined by Murray's from the

Ile d'Orléans, moving up the wide foreshore at low tide, and by Monckton's crossing from Pointe Lévis. Their first objective would be a French redoubt built at the foot of the cliffs to the west of the Falls, in the hope of enticing the main French force down from their defences along the top. The British were in high spirits, rested, fit and scenting victory.

Their exuberance had been set to song by Sergeant Ned Botwood of the Louisbourg Grenadiers, with verses beginning:

Come, each death-doing dog who dares venture his neck,
Come follow the hero that goes to Quebeck …

Up the River St Lawrence our troops shall advance,
To the Grenadiers' March we will teach them to dance …

With powder in his periwig and snuff in his nose,
Monsieur will run down our descent to oppose;
And the Indians will come: but the light infantry
Will soon oblige *them* to betake to a tree.
From such rascals as these may we fear a rebuff?
Advance, Grenadiers, and let fly your Hot Stuff![3]

Accordingly, on the morning of 31 July, French sentries, and then most of the 12,000 French troops manning the Beauport defences, stared across the basin at the gathering flotillas of the new flatboats, each capable of carrying 60 soldiers and a gun in the bows. It was a fine day with the promise of heat to come and the sun caught the red and white of the uniforms and the steel tips of the bayonets of the infantry sitting shoulder-to-shoulder in the boats as the sailors heaved at the oars and they slowly moved across the calm water; in the stern of one sat General Wolfe. Ahead of the flatboats sailed the *Centurion* of 64 guns, with Admiral Saunders on board, and two small, 14-gun ships, which closed the beach and opened fire. From the cliff-top on the east side of the Falls, heavy British guns began to bombard the redoubt below.

By 11 o'clock that morning the mass of flatboats was within a mile of the beach but just out of artillery range and showing no sign of making a landing. Instead they were rowed upstream against the ebbing tide, drifted back with the current and then repeated the move. Finally, at half-past five that afternoon, when the tide was at its lowest, Wolfe made a signal, the bows of the boats swung west and they pulled for the shore. At the same time the French saw, a mile away and beyond the clouds of spray at the foot of the Falls, a solid phalanx of British infantry marching towards them along the beach. The mounting crescendo of the scene was matched in the sky, where dark storm-clouds were gathering over the St Lawrence.

As the flatboats grounded, 13 companies of grenadiers scrambled ashore and raced for the redoubt where the defenders began to abandon their guns. The grenadiers' drums beat the charge and, followed by two infantry regiments and a detachment of the Royal Americans, they jumped over the breastwork to find the enemy gone. But the redoubt was within range of musket-fire from the cliff-top and, stung by unexpected volleys, the grenadiers, their blood up, ran to the foot of the cliff and, without orders, began to climb. The cliff rose nearly 200 feet (61 metres); rocky outcrops and earth bound to the rock by scrub made it difficult to climb at any time but, under fire from the top, it was desperate. As they climbed, the grenadiers hauled themselves up by rocks and branches, to be hit by shot from above and slither down the cliff-face, or hang, caught in the branches of bushes. Then it began to rain: first a few heavy drops, then torrents, turning the slopes into mud slides but wetting the powder of their tormentors above. Soon the ghastly scene was almost blotted out by grey sheets of rain. Amongst the dead on the cliff-face was Sergeant Ned Botwood.

The ascent was impossible, the grenadiers' ammunition was as wet and useless as their enemy's and many were dead or wounded. Finally, the shouted orders of their officers brought the survivors down to what shelter was offered by the earthworks of the redoubt. There Wolfe, seeing that his plan had failed, had taken direct command. The French were not being lured down to the beach; the cliff could not be scaled; and now the tide was turning and would soon cut off Townshend's and Murray's brigades from safety on the far side of the Falls. He ordered an immediate retreat, Monckton's brigade re-embarking in the boats while Wolfe himself and the Highlanders covered the retreat of the other two along the beach, the spray from the great waterfall unnoticed in the rain.

Watching the British attack from his command-post on the cliff-top, Vaudreuil was exultant and wrote to one of his brigadiers: 'I have no more anxiety about Quebec.'[34] Wolfe was angry at the indiscipline that had cost so many lives, jotting in his journal, 'Their disorderly March and Strange Behaviour. Necessity of calling them off and desisting from attack. The delays occasion'd by their rash and inconsiderable Proceedings lost us part of the day and the tide beginning to make the retreat of Br. Townshend's corps a hazardous and precarious affair. Two hundred and 10 killed and 230 wounded. Many excellent Officers hurt in this foolish Business.'[35]

Next day, he put his thoughts into formal but no less forceful language in his orders, without any recognition of the dash and, as it might have been seen, initiative that had been shown. 'The check which the grenadiers met with yesterday will, it is hoped, be a lesson to them for the future', he wrote.

> They ought to know that such impetuous, irregular and unsoldier-like proceedings destroys all order ... The grenadiers could not suppose that they alone could beat the French army and therefore it was necessary that the corps under Monckton and Townshend should have time to join, that the attack might be general. The very first fire of the enemy was sufficient to repulse men who had lost all sense of order and military discipline.[36]

He realised that, humiliating as his defeat had been, it might have been much worse; now he would have to devise a fresh and original plan of attack, writing to Monckton, after a night's rest: 'This check must not discourage us. The loss is not great ... prepare for another and, I hope, more successful attempt.'[37]

The strategy had to be reconsidered. He knew that Amherst had been successful in taking Abercromby's defeated but reinforced army back up the length of Lake George for another attempt against Ticonderoga. Mindful of the first calamity, Amherst had delayed his departure until siege artillery could be brought up, but there had been no need for it, the threat being enough. As the British were preparing for the siege at the end of July, the French had realised that their success could not be repeated and, on 26 July, they had blown up Fort Carillon and retired up Lake Champlain to Crown Point. This, too, had been quickly captured by the British, and Amherst had felt confident enough to detach a force to take the French fort at Niagara, which would open the way to the Great Lakes beyond. He could then concentrate on the main drive north to meet Wolfe on his way south, which prompted Montcalm to send 1,000 troops he could not readily spare to reinforce Montreal. But as this news reached Wolfe through French prisoners and deserters, he realised that Amherst's success would be of little help because he could not hope to take Montreal, let alone reach Quebec, before winter set in. Already the evenings were darker, the leaves beginning to brown and curl, and he now had two months, at the most, to take Quebec.

One possibility remained. A week after the bombardment of the city from Pointe des Pères had begun, a small squadron led by the 50-gun *Sutherland* had slipped past Quebec at night, under fire from its batteries, and gained the upper river. A post had been established on the south-eastern shore by rangers and they were now reinforced by a battalion of the Royal Americans and a detachment of grenadiers. On 5 August, Brigadier Murray was also sent upriver with 1,200 men, charged with raiding the opposite shore to create diversions while new plans for a major attack were made. Such raiding could threaten the passage of supplies overland to Quebec and would have to be countered. Therefore, Montcalm sent the young and able Marquis de Bougainville with 1,600 men to defend the vulnerable 35 miles of the north-west bank above Quebec.

The offensive against Quebec was failing. The brigadiers argued and criticised Wolfe's generalship, particularly Townshend, who used his skill as a caricaturist to sharp, lewd, or scatological effect. One, entitled 'No Mercy to Captives before Quebec', showed Wolfe discussing women prisoners with his officers, 'We will not let one of them escape ... the pretty ones will be punished at Headquarters', while one adds, 'I understand you completely General – strike 'em in their weakest part, Egad', and another, 'I wonder if I shall have my share'. In another, Wolfe peers into latrines through his telescope, complaining of 'Dreadful laxity!' His height was mocked, one sketch showing an immensely tall Wolfe being measured and the caption 'Higher than before! Our General begins his day.'[38] One of Wolfe laying siege to a brothel was shown to the general; he angrily crumpled it and said that, if he survived the campaign, the libel would be the subject of an enquiry. Others laughed but it was not generous laughter and it began to erode morale.

Wolfe had considered an attack on Quebec from the river upstream of the city, but there were major obstacles. First of these were the French batteries commanding the narrows between the city and Pointe des Pères, although these were now being battered by British guns across the water. If a formal attack was to be made on the landward defences, heavy guns would have to be put ashore to batter down a breach for storming. Any landing that was more than a raid would probably be opposed by Bougainville's flying column, and another defeat would mean the end of the year's campaign. Yet, increasingly, this seemed to be the only available option. So, having taken

Admiral Saunders into his confidence, Wolfe circulated a list of other options, based on land attacks, to his brigadiers and, as he expected, they were rejected. By this little ruse he managed, without arousing further argument between these three argumentative officers, to engineer an agreement that the only option was the one he himself favoured.

An offensive across the river would be as difficult as any. During the second week of August, Murray made two trial attacks 25 miles above Quebec at Pointe aux Trembles. Both failed: not only had Bougainville's flying column kept pace with the boats and been ready to oppose the landings, but navigation had been faulty and an unexpected shoal encountered. Then, on the night of the 16th, the brigadier conducted a night raid. While camp fires were lit on the south-eastern shore and Admiral Holmes took his little squadron towards Pointe aux Trembles again, the raiding force silently embarked in flatboats which were carried on the tide to another destination, Portneuf. While Bougainville followed Holmes's movements, the raiders scrambled ashore unopposed to capture and burn a French supply dump at Deschambault. The lesson was that, to achieve success, cunning was as important as dash.

Wolfe had been ill again, his bladder gravel, rheumatism and, probably, feverish tuberculosis worsening. Towards the end of August he rallied but was under no illusions and was said to have told his doctor, 'I know perfectly well you cannot cure my complaint but patch me up so that I may be able to do my duty for the next few days and I shall be content.'[39]

Before deciding upon a detailed plan of attack, Wolfe had to change his strategic stance. The camp at Montmorency on the northwestern shore was abandoned, and only small garrisons left on the Ile d'Orléans and at Pointe Lévis, while the rest of the army – about 5,000 fighting soldiers – was moved to the south-east shore, upstream of Pointe aux Pères. The first problem would be to cross the river and the second to bring the French army to battle. On 2 September, Wolfe wrote a long and pessimistic despatch to Pitt, giving a full account of the campaign, apologising for not having written before as he had been 'so ill and still am so weak'.[40]

The British knew from French deserters that Quebec was short of food, yet starvation seemed unlikely to force its surrender before the onset of winter. So Wolfe tried to encourage more desertion by burning French settlements and farmsteads so that the smoke could be seen from the ramparts of the city in the hope of encouraging militiamen to return to save their families and threatened homes. Townshend found this distasteful and demeaning, writing to his wife that it 'has reduced our operations to scene of skirmishing, cruelty and devastation. It is war of the worst shape. A scene I ought not to be in. Genl. Wolfe's Health is but very bad. His Generalship in my poor opinion – is not a bit better, this only between us.'[41]

Yet Wolfe had given orders forbidding gratuitous cruelty towards individuals, as had General Amherst, the Commander-in-Chief. More atrocities were committed by the enemy because they had made wider alliances with the Indians, and the French-Canadians sometimes adopted Indian customs. This had led to Amherst issuing an order and sending a copy to Montcalm himself.

> No scouting party, or others in the army, are to scalp women or children belonging to the enemy. They are, if possible, to take them prisoners; but not to injure them on any account. The General being determined, should the enemy continue to murder and scalp women and children, who are the subjects of the King of Great Britain, to revenge by the death of two men of the enemy for every woman and child murdered by them.[42]

Yet, inevitably, there was some indiscipline and looting, the latter sometimes condoned. This was illustrated in a caricature by Townshend showing a soldier with a stolen goose under his arm being stopped by an officer, who says: 'You villain, what have you? If lean, I'll hang you, if fat, I'll forgive you. Go to the sutler [provisions quartermaster] – I'll enquire.'[43]

Looking to the future, Wolfe told Pitt that he could not order a direct assault on the city as that would be 'of so dangerous a Nature and promising so little Success'. His general plan was therefore to bring the enemy to action in the open, and he was 'preparing to put it into Execution'.[44] Exactly how this was to be done was not clear. He concluded:

> By the List of Disabled Officers (many of whom are of Rank) you may perceive, Sir, that the Army is much weaken'd. By the Nature of the River, the most formidable part of this Armament is deprived of the Power of Acting. Yet we have almost the whole force of Canada to oppose. In this situation, there is such a Choice of Difficultys that I own myself at a Loss how to determine. The Affairs of Great Britain, I know, require the most vigorous Measures; but then the Courage of a handful of brave Men should be exerted only when there is some Hope of a favourable Event. However,

you may be assured, Sir, that the small part of the campaign which remains shall be employ'd (as far as I am able) for the Honour of His Majesty and the Interest of the Nation.[45]

He also wrote to his mother, putting as brave a face as possible on the outlook:

No personal Evils (worse than defeats and disappointments) have fallen upon me. The enemy puts nothing at risk and I can't in conscience put the whole army to risk. My antagonist has wisely shut himself up in inaccessible entrenchments, so that I can't get at him without spilling a torrent of blood and that, perhaps, to little purpose. The Marquis de Montcalm is at the head of a great number of bad soldiers and I am at the head of a small number of good ones …[46]

On 7 September, most of Wolfe's soldiers embarked in 22 ships and sailed upriver to Pointe aux Trembles-trailed by Bougainville's column – to make a feint landing. The convoy then turned and swept downriver on the tide while the French struggled to keep pace and failed to do so. Rain soaked the men packed on the decks of the transports so that, when they finally returned to the south-east bank, they had to dry their clothes at bonfires. Their discomfort had been worthwhile: Wolfe had realised that by using the tides, waterborne troops could quickly exhaust an enemy trying to keep pace with them on land. The French had, however, learned the wrong lesson, imagining that the British were intent on blockading Quebec by preventing supplies reaching the city by river. They did not expect another landing. So Wolfe, having learned his own lesson, ordered that the moves up the river and down again on the tides should continue. The deception was effective and a French deserter confirmed that a British attack near the city was not expected. Vaudreuil thought the British would, having tried to cut his communications with Montreal, launch another assault against his main defences at Beauport.

On 10 September, Wolfe made the final reconnaissance from the cliffs of the south-east shore, just upstream of the city. He assembled a party of senior officers, including Townshend and Monckton, his chief engineer Major Mackellar and Admiral Saunders; also with them were Commander Chads, an able navigating officer, who was to command the boats in the first landing, and Captain Delaune, also an engineer, who was to lead the first assault. All disguised themselves in long greatcoats borrowed from the Louisbourg

Grenadiers and trained their telescopes on the long, wooded shore across the river. The leaves of the trees were beginning to change into the reds and golds of autumn, reminding them of the approach of winter and of an end to the waging of war for six months.

Wolfe focused his telescope particularly on a fold in the opposite cliffs nearly two miles upstream of Quebec. There, the heights, steep as cliffs, were thickly grown with scrub, rising about 180 feet (55 metres) from a narrow beach. This was a known landing-place, a narrow path slanting from it to the cliff-top, where French tents could be seen, but only enough of them to suggest a guard of less than 100 men. The path itself could be seen to be blocked by felled trees. The shallow cove so formed was known as the Anse de Foulon, and it was there that Wolfe decided to put his army ashore.

The group in greatcoats scanning the opposite shore had not escaped the notice of a French officer, who, watching them through his own telescope, guessed that they were officers in disguise. Yet even his report did not change his superiors' view that an attack so near to the city was unlikely. Otherwise, British security was effective, Wolfe keeping his plans to himself and ordering Holmes to continue sailing and drifting up and down the river. Next day, he returned to the bluff opposite the Anse de Foulon with Monckton, Holmes, Chads and Delaune, but still did not take his brigadiers into his confidence. He did, however, write to the officer commanding his troops at Pointe Lévis, Colonel Burton, who would command the second wave of the attack:

> Tomorrow the troops re-embark. The fleet sails up the river a little higher as if intending to land above upon the north shore, keeping a convenient distance for the boats and arm'd vessels to fall down to the Foulon and we count (if no accident or weather prevents) to make a powerful effort at that spot about four in the morning of the 13th.[47]

Although the brigadiers knew that an attack on the far bank of the river was imminent, they did not know where, or when, they would land and wrote to Wolfe asking for specific orders. On 12 September, less than 24 hours before the landing was to take place, he replied sharply, 'It is not a usual thing to point out in the publick orders the direct spot of an attack, nor for an inferior Officer not charged with a particular duty to ask instructions upon that point'; [48] but he did name the place he had chosen for the landing. Brigadier Monckton thought a night attack too risky, so Wolfe put the timing forward one hour so that the landing would be made in darkness but sunrise would light whatever transpired at the top of the cliffs and outside the city.

Wolfe had deployed 3,600 men upstream of Quebec and ordered Burton to march his 1,200 from Pointe Lévis along the south-east bank after dark, ready to be embarked in boats for the river-crossing. Meanwhile, Admiral Saunders still lay in the basin below Quebec with most of his fleet and, at dusk on the 12th, began an elaborate feint: the big ships slowly sailed along the Beauport shore and opened fire; signals were made, flares lit, and boats were lowered crowded with marines and seamen as if about to land. This deception, too, was successful, convincing the French that a landing was planned there and that whatever was happening upstream was itself a feint. So the bulk of the French army, which outnumbered the British by two to one, remained on the north-west shore below Quebec.

Wolfe himself was on board Holmes's flagship, the *Sutherland*. With him in the stern cabin was a boyhood friend, Captain John Jervis (the future Admiral of the Fleet Earl St Vincent), and to him Wolfe confided that he did not expect to survive the coming battle. Taking a miniature of his fiancée, Katherine Lowther, from his pocket, he asked Jervis to give it to her when he returned to England. At two o'clock in the morning of 13 September, the tide turned and, according to Wolfe's instructions, two lanterns were hoisted to the maintop yardarm of the *Sutherland*. This was the signal for the attack to begin and the crowded boats cast off and floated downstream in the darkness. Then Wolfe, muffled in a caped greatcoat, his tricorne hat set square on his head, clambered down the ship's side into a boat commanded by Midshipman John Robison, and sat with his immediate staff in the stern.

With only the sound of swirling water and the pressure of darkness around him, the general surprised the midshipman by quietly reciting some verse. It was a poem from a book given him by Katherine Lowther and had been written nine years earlier by a fashionable young poet, Thomas Gray. The sombre words of his *Elegy Written in a Country Churchyard* were in harmony with his mood, beginning, 'The Curfew tolls the knell of parting day ... and leaves the world to darkness and to me ...' It was oddly prophetic:

Th' applause of list'ning senates to command,
The threats of pain and ruin to despise,
To scatter plenty o'er a smiling land,

And read their history in a nation's eyes.

It was also charged with high-flown gloom:

> The boast of heraldry, the pomp of pow'r,
> And all that beauty, all that wealth e'er gave,
> Awaits alike th' inevitable hour:
> The paths of glory lead but to the grave.

Wolfe paused, then said, 'Gentlemen, I would rather have written those lines than take Quebec.'[49]

Led by Commander Chads, the boats began to cross the river towards the north bank and the dark mass of the wooded cliffs appeared above them. There were known to be sentries along the heights and suddenly one of them, hearing something unusual out on the dark river, shouted, *'Qui vive?'* A Scottish officer, Captain Donald Mcdonald – a former Jacobite, who had lived in France – instantly replied with a perfect French accent, *'La France!* *'À quel régiment?'* called the sentry. *'De la Reine,'* answered McDonald.[50] The sentry, who had been warned to expect French supply-boats trying to run the British blockade that night, did not bother to ask for the password.

The strong tide had swept the boats as far as the Anse de Foulon and there they pulled for the shore. They ground onto the beach and Wolfe jumped into the shallows with Captain Delaune and 24 volunteers, who were to lead the way up the cliffs. Wolfe ordered those near him to scale the heights as best they could and they vanished into the darkness. Hauling themselves up near-vertical slopes of crumbling earth and rocky outcrops by grabbing bushes and the roots and branches of trees, the soldiers scrambled upward, snagging their muskets and cross-belts in the branches.

Captain McDonald led and, when a French sentry heard the noise of scrambling in the bushes below and shouted a challenge, he answered in French, saying that he was bringing up a stronger detachment to relieve the guard at the top of the path. As the sentry wondered why he had not been warned, he and the tents beyond were rushed by the British. Wakened by the noise, the French fired their muskets before running for the cornfields inland. Not one of the British had been hurt but there was now no need for silence. Word of success was shouted to those below in the darkness and answered with cheers as the main force began their ascent.

The light infantry and the Highlanders, stiff-limbed after six hours sitting in boats on the cold river, climbed next, clambering over abandoned pallisades of tree-trunks like those at Ticonderoga. The boats of the second division had been swept farther downstream and come under fire from the cliffs; Wolfe ordered them to row back to the Anse de Foulon and follow the others up the slippery heights. As dawn lightened the sky, the general himself reached the top and looked across a plateau, draped in morning mist, towards Quebec. The undulating ground, partly cultivated, was known as the Plains of Abraham, after its former owner, a river pilot named Abraham Martin. Wolfe's first orders were to clear enemy snipers from the Heights of Abraham, as the cliffs were called, and, further upstream, silence a battery that had been firing and could hamper the landings as daylight grew. Wolfe feared that those guns might belong to Bougainville, whose riverside force might be nearer than expected and ready to crush his own small force against the defences of Quebec. So, until he heard that this was not the case, landing and climbing were halted. Townshend, whose brigade was still waiting on the river, noted in his diary: 'At that moment he [Wolfe] doubted (and with great reason) of the success of the enterprise.'[51]

Wolfe was well aware of the effect his despatches and letters to the Government – and to his mother – would have had in England. His pessimism had crossed the Atlantic, and Horace Walpole was to write to a friend:

> You must not be surprised that we have failed at Quebec, as we certainly shall … Two days ago came letters from Wolfe, despairing as much as heroes can despair. The town is well victualled, Amherst is not arrived and fifteen thousand men encamped to defend it. We have lost many men … that is, we now call our nine thousand only seven thousand. How this little army will get away from a much larger, and in this season and in this country, I don't guess – yes, I do.[52]

Then Wolfe's spirits rose. All seemed clear and no French soldiers were in sight ahead, or to east or west, so he ordered the landings to continue. Townshend's men came ashore and the empty flatboats were sent across the river to Pointe Lévis to collect the reserve. As the sun came up, the whole of the army due to fight that day – 4,828 regular soldiers in all – had come ashore and was drawn up along the top of the cliffs. Sending patrols to look for Bougainville to the west, the general himself walked with his staff and an escort towards the walls of Quebec, which were hidden by rising ground. He stalked through the mist and dew, his tall, thin figure accentuated by his distinctive uniform; unlike the elaborate red, white and gold uniforms of his brigadiers, his was entirely red but for his white stock and black, brown-topped boots; he affected this, it was said, because he was younger than, and junior to, his immediate subordinates and wanted to assert the essential difference in responsibility.

News came from the patrols that Bougainville's force was nowhere in sight, so the way was clear for a direct challenge to Montcalm before Quebec. Wolfe walked across the Plains of Abraham to the escarpment on the far side, where the plateau fell steeply to the St Charles river. All was quiet, with no sign of the French returning from Beauport across their pontoon bridge to the city. Quebec was still out of sight, hidden by a long, low ridge parallel to the walls named the Buttes à Néveu; he considered occupying this but it was within the range of French artillery and he decided to deploy his army 500 yards (457 metres) farther back. So the army marched across the open ground until the vanguard reached the far escarpment, where it turned right to face the city and two of Townshend's battalions took up positions guarding the left flank. Meanwhile, the main army, with Murray's brigade in the centre, took up battle formation. This was a long line, only two deep, of more than 3,000 men. Monckton's brigade, on the right flank, guarded communications with the beachhead, where sailors were unloading guns and ammunition for manhandling up the heights.

When Montcalm heard guns firing upriver at dawn, he was in his headquarters at Beauport and thought it no more than a customary morning exchange of fire. On the river he could see Saunders's ships and the boats that might bring an assault ashore below the city; across the river, he could still see the tents and campfires on the Ile d'Orléans and on Pointe Lévis. He had taken the precaution of sending an aide-de-camp to Vaudreuil's headquarters near the St Charles bridge to make sure that the gunfire he had heard was as innocuous as he thought. Before an answer could be returned, a messenger galloped up with news that the entire British army was ashore at the Anse de Foulon. 'It is but a small party come to burn a few houses and retire,' he remarked,[53] but even so he mounted his horse and, accompanied by another aide-de-camp – a Scottish Jacobite – set out for Quebec.

Before he had reached the pontoon bridge over the St Charles at a quarter past six, he could see, two miles away, a sight he had never expected to see. There, standing still and ominous across the Plains of Abraham, was a long red and white line of British infantry, touched by the colour of the Highland plaids and the gleam of sun on bayonets. 'I see them where they have no business to be!' said Montcalm and rode to Vaudreuil's headquarters.[54] The Governor-General was willing to order a state of alarm and that 1,500 French-Canadian militia and Indians be sent to snipe at the British flank above the St Charles, but that was all. Montcalm could, and did, order his eight regular battalions inside the city to prepare to meet the British beyond the walls and sent an urgent order to Bougainville, far upriver, to attack the British rear. But Vaudreuil still expected a British attack from the river between Beauport and Montmorency and refused to march his militia and marines – more than 2,000 of them – to the city. So Montcalm rode across the pontoon bridge and into the city to take command in what he knew would be the decisive battle.

Of some 7,000 troops available only about 3,500 regulars and marines, together with about 1,000 Indians, were in position to fight. Montcalm knew that they would have to do so at once: to retire behind the walls would mean that the British could dispose of Bougainville's mobile force of 2,000 men, then bring up heavy artillery and begin a siege in which they would inevitably succeed. But if the small British army, drawn up across the Plains of Abraham, could be swept over the cliffs at once, Quebec could hold out until winter set in. So he ordered his little army to march through the city gates and form line of battle.

The opposing armies were evenly matched in numbers. Six regular infantry battalions – including the 78th Highlanders and the Louisbourg Grenadiers – formed the British line of battle; the French line was formed by five equally well-trained regular regiments with two battalions of French-Canadian marines and militia on either flank. Standing in their two long parallel lines, the British watched the white-coated French regulars form along the crest of the low ridge that hid the city from them; by eight o'clock their dispositions seemed complete. The British, having spent a cold and sleepless night, climbed the cliffs and been standing for two hours, fidgeted with impatience. In front stood their officers and their three brigadiers in their finery, while the gaunt, red-clothed figure of Wolfe stalked to and fro, cane in hand.

The crack of rifle-fire and the sputter of musketry had been spasmodic throughout the morning, and now came the thump of artillery as Montcalm brought up small field-guns and opened fire. So thinly spread were the British that their casualties were few and, when a man was hit, another stepped into line to take his place. Such loss was unnecessary so disregarding the convention of facing the enemy's fire as if on parade, Wolfe ordered his army to lie down and await the French attack.

Montcalm, watching from his black charger, knew that delay would not only be pointless but possibly fatal, so, soon after ten o'clock, he ordered the advance. As the French surged forward in three divisions, six deep, the British rose to their feet, their bayonets fixed, each musket loaded with two bullets to give their first volley maximum impact. No cavalry were fielded by either side and, as the armies closed, the few guns that had kept up a harassing fire fell silent. In contrast to the motionless British, the French advanced rapidly, some running, so that the cohesion of their line was lost. At 350 yards (320 metres) from the British line, the French halted and fired. The range was too great for accurate aim but Wolfe, conspicuous by his height and his red uniform, was hit in the wrist by a bullet and he bound the wound with a handkerchief. Soon after, he was hit again in the groin by a half-spent bullet; he doubled up but did not fall and continued to walk along the front of his battle-line, ordering his men to hold their fire. The French came on again, the militiamen throwing themselves prone to aim and fire before running on, so further distorting their already ragged line of battle.

The British, gripping their muskets, looked anxiously at their officers for the order to fire. At 80 yards (73 metres) the French fire became more effective and the steadfast British infantrymen began to fall. Still Wolfe stood casually 'with a countenance radiant and joyful beyond description', as one of his officers said,[55] until the French came to within 40 yards (36.5 metres), point-blank range.

Below, on the St Lawrence, the British ships' companies could see nothing of the battle on the Plains of Abraham, hearing only the sound of firing. Then they heard what sounded like a single shattering explosion: a volley from more than 2,000 double-shotted muskets. This was the culmination of the British Army's discipline and drill: the bringing to bear of irresistible fire-power at short range when the musket did not miss. As the smoke cleared, the French line could be seen broken and shredded. Then the British had reloaded and a second explosion told the listening seamen that it had happened again. This time, the British did not reload but charged with the bayonet. Those French still on their feet turned and ran, excepting the Royal Roussillon Regiment, Montcalm himself in their midst, which stood its ground and fought on.

As the smoke of the first volley drifted away, Wolfe had been hit again, staggering back into the arms of two grenadiers. A musket-ball had struck him in the chest and, as he was carried to the rear, it was obvious that he was mortally hit. Bleeding from chest and groin, he seemed unconscious and was carried to sheltered ground in a Highlander's plaid held at the four corners. A young soldier, James Henderson, called for a surgeon, but Wolfe told him, 'There's no need now. It's all over with me.' When a surgeon's mate came up, he managed to say, 'Lay me down. I am suffocating.' Then, as Henderson leant over him, he whispered, 'My dear, don't grieve for me. I shall be happy in a few minutes. Take care of yourself as I see you're wounded. Tell me, how goes the battle?'

He heard the shout, 'They run! See how they run!' and managed to whisper, 'Who runs?' 'The enemy, sir, egad, they give way everywhere.' Then, as Henderson remembered, Wolfe, 'raised himself up at the news and smiled in my face'.[56] Summoning his ebbing strength, he gave a final order: 'Go one of you, my lads, to Colonel Burton; tell him to march Webb's regiment with all speed down to Charles's river to cut off the retreat of the fugitives from the bridge.' Then he turned on his side and was heard to whisper, 'Now, God be praised, I will die in peace.'[57] A moment later, he was gone.

The battlefield was ghastly, for it had been cleared with the bayonet and the Highland broadsword: 'The bullet and bayonet are decent deaths compared with the execution of their swords', recalled one shocked survivor.[58] It took hours to gather the wounded in, amongst them Brigadier Monckton, but British losses were amazingly light: 58 killed and 590 wounded. The French had lost nearly 500 killed. Amongst these was the Marquis de Montcalm, who, like Wolfe, had received two light wounds before being hit in the groin. He was taken to a surgeon's house in the city, where he died at four o'clock the next morning.

As the French army died where it stood, or surrendered, or fled, the Marquis de Vaudreuil finally took action, sending the troops he had held at Beauport to the pontoon bridge to meet the fugitives from the battlefield. Then, although he could have marched up the bank of the St Charles river to join Bougainville above Quebec and returned with a fresh, combined force nearly twice the size of the tired British army, he insisted on a retreat to Jacques Cartier, 30 miles south of Quebec on the way to Montreal; he did not even see Bougainville's men by the St Lawrence.

Wolfe was succeeded in command by Townshend, who recalled Murray's brigade from pursuing the French to the pontoon bridge over the St Charles and Monckton's from chasing the rest into the city. Having reassembled the army, he again formed line of battle, facing the opposite direction, to meet Bougainville, who arrived soon after 11. Hearing of the British landing at nine o'clock that morning, he had marched 1,100 men towards Quebec, emerging from the forest onto the Plains of Abraham to see that the battle was over and that the British still stood upon the battlefield. He did not know that his force, if combined with that under Vaudreuil's command, could muster some 7,000 men, outnumbering the British. So, sending 100 horsemen, each carrying a sack of biscuits, round the British flank and into the city, he withdrew into the forest. The city itself was held by the remnant of the French until the 17th and formally surrendered to Townshend on the following day. The British marched into a ruined, famished Quebec. Six hundred regulars surrendered together with 1,000 irregulars and 1,000 French sailors, who had been manning the batteries, and 2,600 civilians.

Townshend began writing his despatch to William Pitt, announcing the victory and the death of Wolfe in such terse style that it was to give the impression that he was trying to belittle the general's achievement. It is unlikely that such was his intention; more probably, it was his own fatigue and his lordly manner that made his report seem detached and laconic. Whatever his intention, it did nothing to diminish the upsurge of emotion – joy at the victory, grief at the death of Wolfe – in the British Isles.

Wolfe had not been known to the British people but the circumstances of the young general's death on the battlefield at the moment of victory struck a romantic, patriotic chord. Apart from the triumph of capturing the capital of New France, the death of Wolfe at the head of his men stirred depths of emotion. It seemed an echo of popular classical and mock-classical myths of heroism and sacrifice and was reflected in crude and flamboyant verse, painting and sculpture:

Her grateful senate o'er thy sacred dust
Bid genius raise the animated bust,
Bid sculpture's ever-living language tell,
'Wolfe nobly conquered, when he greatly fell!'[59]

More than animated busts were to be raised, notably a grandiose memorial in Westminster Abbey.

Townshend's despatch announcing the fall of Quebec had reached London on 16 October, two days after the doom-laden letter Wolfe had written to Pitt six weeks before. Bells rang, flags flew, saluting guns thumped and the sun shone. Five days later, Horace Walpole was writing to a friend:

> It is still all gold. I have not dined or gone to bed ... till the day before yesterday. Instead of the glorious and ever-memorable year 1759, as the newspapers call it, I call it this ever warm and victorious year. We have not had more conquest than fine weather: one would think we had plundered East and West of sunshine. Our bells are worn threadbare with ringing for victories.[60]

The capture of Quebec was the crown of what was already being called 'The Year of Victories': and they had not only been in Canada and the Indian Ocean. In Europe and in European waters the war had reached a succession of climaxes, each seeming more dramatic than the last. As triumphant news crowded into the newspapers from battlefronts far and near, the British forgot how timorous they had been three years before. On the Continent, where they, in alliance with the Prussians, were defending Hanover, the French had, in July, taken the town of Minden, which commanded the approaches to the Electorate; but there, on 1 August, an army of 43,000 British and Hanoverian troops commanded by the Duke of Brunswick had fought and routed 60,000 French.

As on land, so it was at sea. Britain was now seen by France as the principal enemy, and defeat in Canada, India and now at Minden could be redressed by a direct attack on the British Isles themselves. This could only be achieved by gaining command of the sea. So, while an army massed along the Channel coast, the two French fleets in European waters – one at Toulon, the other at Brest – would put to sea, join and sweep the British from the narrow seas. Fear of invasion, which had been unnecessary in 1756, was now justified; the militia was mobilised and, in July, the two battalions that Townshend had helped raise in Norfolk marched to help with the defence of Portsmouth.

In August, the French tried to combine their two main fleets. The Toulon fleet, commanded by Admiral de la Clue, managed to slip out of the Mediterranean, passing Admiral Boscawen's fleet at Gibraltar, where it was refitting and taking on stores. Boscawen scrambled his ships to sea, catching the French off Lagos on the coast of Portugal. After a fierce action, four of the biggest French ships, including the flagship *Océan*, ran into Lagos Bay, where Boscawen burned two and captured two; the survivors ran for Cadiz, where they were blockaded.

There still remained the fleet in Brest, which was being blockaded by Admiral Sir Edward Hawke; amongst his 30-odd captains was Augustus Hervey. In November, a westerly gale blew the British off-station and the French admiral, Hubert de Conflans, took the chance and escaped into the Atlantic with his 21 sail of the line and four frigates, planning to join troop transports ready to sail for the invasion of Ireland. On 20 August, Conflans met Hawke's returning fleet and turned to run for shelter with the British in pursuit. The gales increased, both fleets crowded sail in flight and in pursuit and the French were driven into the wild, rocky waters of Quiberon Bay. Regardless of his own safety, Hawke followed them inshore, where heavy seas were exploding on the rocks, and he fought them until dark. When the first watery daylight illuminated the scene next day, Conflans's fleet had disintegrated. Six French ships had been wrecked, burnt or captured, the rest running for shelter in estuaries; the French flagship, *Soleil Royal*, had been beached and burned by her crew. Two of Hawke's ships of the line were wrecked, a small price to pay for the final elimination of any risk of French invasion.

British euphoria knew no bounds, lampooning the defeated enemy with bloodthirsty glee:

Old Neptune frowns to see his sapphire flood,
So purpl'd o'er with streams of Gallic blood ... [61]

The two naval victories had not only saved Britain from invasion but secured unchallenged command of the seas. However many boastful ballads were sung and witticisms coined – 'What wonders brave *Hawke* and *Boscawen* have done, the one burnt the *Ocean*, the other the *Sun*'[62] – they had given the British deep self-confidence, sweeping away the doubts and insecurity that had beset them three years before. Now Wolfe's triumph at Quebec could be followed by the further reinforcement of his successor, and the command of the Indian Ocean, won by Pocock, could not be challenged.

Nor were the victories at Quebec and Minden, Lagos and Quiberon, at Ticonderoga and in the Indian Ocean the only causes for celebration. In the Caribbean, a force had been despatched to seize the rich French island of Martinique, but, finding it too strongly defended, had instead taken Guadaloupe, the second most productive sugar-island. Increasingly, William Pitt, supported by Anson and Ligonier, became convinced that the use of the

Royal Navy to put the British Army ashore, where it was not expected and could do the most damage, was a potentially decisive strategy. Seaborne attacks had been made on the French coast but had not always been successful: in 1758, one on Cherbourg had been a qualified success but another, against St Malo, ended in disaster when the soldiers were attacked while re-embarking in the Bay of St Cas, losing more than 800 men. But Pitt persevered and more ambitious plans were made, particularly for an amphibious attack on Mauritius, covered by a squadron commanded by Commodore Augustus Keppel; this was cancelled, and the force was then destined for the French coast and finally for the heavily fortified, rocky island of Belle Ile in the Bay of Biscay.

'The Year of Victories' was celebrated throughout the British Isles, the American colonies and the British trading ports of the Caribbean and the coast of India. Every balladeer seemed to join the chorus of jingoism:

Blow the trumpet, strike the lyre,
British hearts with joy inspire,
Voice with instruments combine,
To praise the glorious Fifty-nine.[63]

The *annus mirabilis* was recognised as such by all, and the theme of popular ballad and song was '*Hail glorious, wond'rous Fifty-nine!*'[64] *Rule Britannia!*, composed 20 years earlier by James Thompson, had been the most popular song throughout the year. Now it was succeeded by a new one, *Heart of Oak*, written by the great actor-manager, David Garrick, for his pantomime, *Harlequin's Invasion*, which began:

Come, cheer up, my lads! 'tis to glory we steer,
To add something more to this wonderful year.

'A conquest too dearly obtained'

On 6 January, 1762, seven members of the war cabinet met in the high-ceilinged conference room overlooking Horse Guards Parade in London to discuss the most ambitious operation of war ever considered. Lord Anson and Lord Ligonier were to advise the Earl of Bute (the new Prime Minister, who had succeeded Pitt in the preceding year), the Earl of Egremont (Secretary of State), the Duke of Devonshire (the Lord Chamberlain) and the Duke of Newcastle (First Lord of the Treasury) on the 'most effectual methods of distressing and attacking the Spaniards'.[1] Four days earlier, the British Government had declared war on Spain and was presented with new strategic problems as a result.

Until now, the fortunes of war had increasingly favoured the British. The Royal Navy had nearly 300 ships at sea, manned by more than 82,000 men, and 600,000 tons of merchant shipping with crews numbering 36,000; the Army could now field 120,000 regular soldiers. Success had come to be expected. After Quebec had fallen, it had been held by Murray against a counter-attack and then, in September, 1760, Amherst had captured Montreal:[*] Canada was British.

In India, the sea was still commanded by Pocock's successor, Steevens, and the Comte d'Aché dared not return from Mauritius to the Coromandel coast; so, starved of reinforcements, the Comte de Lally finally surrendered Pondicherry to Colonel Eyre Coote on 15 January, 1761: India was dominated by the British. In the Atlantic, Belle Ile fell on 8 June that year to a British amphibious attack led by Commodore Keppel, in another demonstration of amphibious warfare. At Lagos and Quiberon, the French fleets had been reduced by three-fifths, and all fear of an invasion of Britain had been removed; their one attempt, early in 1760, had put 600 men ashore at Carrickfergus in Northern Ireland, only to be driven off and then captured at sea.

Now all that had changed. The diplomacy of the foreign secretary to King Louis XV, the Duc de Choiseul, had, by invoking the Family Pact between the Bourbon monarchies, persuaded King Carlos III of Spain to support France. Spain had nothing to gain from war with Britain because her wealth depended upon the safe arrival of rich cargoes from Spanish possessions in the Caribbean, the Americas and the Pacific, which would be vulnerable to the Royal Navy. In England, King George II had died in October, 1760, and had been succeeded by his young grandson. King George III had decided to continue the war with France but did not approve of William Pitt's recommendation to declare war on Spain in the early autumn of 1761, once the implications of the Family Pact became apparent. Pitt had resigned and had been replaced by the Earl of Bute, who held the confidence of the King. The King, too, then became aware of the danger from Spain and finally consented to the declaration of war.

This changed the balance of power at sea. The French Navy had been ruined, having lost half its 77 ships of the line since 1758, while the British maintained 120 in active commission. But Spain could offer some 70 sail of the line, about 50 of which were in commission, or available for service; these, combined with the remnant of the French line of battle, could not only challenge the British at sea but again make an invasion of the British Isles a possibility. The immense wealth of the Spanish Empire was defended by a global system of fortified ports and military bases. The most powerful and strategically important of these were Havana (usually known as 'the Havannah'), the capital of Cuba, which was recognised as the strongest naval and military base in the Caribbean and the Americas, and Manila in the Philippines.

Lords Anson and Ligonier, the old sailor and soldier, and the politicians looked at maps of the world in the conference room overlooking Horse Guards Parade that January morning, and it was Anson who focused their attention on distant horizons. They had been discussing a possible attack on Louisiana, the rump of New France surviving to the south-west of British North America, or the sending of an army to Portugal to threaten Spain directly. Anson was in favour of an offensive that did not involve long overland marches such as those made by Braddock, Abercromby and Amherst; much better to make use of the mobility of the sea. Anson then suggested a strategic concept of astonishing originality.

'We began', recorded the Duke of Newcastle, 'with my Lord Anson's project of attacking Havana and, after hearing the facility with which his Lordship and Lord Ligonier apprehended there was in doing it, we all unanimously ordered the undertaking.'[2] Such an intercontinental *coup de main* had been suggested during war with Spain nearly 20 years before, but it had been considered too ambitious. The idea had also been put about by the Duke of Cumberland after listening to old Admiral Sir Charles Knowles, who had fought an action off Havana in 1748. But that was not all. Lord Egremont brought up an equally spectacular plan put forward by Colonel William Draper, who had made his name leading the sortie during the siege of Madras and had recently been chief of staff for the attack on Belle Ile. This was to use ships and troops based in India – both regulars and East India Company mercenaries – to attack Manila, which was to the Pacific what Havana was to the Atlantic.

The concept of two co-ordinated thrusts at the twin hearts of the global Spanish Empire was far more ambitious than anything the councils of war had hitherto considered, but it seemed simple and was immediately authorised. That evening, the King, who had been kept informed but whose grasp of geography was sketchy, wrote to Lord Bute: 'It gives me no small satisfaction that Cuba, Louisiane and the Manillas seem to be agreed on by those who assembl'd today.'[3]

The attacks on Havana and Manila would be co-ordinated and only when the former had succeeded would the forces engaged move to attack Louisiana from the north shore of the Gulf of Mexico. Like Wolfe's attack on Quebec, that against Havana would be a race against the seasons because, just as operations in the St Lawrence would have been halted by the onset of winter, so ships would be unable to operate off the coast of Cuba once the hurricane season began at the end of August. Also, it was well known that, after a few weeks in the tropics, any army was liable to suffer from a grim range of tropical diseases.

Once the decision had been taken, preparations began with astonishing speed and efficiency. First, the commanders had to be appointed. The attack on Havana would involve a vast troop convoy covered by a major fleet and that, decided Anson, would be commanded by Vice-Admiral Sir George Pocock. Now aged fifty-five, still a bachelor, and knighted for his victories in the Indian Ocean, Sir George would be given the 90-gun *Namur*, the finest first-rate in the fleet, as his flagship. Ligonier had listened to the King's preferences in his choice of a military commander and had chosen the Earl of Albemarle, who was not a popular figure in the Army. Bland and plump at thirty-eight and socially well-connected, he was an enthusiastic, reasonably efficient but conventional soldier, but certainly not to be compared with the late Lord Howe; a favourite of the Duke of Cumberland's, Wolfe had described him as 'one of those showy men, who are seen in palaces and courts'.[4] Wolfe's successor, Townshend, had challenged Albemarle to a duel for belittling his achievement at Quebec; this had only been stopped, when pistols were already loaded, on the order of the King. One of Albemarle's brothers, William Keppel, was to take charge of siege operations as an acting major-general. Another brother was Commodore Augustus Keppel, who had tried to save Byng, had captured Goree – the second of two French settlements in West Africa to be taken in 1758 – and had recently made his name at Belle Ile. A specialist in amphibious operations, he was to be Pocock's second-in-command and in charge of the landings. The fleet would be assembled from squadrons currently in home waters, the Caribbean and off North America; the expeditionary force, which could eventually number 16,000, would come from England, the West Indies and the American colonies.

While these seven men were taking decisions on world war in the quiet room off Whitehall, the life of London pulsated around them. The capital had enjoyed a winter of social bustle after the coronation of the young King in September; indeed, some of the guests, invited from Hanover for the occasion, were still there in January, and amongst them was Count Frederick Kielmansegge, who kept a diary of his daily life. After promenading at Ranelagh pleasure-gardens in Chelsea, they had gone on tour, visiting Oxford and Cambridge, taking the waters at Bath and watching the races at Newmarket. Returning to London in November for the ceremonial opening of Parliament by the King and various other entertainments – sightseeing, the launch of a ship at Deptford, a hanging at Tyburn and spending evenings at the theatre –Kielmansegge heard rumours of coming war with Spain. When it was formally declared on 4 January, he was present outside St James's Palace to hear the fanfares and see the heralds, dignitaries and their escort of Life Guards. While the declaration was being read, his eye for detail noted 'The Queen, *en negligée*, leaned on the window-sill, which greatly increased the cheers of the people'.[5] Next month, London was full of talk about 'a secret expedition' being mounted against Spain – 'We have a mighty expedition on the point of sailing', Horace Walpole recorded. 'The destination is not disclosed'[6] – and Lord Anson promised that he would be happy for the Hanoverian visitors to watch it assemble.

The expedition might have to wait for some days before departing until a favourable wind enabled some of the storeships to sail from the Downs anchorage off Deal to Portsmouth, where they would be joined by transports that had taken part in the Belle Ile landings. While waiting in London, the visitors amused themselves at dinner parties, concerts, visits to artists' studios, balls and the opera. On 15 February, Admiral Pocock had taken leave of the King at St James's Palace and left for Portsmouth, hoisting his flag in the *Namur* at Spithead three days later. On the 17th, the names of the senior officers of 'the intended expedition ... victualled for the West Indies' were publicly announced, and that 'the expedition fleet' would be accompanied by four surgeons and 47 surgeons' mates.[7] Finally, on 24 February, word came from Lord Anson that any of the party who wished to see the embarkation of 'the secret expedition' should leave for Portsmouth immediately.

Anson himself left London that afternoon, taking the senior Hanoverians, including Prince Charles of Mecklenburg, with him. Kielmansegge and his friends had been looking forward to two parties on this evening and, 'determined not to give up the anticipated pleasure', chose to leave by carriage at three o'clock next morning. So, first attending a party given by a Miss Speed and then supper with Major-General the Honourable John Barrington, who had been the captor of Guadeloupe and was now to command the troops in Ireland, they boarded the carriage in the chill darkness and set out. At half-past eight they reached Godalming, 38 miles from London, to find that Anson's party, having spent the night there, had only left half an hour before. But they had taken 20 fresh horses and the 14 that remained were reserved for the Duke of York's party, which was due later in the day. The only alternative was to take a 'flying-machine', a fast coach, which made the journey of 72 miles from London to Portsmouth within the day. Four of these left London early each morning, kept their own changes of horses and halts for refreshment along the way, and reached Portsmouth before seven in the evening.

Kielmansegge's party found seats on two 'flying-machines', each of which could take up to a dozen passengers, inside and outside. Boarding his coach, the other passengers reminded him of Henry Fielding's novel *Tom Jones*, 'in which the most ridiculous, but life-like, descriptions are given on such journeys and of the company, conversations and adventures'. He himself found pleasant companions, including a captain in the service of the East India Company and his young wife, but his brother, in another coach, had more mixed company, more reminiscent of Hogarth's satirical engravings, including 'a fat English inn-keeper's wife, who kept her brandy-bottle handy, and two sailors' wives'.[8] The count's journey was not uneventful as a quarrel broke out between the coachman and a carter who had blocked the road, leading to a fight, which was won by the men from the 'flying-machine', although Kielmansegge admitted that he 'as a careful strategist, guarded the baggage and coach with the lady inside, and formed the *corps de reserve*'.

They entered the gates of Portsmouth after dark and rattled along the cobbled High Street between rows of taverns and grogshops, sailors' outfitters and lodging-houses to the coaching inn. The prince, they learned, was staying with Lord Anson at the admiral's house in the naval dockyard, one mile from the town itself, so they decided to join him for breakfast next morning. Then, driving out through the fortifications and entering those around the dockyard, they found the prince, Anson and the Duke of York surrounded by

> the entire General Staff of the expedition, viz. my Lord Albemarle, commanding the troops as Lieutenant-General; the Major-Generals Eliott and Lafaussille; Colonel Keppel, brother of Lord Albemarle, who was serving on this occasion as Major-General, and Howe, as Adjutant-General, with six aides-de-camp of the general's; Admiral Pocock, commanding the entire fleet of the expedition; Commander [Commodore] Keppel, who will command the landing of the troops; and others.

The atmosphere was so cordial that Kielmansegge added:

> Though jealousies between officers in the Army and Navy, which mar the success of the most carefully-arranged undertakings, are no rare occurrence, especially among Englishmen, on this occasion there was no ground for the slightest apprehension, but rather reason to expect a successful issue, as every care seems to have been taken to select the best men whose ability could be depended upon.[9]

The nature of the expected 'successful issue' remained a mystery, however, since none of the officers would divulge the destination, which remained, despite the publicity, secret.

It was nearly eleven before breakfast ended and the company boarded carriages and mounted horses for the journey to Southsea Common on the far side of Portsmouth to watch the embarkation. As soon as the procession passed the fortifications of stone ramparts and earthworks, they could see a stirring panorama of 'the magnificence of the Navy ... a grand subject of contemplation', as Dr Samuel Johnson found at Plymouth that same year.[10]

On the grass of the common which spread south and east to the beach and Southsea Castle, Lord Frederick Cavendish's 34th Regiment of Infantry was drawn up on parade. Along the shingle beach lay a line of flatboats, such as had carried Wolfe's army to the Heights of Abraham. Beyond, out in the Spithead anchorage between Hampshire and the Isle of Wight, lay magnificent ships of the line surrounded by a fleet of sturdy little transports. The visitors were told that the 72nd Regiment had embarked the day before, now it was the turn of the 34th, and two more would follow.

'After the regiment had marched past the Prince in splendid style', Kielmansegge noted,

> it formed up again close to the shore and awaited the signal for entering the boats. Immediately on this being given, each officer marched with his men to the boat, of which he had previously received the number; then he and his drummer entered first and passed right through from the bows on shore to the stern, the whole division following him without breaking their ranks; so that in ten minutes everybody was in the boat. The officers and drummers, with their corporals, sit aft near the rudder, the privates in two, or three, rows behind one another on the thwarts, holding their muskets before them, and two petty officers sit in the bows, but the oarsmen occupy special rows between the soldiers and a little in front of them, so as not to be hampered in the use of the oars. As soon as everything has been arranged in this way, the naval officer commanding the embarkation gives a signal, when all the boats start off at the same time and row to their respective vessels.[11]

The guests passed the afternoon touring the fortifications and playing chess before joining the Duke of York and Lord Albemarle at the Governor's residence for a dinner of 24 courses. Afterwards they moved to the Assembly Room for a ball, dancing until one with a break of half an hour for bread, butter and tea. In the candlelight, the gold braid glittered and the red, white and blue of the uniforms displayed the initial, but short-lived, elegance of war: there was the florid, courtly figure of Albemarle and his naval brother, Augustus, whose weather-beaten face with its long upper lip suggested his Dutch ancestry; there, Admiral Pocock, whose boyish looks, painted when he was a young captain by Thomas Hudson, had been creased and tanned by the Indian sun.

Next morning two more regiments marched past and embarked and the guests watched Commodore Keppel's ship, the *Valiant*, sail out of Portsmouth harbour – having had a leak repaired – to join the other four ships of the line at Spithead. Then they also embarked in boats and were pulled out to the ships of the squadron, which were manned overall: 'It is certainly a wonderful sight to see several hundred sailors at the same time standing upon the yards, especially from a slight distance, where it looks as if a swarm of bees has settled upon the ship.'[12] As saluting guns thumped – 'a splendid sight, as the ships were lying all round us, and gave us some idea of a naval action', thought Kielmansegge – and flags were hoisted, the boats ran alongside the *Namur*. After they had toured the ship, dinner for 25 was served in the great cabin; presiding over the long table, Admiral Pocock proved an attentive host. After dinner, the guests were rowed ashore as again the yards were manned and saluting guns were fired. Ashore, there were refreshments in a Portsmouth coffee-house before Anson, who was now suffering from a heavy cold, left for London and Kielmansegge attended another ball, which he opened by dancing with the pretty young wife of the East India Company officer he had met in the 'flying-machine' from London.

While the Duke of York and the Hanoverians were being 'sumptuously entertained',[13] as the newspapers put it, by Pocock in his flagship, the soldiers they had seen embark were getting accustomed to a different life afloat. More than 4,000 of them, including some officers' servants and some women, were on board 30 transports, which, together with 19 supply ships and eight ordnance and ammunition ships, had assembled in the Solent; they were mostly tubby little ships of between 200 and 400 tons, many of which had been engaged in the landing on Belle Ile. Each warship and each transport was to carry a flatboat, measuring 38 feet by 11 (11.6 × 3.4 metres), on board, but only 18 of the latter had space. So a problem arose when the victualling ships were ordered to take one each – their captains complained that they were being paid by the tonnage of provisions loaded, which would thus be reduced, and demanded extra payment.

Each soldier was to be provided with a straw mattress, a blanket, a coverlet and a pillow, to be laid on the lower deck at night, but those in the ships were dirty, worn, rotten and gnawed by rats; there were no fresh stocks in Portsmouth dockyard, so replacements were bought in London and sent by sea to Spithead. During the voyage to the Caribbean, hot food – mostly stew with vegetables, while stocks lasted – would only be available when the sea was calm enough to allow cooking. Later, meals would be cold, salt meat and biscuit, and tenders came out from Portsmouth with fresh stocks. Pocock and Albemarle worried that the ships from Guernsey, laden with wine for their own table, had not arrived by early March when they were ready to sail.

Only the senior officers and the politicians in London knew where they were going. Impressive as the naval and military concentration was, its size seemed to warrant no more than an attack on some French, or Spanish, island, or a lightly defended port. Indeed, Major Thomas Mante, the engineer officer, was to write of 'The Admiral and the General ... the one was almost without a fleet and the other without an army ... The hopes of the nation were animated from the confidence the people had in the Admiral ... the preserver and guardian of the British possessions in Asia.'[14] So it was generally assumed that the force would be reinforced on passage, probably in the West Indies. It was known that another attempt was being made to take Martinique in the Caribbean with a fleet commanded by Rear-Admiral George Rodney and troops from North America, but news of it was still awaited. 'Our great expedition under Lord Albemarle is not yet sailed', wrote Horace Walpole on 25 February, 'but waits, I believe, for a card from Martinico to know how it will be received there.'[15] Despite the danger of disease to any Caribbean expedition there was enthusiasm amongst naval and military officers to take part, and Pocock complied with a request to join from Lieutenant James Gardner of the marines, who had lost his right hand in one of the admiral's actions in the Indian Ocean and had been put ashore at Chatham.

Finally, on 5 March, Pocock wrote to the Board of Admiralty: 'Honourable Gentlemen: I am to acquaint you that we are now getting under sail.'[16] The whole convoy of five sail of the line and a frigate, escorting a total of 67 transports, supply and hospital ships, moved from Spithead to St Helen's Bay near the eastern headland of the Isle of Wight to catch a wind to carry them down-Channel. At noon it came, sails billowed from the yards and the ships swung south, then west, and, passing St Catherine's Point, steered for the open sea. Taking up a defensive formation – the *Namur* leading and a column of warships on either flank of the convoy – they passed the hills of Dorset and Devon. Two days after the convoy had sailed, citizens of Plymouth taking a Sunday morning walk on the Hoe saw ships out at sea, and it was reported 'The expedition fleet from Portsmouth, under the command of Admiral Pocock ... appeared this morning off Plymouth ... and were joined there by the *Burford* and *St Florentine* [small ships of the line] and were all out of sight by one o'clock with a fine gale at N.E.'[17]

It was only when the flagship was at sea that Pocock, Albemarle and their staffs could relax and talk freely about their objective. When the two commanders had received their instructions in February, Anson and Ligonier had also sent orders to Lord Amherst in North America and Admiral Rodney in the Caribbean to prepare to furnish the expedition with troops and warships respectively. They had also written to the two chosen commanders of the parallel expedition against Manila on the far side of the world; although this was a co-ordinated offensive, they did not have to coincide exactly since communications were so slow that, if tight security was maintained for two or three months, there was no chance of the Spanish in the Philippines receiving news of the threat, let alone of reinforcements being sent from Spain. These two officers were Rear-Admiral Samuel Cornish, who had relieved Admiral Steevens, Pocock's successor in Indian waters, and Colonel William Draper.

Havana was another matter. Speculation would, doubtless, include it amongst the possible destinations of the expedition that had left Portsmouth. The relatively small convoy that had sailed on 5 March would be misleading because the plan was that it would be reinforced on the voyage and on arrival in the Caribbean: first, by the two ships of the line from Plymouth; then by another seven sail of the line and 10,000 troops from the force that had been sent to take Martinique and from several West Indies garrisons in Antigua, Dominica and Guadeloupe; finally, by 4,000 regulars and provincials from New York and South Carolina, a regiment of freed slaves and a labouring force of 2,000 slaves from Jamaica. The force available to Pocock and Albemarle for the attack should therefore include 14 ships of the line and about 16,000 soldiers.

Surprise would be essential to success, so Anson had ordered the final approach to be made from an unexpected direction. Instead of taking the usual, safe route to Havana along the south coast of Cuba and rounding the island's western end, the fleet would approach by the dangerous Old Bahama Passage through innumerable reefs along the north coast. The tactics of the landing and the attack on the city were left to the commanders, and this occupied their time as they sat at a table strewn with charts in the great cabin of the *Namur* while the great ship heaved over the Atlantic swell, the other ships of the line and the transports dipping and wallowing around them.

Success depended upon the core of the expedition combining with other large forces from Martinique, Jamaica, New York and elsewhere. But, although the commanders there had been sent orders to rendezvous with Pocock, no-one knew if the orders had reached them as there had been no time to receive confirmation. Yet the organisation of the expedition in England seemed to have been so efficient that it was expected that they, too, would be ready. So when the convoy from Portsmouth reached Barbados on 20 April, Pocock and Albemarle heard with satisfaction that Admiral Rodney and Major-General the Honourable Robert Monckton – recovered from the serious wound he had suffered while one of Wolfe's brigadiers at Quebec and having subsequently been Governor of New York – had indeed captured Martinique. This was where they expected to be joined by the reinforcements. But, on arrival in Cas de Navires Bay on the 26th, the anchorage looked oddly empty and there was only one ship of the line in sight, instead of the ten they expected as reinforcements; nor was the admiral there to meet them, it being reported that he was 'much indisposed'.[18]

Rodney had the reputation of being a difficult man, as his tense, pinched features suggested; admired but not liked by subordinates, in whom he did not confide, he had already quarrelled with Monckton; yet he was an original and innovative commander, although said to owe his rapid promotion to influential friends. It was therefore assumed that his supposed indisposition was a diplomatic excuse, perhaps because of his annoyance that Pocock, and not himself, had been given command of the expedition. However, earlier that year a French plan to invade Jamaica had been reported, followed by the departure from Brest of eight ships of the line and 3,000 troops, bound for the Caribbean. The Governor of Jamaica had not only held back his own squadron at Port Royal but appealed to Rodney to send him his. His letter had coincided with the orders to Rodney from London to reinforce Pocock with ten sail of the line, some smaller warships, and all the troops that had been engaged in the capture of Martinique. Rodney had decided that Jamaica took priority and had sent all the ships earmarked for Havana to Port Royal under Commodore Sir James Douglas, his second-in-command, leaving only one ship of the line, the *Marlborough*, to fly his flag; he had also sent the French prisoners to France in the transports that should have carried troops to Havana. So Pocock saw the entire global enterprise put at risk, for now his seven sail of the line might have to meet not only the French squadron from Brest plus those already in the West Indies but more than a dozen Spanish ships of the line reported to be at Havana. Monckton, however, had refused to allow his little army to be sent to Jamaica, so at least they were ready to join the expedition, although he himself chose to return to being Governor of New York.

There was a curt exchange of letters with Rodney; Pocock brushing aside protests at his taking Rodney's flagship under his own command. Pocock also sent urgent orders to Douglas to leave Jamaica and meet him with all his ships off Cape St Nicolas, the western headland of Hispaniola (St Domingue, now Haiti), on passage to Havana. Douglas was, however, already convinced that the French were not planning to attack Jamaica and that they and the Spanish had not combined forces at sea. The squadron from Brest had been sent to save Martinique, but, finding that it had already fallen, sailed for the anchorage at Cap François on the north coast of Hispaniola. Douglas had also heard of the coming attack on Havana, so, disregarding Rodney's orders, he sent a small squadron under Captain Augustus Hervey to blockade the French at Cape St Nicolas, and set out with the rest of his ships to meet Pocock.

Meanwhile, Albemarle had more than doubled his command, bringing it to about 11,000 men. Monckton's men were tough, canny veterans from Canada, very different from the rigidly drilled regiments that had paraded on Southsea Common. But, having been in the tropics for several months, they were already sickly from dysentery and heat exhaustion and debilitated by drinking cheap rum; their uniforms and bedding were dirty and their appearance slovenly. Albemarle wrote to his friend Lord Amherst, who had sent the troops to Martinique:

Dear Jeff, it is very strange to me to write to Your Excellency in a formal way ... *Entre nous*, I found everything in the greatest confusion here, the Admiral and the General being upon ill terms, the service suffers ... Your army is a fine one, brave to the last degree, almost spoilt by the expedition up the River St Lawrence. Your officers are all generals, with a thorough contempt for everybody that had not served under *Mr Wolfe*; they either suffer, or cannot prevent, the soldiers doing what they please ... I dare not find fault as yet; I am greatly afraid they will oblige me to tell them my mind when we are better acquainted. They have conquered in a few days the strongest country you ever saw [Martinique], in the American way – running, or with the Indian hoop [whoop]. That manner of fighting will not always succeed and I dread their meeting of troops that will stand their ground. They are certainly brave and will be cut to pieces.[19]

At Martinique, Albemarle tried to re-organise his army and hired 600 African slaves to help with the heavy labour expected in constructing roads and siege-works at Havana in summer heat. Although a regiment of freed slaves and several thousand labouring slaves had been ordered from Jamaica, Albemarle rightly forecast that the former would not want to enlist for fear of being enslaved again while away, and that the planters would not agree to losing large numbers of their own workers. At the beginning of May the whole army re-embarked in transports, which had been scrubbed clean and aired, and they sailed on the 6th. They were joined by a trade convoy bound for Jamaica which took advantage of such an escort, so that the whole fleet numbered 13 warships and more than 200 military and civilian transports and merchantmen. On 25 May, Commodore Douglas's command joined Pocock's off Cape St Nicolas.

The huge fleet made its stately progress from Martinique, past the dark green hills of Guadeloupe and Monserrat, along the southern shores of Puerto Rico, north through the Mona Passage into the Atlantic and westward past the northern coast of Hispaniola to Cape St Nicolas, where the squadrons commanded by Douglas and Hervey finally joined it. The expeditionary force was embarked in 156 ships, each of the three divisions being identified by flags and each ship flying pennants to identify the troops, ordnance, or stores embarked. Albemarle used a book of 39 signals to summon army officers across to the flagship in calm weather, either singly, or in groups. In the crowded transports, the soldiers and slaves formed a strangely mixed army. There were regulars who had begun the year in chilly Hampshire, now sweating in tropical heat which, they were told, would be far worse ashore; a few, indeed, who had been enjoying the robust social life of London less than six months before. Amongst these was Dr Richard Bathurst, a friend of Dr Samuel Johnson, whose company he had kept in Fleet Street taverns and who had noted: 'Bathurst went physician to the army'.[20]

There was apprehension, not only of the enemy they would soon meet but of the climate and tropical disease. The soldiers from England saw the condition of those they met at Martinique, and, in England, Horace Walpole wrote of his own greatest fear of warfare in the Caribbean:

It cannot be an article of surrender that the climate should only kill its enemies, not its masters. This is a vast event and must be signally so to Lord Albemarle ... Well! I wish we had conquered the world and had done! I think we were full as happy when we were a peaceable, quiet set of tradesfolks as now we are heir-apparent to the Romans and overrunning the East and West Indies.[21]

As the fleet slowly moved along the coast of Hispaniola, a young officer, Lieutenant Daniel Holroyd, of the 18th Foot, who had fought at Belle Ile, noted 'nothing but hills and trees'. Remembering several young women he had courted, he wrote home:

Dear Jack, The probability of a man being knocked on the head some time or other makes me think to leave this letter for you (with a few belongings like regimental accoutrements). If you meet a ring with hair in it, preserve it carefully as it is the hair of Miss Mary Carleton, daughter of Francis Carleton of Cork. There is also a gold locket with Miss B——'s hair in it and a pocket I got from her sister, Miss H—— ... If anything occurs in the epistolary way, be dumb and burn the letters.

By now all could be as sure as he was that 'we surmise we are going to the Havannah'.[22] They now knew in England, too, and Horace Walpole had already written to a friend: 'Lord Albemarle takes up the victorious grenadiers at Martinico and in six weeks will conquer Havannah.'[23] There was no need for security now in Europe, only in the Caribbean.

The task before them was vague but daunting, even to their commanders. Little was known of Havana beyond the fact that it was an immensely strong, fortified city and naval base. The walled city lay to the west of the deep, natural harbour on the north coast of Cuba and was defended by its citadel, the Castillo de la Real Fuerza, and, outside the walls, a fort named La Punta. On the opposite side of the harbour mouth, a massive fortress, El Morro, dominated all, and the entrance to the harbour was itself covered by a heavy battery at the water's edge called 'The Twelve Apostles'. A few miles to either side of the city were smaller forts at the coastal villages of Cojimar and Chorera. The acknowledged authority on Havana was old Admiral Charles Knowles[*], who had fought an action off Havana and visited the city in 1756 when Governor of Jamaica. He had long been an enthusiast for attacking Havana and, as was requested:

To Admiral Knowles is due the most of the original project for the reduction of the Havannah ... [and he] submitted to Mr Pitt a plan – probably the same which he laid before the cabinet at the time of his resignation. [He] afterwards showed his papers to the Duke of Cumberland. He had observed the Morro castle from the shrouds of a ship entering the harbour and had concluded 'I look upon the town as certainly conquered whenever the Morro is taken.'[24]

He had noted details of the walls and batteries of the fortress, the lie of the land and the extent of the harbour beyond, and he had proposed various methods of attack. On reading them, the Duke of Cumberland had written to Albemarle at the end of February, while the expedition was still at Portsmouth awaiting a wind. 'I dread the loss of one single day at present and that not the less for Knowles's company, who is here croaking every day at dinner. Any bystander would think me the projector and fitter-out of the expedition ...'[25] So Knowles's plan was the only one by a professional naval, or military, officer with experience of the ground on which Albemarle's staff could base their own. Even now, plans could not be as first envisaged because there was no news of the contingent from New York. Orders to send troops to Havana had not reached Amherst until 1 April, and he had set about embarking some 4,000 regulars and American provincial troops.

While shepherding his fleet through the Caribbean islands, Pocock was thinking ahead. On 19 May, he wrote to the naval storekeepers at Jamaica to ensure a steady flow of supplies in the weeks ahead: 'As some of His Majesty's ships under my command are now in want of bread, peas and rum and the whole fleet will soon be in want of provisions of all species, it will be absolutely necessary for you to send provisions of all species to the fleet off the Havannah [together with] fresh meat for the sick during the siege.'[26]

On 28 May, the most easterly point of Cuba was sighted – beyond the dark blue sea, white beaches, deep green forest with shadowy mountains beyond – and the final approach was about to begin. The way ahead that Pocock had chosen was through the long and virtually uncharted Old Bahama Passage, which was cluttered with reefs, shoals and islands. Attempts to find pilots in Martinique and Jamaica had failed; others recruited in the Bahamas had proved hopelessly inexperienced on this coast. Without pilots, or charts, the admiral was to exclaim, 'What a prospect I had before me!'[27] But this was not only the shortest route, but the least likely to be watched by the Spaniards, and the one by which the French might try to reinforce Havana. So, to save time and achieve surprise, he had decided to take the risk, sending

Douglas to escort the convoy bound for Jamaica as the invasion force of about 200 sail, pressed onwards behind a screen of frigates, sloops and cutters. On 30 May, Pocock formed his fleet into seven divisions for the dangerous passage, each led by a ship of the line – the first by the *Namur* – with two or three more warships on the flank of each. The invasion force was now well balanced for, in addition to the transports carrying troops, artillery and ammunition, there were two bringing slaves, three loaded with horses, four with wicker fascines for building siege-works, six laden with the baggage of senior officers and eight hospital ships. The procession of ships then steered west into the beautiful, perilous water of the channel – aquamarine, cobalt and peacock-green edged with white surf.

Pocock had sent cutters, tenders, longboats and other small craft ahead of the fleet to take soundings and then mark the shoals by anchoring over them or mooring buoys and, where the reefs broke the surface as cays, by lighting fires on them at night. Meanwhile, Captain John Elphinston had gone farther ahead in the frigate *Richmond* and successfully passed the most hazardous narrows. On 1 June, the flagship passed a huge bonfire burning on Cay Lobos and next day sailed into deep water at the western end of the channel.

The passage had lasted nearly a week, during which the fleet had been in sight of the distant hills of Cuba to the south, secure in the knowledge that they would be off Havana before news of their approach could reach the city overland. However, there remained the risk of encountering Spanish frigates which might be on patrol in its approaches. Sure enough, on the day the fleet passed the Old Bahama Channel, sails were sighted to the north-west and frigates sent in chase. Watching from his quarterdeck, Pocock saw his frigates close in and the *Alarm* engage what looked like another frigate; after half an hour, the gunfire ceased. As the *Alarm's* signals were read, it was discovered that she had captured the Spanish frigate *Thetis* of 22 guns and the sloop *Fenix* of 18; a brig and a schooner under their escort were also taken. More important, British officers had interrogated the captured Spanish captains and learned that 14 Spanish ships of the line lay at Havana, some of them ready for sea, but that the Spanish commanders in the fleet and the city seemed not to know that they were at war with Britain. Two schooners in the little Spanish convoy had escaped towards the Atlantic and it was not thought that they would try to return to Havana so that, so far, surprise had been achieved.

The navigating masters forecast that the fleet would be off Havana early on the morning of 6 June. Tension and wariness increased. Yet, in the flagship, Pocock and Albemarle held a conference that was of concern to all: the distribution of the booty once Havana had been taken. They drew up and signed a long agreement, under which the two of them would receive a third of the proceeds and from their allocations would make donations to the wounded and to the widows of those killed. The naval and military second-in-command – Commodore Augustus Keppel and Lieutenant-General George Eliott – would share a fifteenth part; the remaining nine-fifteenths would be divided between the rest, according to rank.

On that day, Pocock recorded in his log: 'Light Airs and Fair Weather'.[28] In the transports, the soldiers began assembling their equipment in readiness for landing, and in the warships, gunners checked their stocks of roundshot and charges of gunpowder, made up in bags, were put ready in wooden cartridge-cases for delivery by boy 'powder-monkeys' to the gun-decks. By seven in the evening, as darkness fell off the Bay of Matanzas, the fleet turned towards the land. All was ready, except for the still-awaited ships and troops from New York; Pocock's fleet and Albemarle's army of more than 11,000 soldiers prepared themselves for battle.

Lieutenant Alexander Farquarson sat by his weapons and pack on the deck of the transport *Felicity*, opened his copy of *Hutchin's Improved Almanack and Ephemeris of the Motions of the Sun and Moon, etc., for 1762*, which had been published in New York, and wrote on the fly-leaf:

Fruits and blossoms blow
In social sweetness of the self-same bough.

Less obscurely, he added: 'I desire that in case of my death, my shirts and whatever else of my cloathing as found may be delivered to William Simpson, my servant; my other affects to be disposed of on behalf of my family, or for the pay of what debts I may found to be due.'[29]

The little fort at Cojimar, a few miles to the east of Havana, the first landmark to be recognised, was sighted from the masthead of the *Valiant*, and Keppel at once made a signal to the flagship. Then, as a satirical writer was to report or imagine, he mustered the ship's company, waved his hat and told them,

Courage, my lads! The day is ours. The Admiral has given us leave to take yonder town, with all the treasure in it; so we have nothing to do now but make our fortune as fast as we can for the place can never hold out against us. The purser will give every brave fellow a can of punch to drink prosperity to Old England. We shall all be rich as Jews. The place is paved with gold!

The commodore then gave the look-out, who had made the first sighting, a guinea, and the crew were 'skipping and dancing for joy'.[30] Soldiers crowded the decks of the transports, gazing westward as the pale limestone walls and bastions of the great fortress of El Morro and then the distant towers of Havana came into view; Captain Nicholas Delacherois, a Huguenot, noted that it was a very fine town ... as large, if not larger, than Cork'.[31]

At the same time, a Spanish sentry on one of the seaward bastions of the Morro looked east and saw sails against the morning sunlight. He called the duty officer, who estimated that they were about 20 miles distant. The ships could not be identified beyond the probability that they were the large British convoy bound from Jamaica to England that was thought to have passed Havana in the night after rounding the westerly cape of Cuba. He watched as the number of sails upon the horizon grew and it became apparent that they were not moving east but west and so approaching. So, at eight, he ordered the firing of a signal gun to alert the city. It was Sunday morning and Havana was wakened by the thump of the cannon on the ramparts of the fortress above and beyond the harbour mouth as its smoke drifted across the towers, turrets, belfries and the low-pitched roofs of russet tiles of the city. The Governor, Don Juan de Prado, was wakened and hurriedly dressed and walked from his residence, the Palacia de los Capitanes Generales, to the waterfront, where he boarded his barge and was rowed across to the watergate of the castle. He, too, thought that this must be the Jamaica convoy and was not alarmed. However, he had known since late February of the rift with Britain and, on 4 April, had heard an unofficial report that war had been declared. The official despatches from Madrid had been intercepted at sea by the British, but survivors of the courier-ship had landed at the far end of Cuba and the first warning of the crisis had reached him overland; a report of the outbreak of war had been brought by one of the French warships that had broken out of Brest, when her captain arrived to propose combined action against the British. Even so, the Governor was not unduly alarmed. He had first been told that the British attack on Martinique had failed but, even on hearing that the island had fallen, he remained confident that no nation would dare to contemplate attacking Havana. Its defences, built in the late sixteenth century to protect the city from the marauding of Sir Francis Drake, had defied all threats: in addition to the Morro, there was the fort of La Punta between the city and the shore, and the moated Castillo de la Real Fuerza on the harbour side of the city, which was itself surrounded by bastions and curtain walls. Writing to the Minister of the Indies in Madrid on 20 June, he had boasted that the defences were so formidable that the British would not 'even think of coming here as they cannot but be aware of our readiness to receive them'.[32]

As he looked out to sea, Prado, his staff and his naval commander, Don Gutiriez de Heveia, the Marqués de Reale Transporte (the son-in-law to the commander-in-chief of the Spanish navy), looked from the walls of the Morro at the growing mass of sails to the east and counted 150 individual ships which they identified as British. It was a daunting sight, particularly as seen against a sky now dramatic with black thunderclouds towering over Hispaniola. But as less than a dozen ships of the line could yet be seen, he still assumed that this was, indeed, the Jamaica convoy. So he ordered the garrison to stand down and led his staff down the stone steps to the watergate and was rowed back to the city. Having dismissed his staff, the Governor found a party of civic dignitaries awaiting him to ask the reason for the alarm; he dismissed them, too, with assurances that all was well. An hour later he was robed and ready to take his seat for high mass in the Catedral de la Virgen de la Concepción Immaculada; it was Pentecost and the feast was to be celebrated with full pomp.

At seven o'clock that morning, Admiral Pocock gave his orders. Sending the *Richmond* and the sloop *Cygnet* to make directly for Havana and report what they saw, he made the signal for the captains and masters of the transports and gave them final orders for the landing next morning. The plans they were about to follow had been made final the night before by the sea and land commanders, their staffs and, notably, the chief engineer of the expedition, Lieutenant-Colonel Patrick Mackellar, who had been with Wolfe at Quebec. They were assuming not only that the harbour mouth would be blocked – the frigate captain soon confirmed that it had been sealed by a massive chain – but that it would be commanded by heavy guns from both shores. However, there were landing-places a few miles to either side of the city: at Cojimar in the east and Chorera to the west, each of which was defended by a fort at the mouth of a little river. It had therefore been decided, on Mackellar's recommendation, to make a feint against the latter, while the main landing would be at the former. From Cojimar it should be a march of about five miles to the Morro and then around the head of the harbour to cut off Havana from its hinterland.

Having issued his orders, Pocock sent the captains and masters on their way under the orders of Commodore Keppel, who would command the main landing from the *Valiant*. At two o'clock that afternoon, leaving the troop transports off Cojimar, the admiral sailed west in a confident display of sea power. His flagship led 12 other ships of the line, frigates, bomb-ketches and 36 storeships towards Havana, passing the Morro and the city and continuing four miles further to the anchorage off Chorera and what the Spanish would surely assume was to be the main landing. As they swept past the city, masthead look-outs reported 12 Spanish ships of the line trapped within the harbour and two on the stocks.

The spectacle had been watched by Spanish soldiers crowded on the seaward bastions of the Morro, and an urgent message was sent across the habour mouth to the town. But when the messengers arrived at the cathedral, where high mass progressed in a haze of incense, no-one dared disturb the Governor's devotions and they waited until the service ended. Pocock's feint succeeded: not only did Prado send cavalry followed by infantry to Chorera, but, fearful of a direct naval attack on the harbour, he ordered three ships of the line to be sunk as blockships in the entrance.

At dawn next morning, Pocock, lying off Chorera, embarked all his marines in ships' boats and ordered them to pull towards the shore as if about to land. Meanwhile, some ten miles to the east, Lord Albemarle had joined his brothers, Augustus and William, to watch the landing on the long, wooded shore between Cojimar and the Morro. Each soldier had been issued with one day's rations, 40 rounds of ammunition for his musket, two spare flints for the firelock, a cloth, or canvas, cover to keep this dry and a screwdriver for tightening the mechanism. At first light, the troops had clambered down the sides of the transports and into the flatboats, which formed into two waves, each of two parallel lines abreast. The commanders went with them, Generals Eliott and Keppel sitting in the stern of a flatboat and Albemarle himself planning to go when the beachhead had been secured. Three ships of the line sailed ahead, with two more on either flank commanded by Augustus Hervey in the *Dragon*, leading the first wave of 49 flatboats. Each carried more than

50 soldiers; six regiments made up the first wave, the grenadiers in the centre and the light infantry on the right so that they could lead the advance on the Morro. At a signal, the whole array moved forward, sails filling and oars dipping; at six o'clock, the first boats touched shore. A grapnel was thrown over the stern of each as a kedge-anchor for hauling out to sea again, while two sailors jumped over the bows into waist-deep water to guide the boat past rocks. The soldiers followed, holding their muskets above their heads, wading through the surf onto the flat, gently shelving rock, slippery with seaweed, and headed for the scrubby woods beyond. The flatboats were kedged into deep water and pulled for those transports flying a naval ensign, indicating that troops were waiting to disembark. The second wave of 27 flatboats, led by another ship of the line, bore one battalion of grenadiers and another of the Royal Americans.

Meanwhile, Hervey had sailed close inshore, followed by a sloop and two bomb-ketches, to bombard the fort at Cojimar, then land marines and drive a crowd of Spanish defenders – regulars, local militia and slaves – into the surrounding woods. Out at sea, artillery, ammunition, horses and rations were being unloaded from transports into tenders, to be joined by the storeships from Chorera. As the landing-craft emptied, they were rowed back to the anchorage to embark more men. By mid-morning, 4,000 soldiers were ashore.

Up to this time, the entire operation had been naval. Indeed, it was ordered that 'officers of the troops were, upon no account, to interfere with the manoeuvres performed on the water, the Commodore being the sole direction of everything to be done on that element'.[33] As the *Namur* came to anchor off Chorera, Pocock could be proud of his achievement. A huge fleet had brought a large army to an enemy shore and taken that enemy by surprise. Both ships and soldiers were in good health and spirits and ready to fight. If any single naval operation could have redeemed the shame of unpreparedness, indecision and dithering in the face of the enemy at the beginning of the war, when John Byng had had to take the blame, it was this.

From the moment the first section of light infantry ran up the shelving shore and into the trees, the nature of the attack on Havana changed. Up to that point it had been the responsibility of the Royal Navy; now it would be in the hands of the British Army. Lord Albemarle had based his plans on those of Admiral Knowles and Colonel Mackellar, accepting their view that the Morro dominated the entrance to the harbour and the city beyond: 'I look upon the

Town as certainly Conquered whenever the Morro is taken,' Knowles had said.[34] He had written, and Mackellar agreed, that 'El Morro commands the town'.[35] Albemarle had discounted a siege of the city itself because he had not enough troops to invest its walls and the harbour and its defences would be supported by the guns of the Morro and the ships of the line at anchor; he did not seem to consider the chances of a *coup de main*, an immediate assault upon the city. So he decided that the capture of the Morro must take priority.

There was another view. Captain Augustus Hervey, on first approaching Havana in the *Dragon*, studied the defences and sent a report to Pocock, concluding:

> El Morro Castle in appearance and to strength does not answer the reports I have heard of it, nor, in my opinion, does it at all command or influence the town, and very little the harbour. But the land laying to the southward of this, tho' uncleared, appears to command the whole. This is all I can say of the eastern side. The western appears to be a very fine coast, cleared and very easy for a descent, level to the town, and not the least obstruction to any approaches towards it, and, in my opinion, an attack that way could not fail of success.[36]

In his view, a sudden attack on the city itself might succeed quickly.

The two salient points were the strategic importance of La Cabaña ridge – the high ground above the harbour and immediately to the south of the Morro (named after a cluster of wooden cabins there), from which both the castle, the harbour mouth and the city could be bombarded – and the possibility of attacking the city from a beachhead at Chorera in the west. The value of the ridge had been recognised by Knowles, who had noted that it was 'as high as a 20-gun ship's maintopgallant mast-head',[37] and Mackellar had agreed that its dominant position made it an important objective as a site for mounting siege batteries. The engineer had also noted that the terrain inland of the Morro was rocky, so that the construction of siege-works would be difficult, and that there was little or no water. However, an attack from the east seemed easiest as the distance between the beachhead and the objective was shortest; also, the Spanish capacity for counter-attacking from the Morro would be far less than that from the city itself were the attempt to be in the west. Mackellar concluded that a direct attack on the city from the west would be preferable only if its garrison was not larger than a quarter of the attacking force – say

3,000 men. If the landing were made to the east at Cojimar, it would be possible to advance on the city round the head of the harbour, which would initially involve the capture of the 'considerable large village'[38] of Guanabacoa at the intersection of roads and tracks on high ground to the south-east of the harbour.

Albemarle weighed up these two opinions and, since he, as a soldier, also preferred the formal siege of a fortress, he finally decided that the Morro must be taken first. But to guard against a Spanish attack on the besiegers from the rear, Guanabacoa would have to be taken before that. Accordingly, he ordered the main force to march inland for the latter objective, while the vanguard of the besieging force cut through the dense thickets towards the Morro.

On their first night ashore, the soldiers had their first experience of what was to come. The storm clouds that had been building up to the east had moved towards them and the heat and humidity increased. Then, as they rigged bivouacs at the edge of the woods, mosquitoes swarmed, and fires were lit in the hope that the smoke would keep them away. Then the whine of the mosquitoes was obliterated by the thunder and tropical rain put out the fires and drenched the soldiers. Lord Albemarle, who complained that 'a hot climate does not agree at any time with my constitution', was soon 'much fatigued',[39] and Commodore Keppel was suffering from an agonising headache. It was a long, uncomfortable night.

Next morning, the British marched south along the track to Guanabacoa, led by Colonel Guy Carleton's light infantry, and it was there that they met the first serious opposition. On the high, open ground in front of the village, Spanish cavalry and infantry were deployed – 6,000 of them, according to the British; a few squadrons of dragoons and several companies of infantry, according to the Spanish – and the cavalry charged. The British infantry formed, shoulder to shoulder; a few volleys and the threat of the bayonet sent the cavalry hurtling away, and the soldiers marched into the wide streets of the village. While a small garrison fortified Guanabacoa in case of counter-attack, Carleton turned back towards the Morro and another force, under Colonel Howe, advanced on it by the more direct route through the woods from Cojimar. It was hard going: the scrubby woodland was dense and thorny and the trees, bushes and brambles were reinforced by cactus, both 'prickly pear' and the hard, sharp, pointed leaves of the apppropriately named 'Spanish bayonets'. Lord Albemarle had taken his first look at the undergrowth and accurately forecast: 'We have a terrible wood to pass.'[40]

On 8 June, the first of the big blockships that had been moved into the harbour mouth was sunk, followed by two more next morning. Now aspects of the terrain which had escaped the notice of Admiral Knowles and Colonel Mackellar became apparent. There was no fresh water, and as the summer heat and the amount of laborious ground-clearing increased, this had to be carried from Cojimar to the sweating soldiers hacking at the undergrowth. Then, as they neared the castle, it was seen that the ground was solid rock thinly covered with earth, so that it would be impossible to dig trenches or raise earthworks; nor would it be possible to fill sandbags or the wicker fascines they had brought from England, let alone bury the dead. Most ominous of all was the sight that met patrols that reached the western edge of the wood and looked directly at the limestone walls of the Morro. Admiral Knowles had accurately described the massive bastions and curtain-walls and counted the gun embrasures, but he had made no mention of any moat. Now it could be seen that the fortress was protected by a gulf of dry moat cut in the solid rock, more than 60 feet (18 metres) deep and, in places, more than a 100 feet (30 metres) wide. Because it was designed to be dry, a high, thin, knife-edge of rock had been left to keep out the sea, and this had prevented Knowles seeing it from his passing ship. Now it seemed impassable and the fortress impregnable. Albemarle decided it was too late to change, or much modify, plans and the siege must go ahead as envisaged.

The approach to the castle was difficult. When heavy naval guns were landed at Cojimar, they had to be dragged along the foreshore on wooden sledges and then inland over steep, dusty tracks along which soldiers and slaves also hauled ammunition, rations and kegs of water. Commodore Keppel asked Pocock for leave to double the rum ration for sailors working ashore but was told that the fleet itself was in short supply because a convoy from Jamaica was overdue. Inland, Carleton had rounded up 100 Spanish horses and, having shipped extra saddles and horses from England, was able to achieve some mobility for his patrols and dominate the open country south of Havana.

On 10 June, Albemarle marched the main army north from Guanabacoa and camped in the woods facing La Cabaña and the Morro. At his request, Pocock made another feint in the west, again embarking his marines in boats as if to land that night, and next day, eight of his ships sailed close inshore to bombard the fort at Chorera. Meanwhile, Carleton's light infantry moved towards La Cabaña, where the huts had been burned and the gun emplacement built on its highest point, called the Spanish Redoubt. It was a hot, cloudy morning and at noon the thudding of naval guns from the coast at Chorera six miles away ceased as the Spanish abandoned the fort there. An hour later, as it began to rain, Carleton's light infantry fixed bayonets and they and the grenadiers rushed the heights; the Spanish Redoubt proved to be lightly held and what defenders there had been scrambled down the cliffs to boats waiting to evacuate them to the city. 'I give your Lordship joy in this first success in gaining La Cabaña hill, and that with little loss', wrote Pocock to Albemarle. 'I perceived the attack just before the heavy rain came on; I thought the shower must be in the faces of the enemy and that would be of favour to our troops.'[41] Now the British held the strategic key to Havana, 'as these heights partly commanded El Morro but entirely the town and harbour'.[42]

Within the city, the initial shock had given way to mingled fear and defiance. On the day after the British landing, Prado had ordered the evacuation of all women and children and their precipitate departure in a thunderstorm added an infectious panic. But, once they had gone and no attack on the city had been made, the defenders recovered their confidence. Like Montcalm at Quebec, Prado could reach an encouraging prognosis: he need only hold the besiegers for two months before they would be laid low by the inevitable tropical sicknesses and the seasonal hurricanes would sweep their ships from the coast. He was confident that the Morro could survive, particularly since it would be reinforced and supplied across the narrow mouth of the harbour. More worrying was the loss of La Cabaña, because the designer of Havana's defences in the sixteenth century, Battista Antonelli, had said: 'The city will be mastered if La Cabaña is.'[43] It would now only be a matter of time before British guns would be bombarding the city from those heights, and a counter-attack would have to be mounted to dislodge them. Meanwhile, the command of the Morro was given to a brave and efficient naval captain, Don Luis de Velasco.

His direct opponent would be Major-General the Honourable William Keppel, who was to command operations against the castle. The first necessity had been to cut paths through the woods from the beachhead and then widen them into roads surfaced with logs. Guns weighing several tons had to be hauled along these roads in the heavy heat and, as they reached the sites of the batteries a few hundred yards from the Morro, Spanish cannon-balls whirred overhead. The lack of topsoil meant that sandbags made of sailcloth, or any available fabric, had to be filled two miles from the batteries and carried forward. Water had to be carried from the beach three miles away, or from an even more distant stream, though now a new source was discovered on the far side of the city. Once La Cabaña had been taken, 2,000 grenadiers and light infantry and 800 marines, commanded by Colonel Howe, were re-embarked and, on 15 June, landed at Chorera. There, they expanded the existing beachhead, including the mouth of the Chorera river, and filled casks with fresh water for shipping to the beachhead at Cojimar and manhandling to the batteries; but it was not enough to slake the thirst of thousands of men labouring in the sun.

The heavy rain showers had stopped, the sun burned hot in a clear sky and, when water supplies failed, suffering followed. 'The fatigues on shore were excessive', complained James Miller, a private soldier, 'the bad waters brought on disorders, which were mortal, you would see the men's tongues hanging out parched, like a mad dog's, a dollar was frequently given for a pint of water.'[44] On 20 June, Albemarle was writing to Pocock: 'We are so distressed for water with this dry weather that, unless you are so good as to assist us, I don't know what we shall do … If we had rain, which I almost wish for, the rocks would supply us again. I am sorry to say we go on very slowly at the batteries.'[45] When water was available it was often tainted, causing dysentery, and Augustus Keppel complained to Pocock that 'our men are … fluxed and some lay it to the water but I think it may come from any other cause as likely as that'.[46] 'The hardships, which English troops sustained in forwarding their approaches against the Morro, are altogether inexpressible', Major Mante was to write, and several 'dropped down dead with heat, thirst and fatigue'.[47]

When Captain Delacherois first landed he noticed 'wild cattle running in droves through the woods' which could be shot for fresh meat, but then 'the destruction and waste wherever an army appears has obliged us to return to our former subsistence, salt beef, pork and biscuit. As for herbage, we have found very little except the cabbage-tree and no roots.' They did see 'wild turkeys, parrots and pigeons in great abundance',[48] but were ordered not to waste time on hunting expeditions. The whole coastline, beautiful and wooded, was rank and reeking with unseen pestilence, but late in June a new and healthier anchorage became available. Two British warships, on passage from Jamaica to join Pocock, captured two Spanish frigates in the harbour of Mariel west of Havana and this became the new base for the transports and storeships.

There was growing awareness of disease. Some of the troops embarked at Martinique and other Caribbean islands were already incubating a variety of tropical infections, and it was learned that, recently, a ship from Mexico had brought yellow fever to Havana. This, known as 'the terror of Europeans in the West Indies', began with 'a faintness and generally a giddiness of the head with a degree of chilliness and horror'; this led to 'a high degree of fever, great heat and a strong beating in all the arteries ... flushings in the face, gasping for cool air ... excessive thirst' and then an apparent easing.[49] Finally, the body became tinged yellow, the eyes glazed, delirium began, excreted bodily fluids turned black and the disease earned its name of 'yellow jack', or 'the black vomit'. Death followed swiftly.

The trials of those building the siege-works before the Morro were not confined to heat, thirst, exhaustion and disease. When not under fire, it was easy, despite warnings to exercise caution, to be careless, become lost in the woods and be captured. The Army complained that they could not stop sailors roaming the countryside in search of loot and excitement: 'The jolly dogs apprehended no danger and I do not know if their pikes did not contribute a little towards their advancing as they talked of charging the villains', wrote one colonel to Pocock.[50] In a grisly reminder of the North American Indians to those who had served on the St Lawrence, the Cuban irregulars, Commodore Keppel reported, 'murder many of them and leave them in the woods mangled to pieces'.[51]

One particular atrocity shocked the British when it was reported:

A party of sailors belonging to an English frigate going on shore at the Havannah in search of fresh provisions were surrounded by the enemy and thirteen of them cut to pieces in a very inhuman manner; and a lieutenant of the rangers had his nose and ears cut off and otherwise used very barbarously by the Spaniards and sent to the British camp by way of derision.[52]

Pocock protested to Prado after a naval captain and a lieutenant were reported missing, trying to shame him by sending his letter by an officer escorting a prominent Spanish merchant, who had been captured at Chorera and was being returned to his family. Prado replied, claiming that he was 'entirely ignorant' of the atrocities, adding that he only knew of two British captured naval officers, whom Pocock had named, and they 'by their outward appearance did not answer the character of officers';[53] despite this they were being detained in a Spanish ship and eating at the captain's table.

A week after the landing, teams of 1,000 men had dragged ten 24-pounder guns, four howitzers, six 12-pounders and two heavy mortars to the batteries. More guns were ordered, and Keppel asked for twenty 32-pounder naval guns to batter a breach in the castle walls and a battery of 17 mortars was sited opposite their seaward end. Once in place, the mortars on La Cabaña tossed shells at the Spanish ships within range, driving them farther up the harbour, and into the city at night to keep the garrison awake, their glowing fuses arching high over the harbour mouth. The bombardment of the Morro was to await the completion of the Grand Battery less than 200 yards (183 metres) from the chasm of the dry moat.

The mortars and the threat of the gun batteries stung the Spanish into a counter-attack. Before dawn on 29 June, more than 500 regulars crept out of a sally-port of the Morro to attack the British batteries near the coast, while another 500 crossed the harbour and climbed the cliff towards La Cabaña. The British were alert, their pickets opened fire and soon there was skirmishing across half a mile of rocky hillside. When the sun rose, the British found the battlefield deserted but for nearly 200 Spanish dead, wounded and stragglers ready to surrender. Later a Spanish naval lieutenant was found wandering and made prisoner, and Albemarle, with a flourish to match Pocock's, ordered that this should be made known to Prado and the officer's servant and clothes be sent across to him from the city. The final touches to the building of the batteries were made that day.

The attack on the Morro was to open with a bombardment by all the batteries to the east and south and another from the sea. Since his arrival off Havana, Augustus Hervey had burned with zeal. Having tried to save Pocock's kinsman, Byng, he felt sure that the admiral was keeping a friendly eye on him; even before the expedition had sailed from Portsmouth, his mother had been getting to know the admiral, writing to her son about friends who had been drinking soup in her dressing-room – for she was convalescent – and adding: 'Sir G. Pocock, who came and sat two hours with me last night is to do the same in a few days. You see, my dear, how I cultivate my marine acquaintances.'[54] Now far from London boudoirs, Hervey planned to make his mark with professionalism and dash.

Soon after his arrival off Havana, he had taken the *Dragon* close to the walls of the Morro on a dark night to take soundings. The castle had opened fire, forcing him to sheer away, but he was convinced that there was nothing to stop warships running alongside to bombard and possibly batter a breach in the walls for an assault from the sea. Augustus Keppel supported his idea, although he worried about flanking fire from La Punta across the harbour mouth; he told Pocock that such an attack by two or three heavy ships would 'soon dismount the guns'[55] of the castle. On the night of 11 June, boats had gone close to the Morro without being fired upon, and their soundings showed that it would be possible for ships of the line to anchor within point-blank range. However, the navigating master of the *Cambridge*, who undertook the work, added that 'The night being so dark that I could not adjust the height of the castle'.[56] What was also unreported was the rise and fall of the tide and whether the ships' guns would be able to hit the enemy embrasures even when at maximum elevation.

At first, Albemarle had shown no interest but Pocock, remembering the effect of naval gunfire at Geriah and Chandernagore, ordered Hervey to prepare to take command of a bombardment from the sea. Finally, on 28 June, when the land batteries were almost ready for action, Augustus Keppel wrote in his journal: 'The generals of the army seeming to wish that some shipping should be employed to cannonade El Morro when the land batteries opened, Sir George Pocock gave me orders to direct Captain Hervey to take charge of that service.'[57]

At dawn on 1 July, four batteries – twelve 24-pounder cannon and 35 mortars – opened fire on the Morro. Then, as planned, four ships began to approach the castle from the east. The *Stirling Castle* was to lead and draw the enemy fire, while the *Dragon*, *Cambridge* and *Marlborough* anchored alongside the castle walls and began to bombard. But there were delays: first, the *Dragon* lost her anchor when weighing; then the wind dropped. Worse, the *Stirling Castle*, which should have led the way, lagged astern and Hervey could see that some of her sails were furled; he signalled urgently to Captain James Campbell to move ahead but there was no response. At eight, Hervey sent Lieutenant Dandy Kidd across to remonstrate with Campbell; Kidd reported, 'I told him that Captain Hervey was surprised he had not set more sail', and Campbell had replied 'that no man was more desirous to get into his station than he was'[58] but blamed his ship's poor sailing and steering. At last, at ten past nine, the *Cambridge* anchored below the walls and opened fire, followed by the other two ships. In a moment, billows of gunsmoke, stabbed with flame, hid all but the masts and yards of the ships. It was soon obvious that, while most of the Spanish guns could not be depressed enough to hit the hulls of the ships, the British guns could not be elevated sufficiently to hit above the thick lower walls of the castle.

But yards and sails, their stays and rigging shot away, crashed to the decks of the ships and some Spanish guns could reach lower, killing men and dismounting guns. The *Dragon* was hit and an officer and 13 seamen killed and 39 wounded. After two hours of fighting, the ship drifted, temporarily out of control, on to a ledge of rock. Asking Keppel for help in refloating her, Hervey characteristically pencilled in his note to be sent across by boat:

> Sir, I have the misfortune to be aground. Pray send a frigate to drop a bower [anchor] off and send one end of the cable on board here. We luckily are in a good line for our fire at the fort but the smoke is so great and that makes it impossible to see the effect we have had, or likely to have. Often duller, Ever yours, A. Hervey.[59]

While the three battered ships fought on, the *Stirling Castle* hung back until Hervey ordered her, as the support ship, to lay a heavy kedge anchor and pass the cable to the *Dragon* so that she could be hauled free by capstan. Campbell only sent a light one across by boat so, when this anchor did not hold, Hervey had casks brought up from the hold and emptied of water, wine and spirits and heavy stores thrown overboard to lighten the ship. Using both capstans to haul on two of her own anchors, she eventually floated free.

The *Cambridge* had also been badly hit, her captain, William Goostrey, and 25 others killed and nearly 100 wounded. An hour after the action began, Keppel sent Captain John Lendrick in the frigate *Echo* into the drifting smoke to report its progress, first coming alongside the *Dragon*, then the *Stirling Castle*, which he hailed through his speaking-trumpet. 'Captain Campbell, sir,' shouted Lendrick, 'I have been on board Captain Hervey by the commodore's orders, who has ordered the *Cambridge* to cut and get out. She had lost her captain and a great number of her men. The ship is cut to pieces, you must go to her assistance either by taking her in tow, or covering her or she must perish inevitably.' There was no response and Lendrick tried again. 'Captain Campbell, sir, this is not a time to make difficulties. If you don't assist the *Cambridge*, she must perish. For God's sake, Captain Campbell, make sail to the *Cambridge's* assistance, or she must perish!'

Finally, as the *Cambridge* drifted away from the Morro, Campbell offered to tow her out to sea and himself opened fire at long range. Midshipman John Buchanan of the *Stirling Castle* was to report that 'Captain Campbell sent me off the quarterdeck to the officer that commanded the lower-deck guns to know the reason why they did not fire brisker. When I came upon the quarterdeck again, I observed Captain Campbell leaning his hands upon his knees under the breastwork, or barricado. On seeing me, he drew out about two, or three feet.' The *Cambridge* refused the tow, an officer shouting to Campbell to get out of her way. Then, William Holman, the *Stirling Castle's* sailing master, reported, the guns of the Morro opened fire on them, too, hitting the ship, killing two and wounding eight. Campbell had 'bobbed and sometimes fell down on his knees' and said, 'I'll be damned if my knees are not tired with stooping.'[60] Thereupon the *Stirling Castle* bore away out of range, leaving Campbell's fellow-captains determined on bringing him to court-martial.[*]

Three hours after the battle began, Commodore Keppel, watching from the *Valiant*, realised nothing had been, or would be, achieved and ordered Hervey to disengage. So, at a quarter past two, he cut his cables, made sail and steered for Cojimar in company with the *Marlborough*. There, they reported to Keppel before returning to the anchorage off Chorera next morning. Nearly 200 British officers and ratings had been killed or wounded, but the north face of the Morro had only been pitted with shot and was otherwise undamaged.

Yet the effort had not been totally wasted: the Spanish, imagining that such an attack must be a prelude to something more – perhaps an assault from the sea – had concentrated on the seaward defences of the Morro while the British batteries ashore had been able to fire without retaliation. Within 24 hours, all but two of the Morro's guns on the landward side had been dismounted, embrasures had been battered and roofs of the barracks shattered, although the main southfacing walls had only been scarred by cannon-balls. The garrison was so exhausted that many had to be evacuated to the city that night and replaced by nearly 600 fresh men.

As the bombardment continued, General Keppel and Lord Albemarle conferred with their staffs about means to capture the Morro. It could not be reduced by starvation since it could be supplied from the city and across the harbour by night, therefore it had to be stormed. Yet in front of that impassable dry moat spread a stone glacis, which would prevent the usual process of driving trenches and saps forward. Instead, a breastwork would have to be built on the surface stretching diagonally from the British batteries across the open ground and the glacis to the edge of the moat. Because of the intense fire from the castle this did not begin until 17 July, by which time it had been reduced by the continual battering by British guns. So, in addition to the carrying of shot, powder and wads for the guns, more sandbags and earth for fascines had to be manhandled.

This heavy work was increasingly given to African slaves, and Mante noted: 'the hardships with which the English troops are sustained in forwarding their approaches against the Morro are altogether inexpressible', [61] and 'It would have been absolutely impossible to carry on these batteries without the assistance of the Negroes.'[62] Commodore Douglas had just arrived from Jamaica with a convoy bound for England and was able to add to the number of slaves. Some of the merchantmen under his escort were loaded with bales of cotton and wool-packs and these were commandeered for use as barricades before the glacis and, later perhaps, to help build a causeway across the moat.

Exhausted and depressed, Albemarle wrote on 13 July to Lord Egremont, the Secretary of State, from his headquarters at Cojimar: 'The increasing sickness of the troops, the intense heat of the weather and the approaching rainy season are circumstances which prevent my being too sanguine as to our future success against the town, particularly as we have no news of the American reinforcement,'[63]

The 4,000 men, including regulars and provincial regiments from New York, Connecticut, Rhode Island, New Jersey and South Carolina, known to have been sent by General Amherst, were thought to have sailed from New York on 11 June but were long overdue. They were now desperately needed because the British had been struck with full force by yellow fever, malaria and dysentery. It was reckoned that 5,000 soldiers and 3,000 sailors were sick and hundreds were dying. 'From the appearance of perfect health', wrote Mante, 'three or four hours robbed them of existence. Many there were, who endured a loathesome disease for days, nay weeks together, living in a state of putrefaction, their bodies full of vermin and almost eaten away before the spark of life was extinguished.'[64]

The hospital tents and the hospital ships were full. Nobody was safe; doctors and surgeons' mates died with their patients, one of them being Dr

Johnson's friend, Dr Bathurst. Over the stricken camps

the carrion crows of the country kept constantly hovering over the graves, which hid rather than buried the dead, and frequently scratched away the scanty earth, leaving in every mangled corpse a spectacle of unspeakable loathesomeness and terrors for those, who, by being engaged in the same enterprise, were exposed to the same fate. Hundreds of carcases were seen floating on the ocean. Yet all these accumulated horrors damped not the ardour of the survivors.[65]

At Guanabacoa, General Eliott's 2,500 men had been reduced to 400 and he was forced to abandon the village and its commanding position and fall back on the defences of La Cabaña. The attack on Havana had become a race against disease as much as against the seasons.

The summer was now at its hottest. Lord Albemarle, although able to sleep on board ship, was covered with the red pimples of prickly heat, and Admiral Pocock, experienced in the tropics, had awnings of sailcloth, soaked with sea water, rigged above the windows of his cabins. Lieutenant Daniel Holroyd of the 90th Foot, who had been so worried about his complicated love affairs, wrote in a letter home: 'We have seen much danger and infinite fatigue ... I still keep my health most wonderfully tho' I lie every night in the fields, which in this country is very unhealthy on account of the Violent Dews. I am heartily sick of this climate.' Grieved by the death of his commanding officer, Colonel Morgan, he found himself one of only four officers and 36 men of his company alive and not in hospital; he added: 'I am likely to have a finishing stroke put to my disappointments.'[66]

After there had been no rain for a fortnight and the wicker of the fascines before the British batteries was dried out, muzzle-flashes set them alight and, as there was no water to extinguish the flames, they smouldered for days. Despite this, a routine of bombardment began from a total of 49 guns, five howitzers and ten mortars, which dismounted the guns on the Morro's ramparts and gradually blew away the parapet and embrasures. Even so, the castle appeared impregnable because of the gulf of the dry moat.

Despite their troubles, the British managed to build the barricade across the glacis to the lip of the moat in two days. From its shelter they could direct small arms fire at Spanish gunners on the battered ramparts, and two cannon were dragged forward to fire at the walls from a distance of only about 100 feet (30 metres). The British could also look down the sheer sides of the moat, and there they saw something of which they had not hitherto been fully aware. To keep the sea from the dry moat, the ridge of rock that had been left at the seaward end – about 60 feet (18 metres) long, 40 feet high and 20–30 inches (51–76 centimetres) wide along its rough and ragged edge – looked just wide enough for men to scramble across in single file. Once across, however, they would be faced by the vast, unclimbable seaward bastion of the castle.

Colonel Mackellar and his engineers studied this view and saw that it might be possible to lay mines at either end of the ridge, one to blow a breach in the bastion, the other to blast the opposite side of the moat into rubble that might form a rocky causeway across which an assault could be mounted. Yet shafts would have to be cut in solid rock and masonry and that seemed beyond the capabilities of the sappers. Then it was remembered that when Pocock's flagship, the *Namur*, had flown the flag of Admiral Boscawen off Louisbourg, he had had on board numbers of tin-miners whom he, a Cornishman, had recruited in his native county. Some were still on board and they were brought ashore and asked whether a mine beneath the Morro was feasible; they said that it was and were given the task of digging it.

On 20 July, the tin-miners and sappers crossed the ridge to the bastion. British infantry gave them covering fire but Spanish musketry killed four of them before they could shelter under the lee of the castle. At the same time, other miners began cutting into the opposite side of the moat – the counterscarp – and, slowly, they began chipping into the rock and the masonry. Aware of what was afoot, the Spanish knew the miners had to be dislodged quickly, and, two days later, they counter-attacked at three o'clock in the morning with 1,300 men in three separate attacks. Two made for the British batteries bombarding the Morro but were held by an advance platoon of infantry and then thrown back by a battalion of the Royal Americans. A third party tried to reach the miners below the seaward bastion of the Morro but were beaten off. Both sides suffered losses but the British mines and batteries were unharmed.

On 28 July, the first convoy of six transports bringing American troops arrived from New York. They had indeed sailed on 11 June but five ships had run aground on the same shoals that Pocock had negotiated so carefully, although no lives had been lost. Commanded by Brigadier Burton, who had fought with Wolfe at Quebec, they were healthy and vigorous after the voyage and they were put ashore to camp at Chorera, west of Havana. More ships were awaited.

By 29 July, both mines were complete and massive charges laid under the bastion and in the counterscarp. It was planned to explode them at dawn on the following day. Even so, an assault would be a forlorn hope, and, even if it reached the top of the castle walls, it would have to face 600–700 defenders, probably well-armed and freshly ferried over from the city. Albemarle expected that the Spanish knew an assault was imminent, so he attempted a bluff. On the day before the mines were ready, prearranged signals were made – rockets fired from the British lines answered by signal guns from the *Namur* – to see 'if a panick should take them';[67] it did not. Albemarle, formal soldier that he was, tried sending a courteous ultimatum to Velasco 'conceived in the most flattering terms ... explaining to him the hopelessness of continuing the defence and expressing his fears that, when the fortress should be taken by assault, it would be impossible to restrain the victorious soldiery from a general slaughter'. Velasco's refusal was 'not less chivalrous in character, assuring Lord Albemarle that he did not think his situation by any means so desperate as his Lordship had represented'.[68]

Putting their defiance into practice, the Spanish tried to attack the miners from the sea at two o'clock next morning, sending two gunboats around the walls of the Morro and opening fire with grapeshot and musketry; again no damage was done. But plans to explode the mines at dawn that day had to be postponed. The engineers, infantry and artillery were ordered to stand ready for an attack in the heat of the day at two o'clock that afternoon.

However low morale might be in the city, it seemed high in the Morro. Don Luis de Velasco and his two immediate subordinates, Colonel the Marqués Gonzales and Captain Don Manuel de Cordova, had 32 officers of high quality, 600 soldiers and marines and nearly 100 armed Negro labourers under their command. They were capable of making another sortie and Commodore Keppel, to prevent another attack from the sea, anchored the 64-gun *Alcide* off the Morro, while boats manned by armed seamen and marines stood by. Keppel had wanted his sailors to take part in the coming assault but his brother William insisted that this was work for soldiers and had chosen his men. If a breach could be blown in the angle of the seaward bastion, three parties of 12, each led by a lieutenant, would try to scramble across the ridge of rock, followed by 300 men of the 1st Foot (the Royals), hand-picked marksmen from the late Colonel Morgan's 90th. They would be supported by 150 men of the 35th and 150 sappers would help clear the breach and attempt to bridge the moat from the counterscarp. The whole of the First Brigade, under the direct command of General Keppel, would be ready to follow. Even if the assaulting troops managed to cross the ridge, they would have to do so in single file in the face of the defenders' fire and steel. It seemed even more of a forlorn hope and, if it failed, there might be no other chance of taking Havana before disease and hurricanes ended the attempt.

After the firing offshore before dawn, the morning of 30 July was as hot as usual and silence hung over the battlefield, broken by an occasional shot. The dark hours between midnight and sunrise were favoured for attacks, so the defenders of the Morro allowed themselves some relaxation and the officers retired to their mess. One of them, Don Bartolomeo Montez, remembered:

> While the whole of the officers were at dinner between twelve and one o'clock, the Constable [de Cordova] entered and said that he had just been to the battery of San Nicolas, from whence he had seen one of the English frigates moving round the point and that one of her boats had been sent out to sound, from which he supposed an attack on that side might be expected. On this the Commander-in-Chief [Velasco] directed me to take the spy-glass and watch the movements of the ship, giving orders at the same time to fire upon her as soon as she should come within range of our guns.[69]

Stepping out of the cool gloom of the vaulted rooms into the glaring light and hot air on the ramparts, Montez looked out across the dark blue water to a motionless frigate, becalmed against the hard line of the horizon. No attack could be expected from that direction that afternoon. As he gazed out at the sunlit sea, the mines exploded.

It was two o'clock. The explosion shook the fortress, the city and the coast from Cojimar to Chorera, tossing rock, masonry and bodies in an eruption of flame. From the forward breastwork, General Keppel and Colonel Mackellar peered through the smoke. The angle of the bastion had been brought down, leaving a cleft in the ramparts, but the mine in the counterscarp had failed to collapse the outer wall of the moat. However, a storming party would be able to cross the rock ridge and climb into the breach, so Keppel ordered them forward. Colonel Stuart gave the signal and the party of 12, led by Lieutenant Charles Forbes of the Royals rushed the glacis, scrambled across the ridge and clawed their way over the rubble to the top of the wall, followed by another, commanded by Lieutenant Daniel Holroyd, and a third led by Lieutenant Nugent.

A British sailor who had been allowed to accompany the assault in recognition of having saved an army captain from drowning wrote in a letter home:

There was a high rock for us English to clamber first and foremost and the ladder which I and Will Jones had stowed ourselves on broke and overboard we went down the rock again and there was a Spanish twenty-four-pounder came rolling after us – no harm done however. Well, we got up again ... and clapped ourselves upon our hands and knees and made sail up the rock that way and when we came up to the walls our people were at it, yard-arm to yard-arm, alongside the Spaniards ... When our soldiers had drove the senors from the hole in the wall (the breach I think they call it), away our men launched into the castle, and we two with them, all helter-skelter like people going to see a show at fair time.[70]

Inside the Morro, Montez reported:

The mine, which the enemy had established in the corner of the Caballero de la Mar, had exploded, blowing up some of our advanced sentinels among its ruins and also some of the seamen employed in the Orejon de la Mar in the charging of hand-grenades ... Of all this I sent an account to the commander without leaving the spot; from whence also I despatched Don Lorenzo de Milla, captain of the battalion de España, to ascertain if the explosion had produced a practicable breach, when he brought back for answer that the breach was not practicable ... At this moment the Commander-in-Chief arrived in his undress uniform with his sword by his side ...

Still there were no British to be seen in the smoke on the walls, but then

no sooner had a dozen English soldiers entered the bastion, than the whole of the seamen, gunners and soldiers made the best of their way out of it. On the crest of the rampart ... a curtain had been formed with bags of sand, under the shelter of which a picket of forty seamen with their officers had been posted, to whom I made known that I had seen four English soldiers enter and desired that the picket ... might be advanced to oppose them. This the officers could not effect, only two of the men coming forward, the rest concealing themselves behind the sand-bags. The English were in consequence enabled to advance and form without opposition.[71]

Velasco and his officers, swords in hands, rallied the defenders, ordering ladders to be cut away from the rear of the fortifications so that they had to stand and fight. But the British had already taken up battle formation on the ramparts and at their first volley, Velasco, leading his men up the ramp to meet them, was shot through the chest. Colonel Gonzales, his second-in-command, was killed, and Montez, seeing, as he put it, 'the number of the enemy increased so much as to enable them to crush our disheartened troops', ordered Captain de Milla to show a white flag and surrender. But events moved too quickly as the British ran with fixed bayonets through the deep alleys between the barrack-blocks, driving the defenders before them. The white flag produced confusion. Some Spaniards fled for the shelter of the lighthouse at the far side of the castle, above the harbour mouth, and, seeing three young British officers congratulating each other on their success, fired their muskets. Two fell dying: Lieutenants Holroyd and Nugent. The third, Lieutenant Forbes, 'exasperated at the death of his companions, immediately marched, attacked and forced the lighthouse and put all in it to the sword'.[72]

It was almost over. A hundred and thirty Spaniards lay dead on the ramparts and ramps and in the alleys, some 40 had been wounded and 326 surrendered. More than 200 tried to escape across the harbour, to be shot, or drowned, as they tried to board boats or swim. The British had lost the two lieutenants and a dozen soldiers killed and 28 wounded. Albemarle immediately wrote to Pocock, who, watching from the sea, had seen the huge plume of smoke and felt the concussion of the mine: 'I congratulate you on the possession of the Morro and tho' we have been long about it and (tho' it is not very becoming in me to say so) it was handsomely taken.' The admiral replied that he had seen from his flagship the storming parties 'march up with a determined and (as it appeared to me) calm and undaunted spirit', adding that 'every ship testified their joy by following the *Namur* and giving three cheers'.[73] Commodore Keppel also wrote to Pocock that day: 'Poor Velasco is so wounded that he must die'; then, cheerfully, '*Water* is found in the castle … In short, the day is a great one and I sincerely give you joy of it with all my heart.'[74]

An hour after the mine had exploded, the British flag was hoisted over the fortress and a British major was rowed across the harbour mouth in a boat, flying a flag of truce, and taking Don Luis de Velasco home to die. 'A brave officer, mortally wounded in defending the colours, sword in hand', as Pocock wrote of him,[75] Velasco was carried into the city and given the last rites; two days after being wounded, he died[*]. On the day of his funeral, Lord Albemarle kept his guns silent.

Within the Morro, the British found a vast arsenal of artillery and ammunition which had been expected to have rendered it impregnable. Now some of these could augment the British batteries, which were being dismantled along the siege-works and remounted along the heights rising to La Cabaña and facing Havana. It was now the city's turn to suffer.

More British regulars and American provincial troops arrived from New York, bringing their total to 3,188 but it was learned that another convoy of five ships, carrying more than 500 men, had been captured by the French in the Caicos Passage. The new arrivals, too, were landed at Chorera to help with the further expansion of the beachhead and the setting up of new batteries to bombard the fort of La Punta and the city from the west. Infantry which were no longer needed to the east of the harbour were also shipped to the west, and Albemarle himself moved his headquarters from Cojimar to Chorera.

The storming of the Morro had distracted attention from what had become the main preoccupation of the army: yellow fever. On 8 August, Albemarle was writing to Pocock:

> The poor Highlanders [42nd Foot] die in numbers. I wish you could spare a frigate to send them to North America; it would, perhaps, be the only means of saving the remains of these poor people. In the meantime, I must beg about some conveyance for an officer to go to Sir Clive [Wintringham, the expedition's chief physician] for medicines, as these poor wretches have none and their situation is most melancholy.[76]

The Royal Highland Regiment had suffered particularly badly. When they had sailed from New York for Martinique a year before they had been 'about 6,000 men, extremely well-disciplined, full of life and courage ... and in every respect, the best troops in the world'. Their decline began on the voyage to Havana when 'being close stowed and the heat being intense, their spirits sunk'. Then, 'during the long siege in that sultry climate, the labour was so great and so constant that it was impossible to be supported; and the greatest number died of mere fatigue'.[77]

The admiral then reported to the Admiralty: 'Soldiers and seamen fall down in great Numbers by Sickness in this very unhealthy season but they do not abate in Courage and Constancy … and show a noble ardour to conquer.'[78] Many were shipped to North America, Pocock recording that 'three Regiments with scarcely a man well among them are gone to New York, where it is hoped the men will recover'.[79]

Yet the end was in sight. Havana was commanded by the batteries from the Morro to La Cabaña and around the western perimeter of the city walls. The roads radiating from the city were cut, as was the stream supplying it with fresh water. The fresh troops from New York worked at the new batteries to the west, building wooden gun-platforms and filling fascines. It would, after all, be possible to take the city before the hurricane season began at the end of August, and on 10 August all was ready. Again Lord Albemarle delivered an ultimatum, this time to Prado himself:

> My dispositions for the reduction of the Havannah are made. Motives of humanity induce me to acquaint your Excellency herewith that you may have an opportunity of making your proposals to surrender the Havannah to His Britannic Majesty and thereby prevent the fetal calamities, which always attend the storming of a town … I am the master of La Cabaña and El Morro, which Your Excellency, in a letter to Don Luis de Velasco, acknowledges to be the key to Havannah.[80]

The aide-de-camp who took the letter to the gates of the city, under a white flag and accompanied by a drummer, was kept waiting 100 yards (91 metres) outside the walls for several hours. Finally the reply was handed to him; as he walked back to the British lines Spanish guns opened fire, endorsing Prado's words in his letter that 'I find myself well assured of carrying on the defence, with strong hopes of a happy exit, and capable of preserving it [Havana] under the dominion of His Most Catholic Majesty'.[81] Albemarle read this and ordered a heavy bombardment of the city to begin at five o'clock next morning.

'Moderate and fair weather', wrote Augustus Keppel in his journal on 11 August.

> Five a.m., the batteries along La Cabaña and upon the glacis of the Morro, consisting of 43 pieces of cannon and 10 mortars, began to fire against La Punta Fort, the north bastion, La Fuerza and other defences of the Havannah. The enemy at first returned fire smartly; at 9 they ceased firing from La Punta and abandoned it and the fire from the town abated very

much.[82]

Also watching was Colonel Mackellar, who recorded: 'About two o'clock there were flags of truce hung out all round the garrison.' Soon after, a Spanish officer emerged from the gates under a white flag and was conducted to Albemarle's headquarters; Admiral Pocock was summoned from his flagship. This time, Prado had written that 'the considerations of humanity ... have induced me to modify the intention I had formed of continuing the defence of the city ...'.[83] But, in his proposals for capitulation, Prado was willing to surrender the city but not the ships in the harbour. Pocock and Albemarle replied jointly next day that they found these proposals 'so repugnant to the customs of war and your present situation that we are under a necessity of returning them'.[84] Orders for the resumption of the bombardment next morning were sent to the batteries but, before dark, terms for the surrender of both the city and the ships were agreed, and the guns remained silent. On 13 August, 1762, Havana formally surrendered.

The terms insisted upon by the victors were generous in their periphery. Surrendered Spanish troops would be allowed to march out of Havana with colours flying and their officers could take their money and belongings before being repatriated. Senior officers would be sent to Spain in a British frigate. If citizens of Havana did not return to Spain within four years, they would automatically become British citizens, although they would be permitted to practise the Roman Catholic faith. In the city, the church of San Francisco would be taken over by the Church of England.

At ten o'clock on the morning of 14 August, General Keppel led a detachment across to La Punta, entered and hoisted British colours on the flagstaff. Two hours later, he took possession of the La Punta Gate and bastion in the walls of Havana and, at the same time, Colonel the Honourable William Howe marched through the Land Gate with two battalions of grenadiers and British colours were hoisted over both. The city within the walls was not badly damaged; there were smashed roofs and pitted walls but not the devastation wrought by a prolonged siege. It was still magnificent with its cathedral and a dozen other churches and monasteries, palaces for the Captain-General and the Archbishop, two hospitals and grandees' houses described as 'elegant, not lofty, built of stone'.[85] Many of its 30,000 inhabitants had fled into the country and the city seemed empty of women, children and the old. Of the 3,000 regular troops, the same number of seamen from the ships in the harbour and unnumbered militia of the garrison, only about 1,000 regulars and 1,200 seamen remained within the walls to surrender. Now it could be seen how dilapidated were the defences and how thin the city walls, so that those who remembered Howe and Wolfe realised that, had Lord Albemarle decided upon a direct assault immediately after landing, Havana must have fallen quickly.

Of the British army that had landed on 7 June and been reinforced at the end of July and early in August, bringing it to about 14,000 men, only about 3,000 were still on their feet. During the nine weeks of the campaign, the Royal Navy had lost 86 killed and the Army 305, with about the same number dead or dying of wounds and about 100 missing or deserted. The remaining 10,000 were either sick, or dead of tropical sickness or disease, heat exhaustion, dysentery and malaria but mostly of yellow fever.

On 19 August, Admiral Pocock completed his report to the Admiralty. His achievement had been assembling a large invasion fleet from a dozen different sources, then landing and maintaining an army on a hostile shore; it had been crowned by the capture of nine Spanish ships of the line fit for sea, the three sunk as blockships and two still on the stocks. No other British admiral could claim such a capture in the current war.

He entrusted his despatch to Captain Hervey – 'a brave and deserving officer in this expedition'[86] – in recognition of his zeal, particularly in his attack on the Morro. In a letter to General Amherst, written next day, he admitted that he and Albemarle agreed that the expeditionary force was so ruined by sickness and fatigue that 'no further operations can possibly be carried on in this season'.[87]

News from Havana was eagerly awaited in London, particularly after the first reports of the successful landing had arrived, followed by doom-laden accounts of sickness. In August, Horace Walpole had written: 'Of the Havannah I could tell you nothing if I would; people get impatient at not hearing from thence.'[88] On 26 September, he was writing: 'We do not take the Havannah, or make the Peace ... We do not doubt but there is great sickness among our troops, nor do the Spaniards seem so terrified at the name of an Englishman as the French are.'[89]

The uncertainty was about to end. Capturing a French frigate on the way, Augustus Hervey reached Portsmouth on 27 September and took the road down which he had once ridden in the hope of rescuing Admiral Byng. Passing Cobham, he sent word of the victory to the retired Duke of

Newcastle at Claremont Park and rode up to the Admiralty just before eight o'clock in the evening. From there he called on the Prime Minister, Lord Bute, and ended the evening drinking with his cronies at White's Club in St James's Street. The news spread through London and, by the stagecoaches, across the country. Three days later, Horace Walpole was writing: 'Io, Havannah! Io, Albemarle! ... The Havannah surrendered on 13 August ... the news came last night. I do not know a particular more. God grant no more blood be shed!'[90]

Few, if any, questioned Albemarle's generalship; the victory was enough. The Duke of Cumberland, a spent force since his defeat by the French on the Continent five years earlier, swiftly claimed credit for suggesting the idea, writing to Albemarle: 'No joy can equal mine. I strut and plume myself as if it was I that had taken the Havannah. I take your siege to have been the most difficult since the invention of artillery: 68 days in that climate alone is prodigious.'[91]

The balladeers were quick to compose:

Now England's victorious,
Our conquests more glorious,
Than those of Eliza or Anna;
Freedom drew honour's sword,
Courage gave us the word,
And our Hearts of Oak storm'd the Havannah![92]

Horace Walpole again put the mood of the euphoric British into words. He wrote in a letter:

As this age is to be historic, so, of course, it will be a standard of virtue, too; and we, like our wicked predecessors, the Romans, shall be quoted till our very ghosts blush as models of patriotism and magnanimity. What lectures will be read to poor children on this era? Europe taught to tremble, the great King [Louis XV] humbled, the treasures of Peru diverted into the Thames, Asia subdued by the gigantic Clive! For in that age men were seven feet high ... Oh! I am out of breath with eloquence and prophecy, and truth and lies: my narrow chest was not formed to hold inspiration ... those lofty subjects are too much for me.[93]

As the news spread east from Whitehall and St James's through the taverns of

Fleet Street to the banking-houses of the City of London, a realistic and personal view was sometimes taken. A sad Dr Samuel Johnson wrote of a lost friend: 'The Havannah is taken – a conquest too dearly obtained; for Bathurst died before it'; another friend, James Boswell, added that he 'fell a sacrifice to the destructive climate'.[94] There had been another death caused, less directly, by the attack on Havana, and only now could it be seen to have been a poignant coincidence. Admiral of the Fleet Lord Anson, the driving force behind that and the attempt on Manila, had caught a cold at the beginning of the year at Portsmouth, when sitting in an open boat and watching the soldiers embark for the 'secret expedition'. This had led to complications, vaguely diagnosed as gout, and a general decline. After drinking medicinal waters at Bath, he had returned to his country house, Moor Park in Hertfordshire, and had been walking in his garden when he suffered what was probably a heart attack and died; he was aged sixty-five. The date was 6 June, 1762, the day on which the fleet he had launched across the Atlantic appeared before Havana.

'Decided by a Peace'

On the day that the Morro castle was stormed at Havana, other British soldiers were embarking for Manila. The possibility of reaching the Philippines to attack the second keystone of the Spanish Empire had been discussed nearly 20 years before when war with Spain had taken Anson marauding in the Pacific. Then it would have meant sending an expedition round Cape Horn and that was seen as an unacceptable risk. But the commander of this new expedition, Colonel William Draper, had suggested a simpler alternative. Once the British had prevailed over the French in India, such an expedition could be mounted from Madras. So it was that, at the end of July in 1762, a small expeditionary force assembled there.

The genesis of this lay in Draper's enquiring mind. While on sick leave after the successful defence of Madras in 1758, he had taken passage in a Company ship to Canton and back. There, for the first time, he had heard about, and then seen, the rich trade of China and the part played in it by Manila. Twice a year a great galleon arrived there from Acapulco in Mexico laden with manufactured goods from Spain, wine and, above all, silver from the mines of Mexico and Peru. This was exchanged for the luxuries of eastern Asia for the European market which had been collected at Canton and Macao: silk and porcelain from China, spices and fabrics from India, lacquered cabinets from Japan. Manila was the great clearing-house, remote, rich and, it was rumoured, impregnable.

It was Draper's memorandum to the Cabinet, written after the Belle Ile campaign, that had caught Anson's imagination and had been combined with the attempt on Havana in the most ambitious strategy yet proposed. One of the attractions of the idea was that it would be relatively cheap to execute: all the troops would be sent from India and many, if not most, would be supplied by the East India Company. Draper himself had been chosen to command the land forces and, embarking in the frigate *Argo* at Portsmouth, he sailed in March and reached Madras three months later.

At first, the council of Fort St George and the Governor, George Pigot, were enthusiastic; the British were the dominant Europeans in India and had commanded the Indian Ocean since Pocock's three battles with d'Aché. But the army commander, Major-General Stringer Lawrence, was less enthusiastic, for he feared that, once a large force had been sent into the Pacific, the French could take advantage of their absence and might again be building up their forces in Mauritius. So, in the event, Draper was only allowed half the numbers he considered essential. Less than 600 regulars of his own 79th Regiment, less than 100 artillerymen, just over 300 East India Company troops – including Eurasians and two companies of French deserters – 600 sepoys and about 50 Indian irregulars boarded transports anchored in Madras roadstead. In addition there would be 270 marines and 550 seamen in the warships. 'Such a banditti never assembled since the time of Spartacus[*], who differed as much in sentiment and language as in dress and complexion', remarked their classically educated colonel.[1]

But the embarkation was as efficient as Pocock's and Albemarle's had been at Portsmouth earlier in the year; because there was no harbour, the problems of loading and boarding were extraordinary and Draper praised the 'activity and despatch'. This feat was said to be 'almost incredible to those who are acquainted with the difficulties that are to be surmounted in shipping stores from the great and perpetual surf that rages against the shore. Everything is obliged to be carried in the boats of the country without the assistance of wharfs, cranes and other conveniences made use of in England'.[2]

The naval commander would be Rear-Admiral Samuel Cornish, who had succeeded Pocock and Steevens in the Indian Ocean. Now past fifty, he had served at sea on the lower deck for the East India Company and the Royal Navy before achieving commissioned rank through merit as a seaman, although his solemn looks suggested a cleric; his final promotion had come through the death of a superior rather than by the choice of the Admiralty. His second-in-command was Commodore Richard Tiddeman and his best flag-captain was Richard Kempenfelt[*], who had served Pocock so intelligently. Cornish flew his flag in the 74-gun *Norfolk*, but his other seven ships of the line and three frigates were mostly worn out, three of them, the *Elizabeth*, the *Grafton* and *Weymouth*, having fought in Pocock's battles. There was to be a single store-ship and all the troops and weaponry were to be embarked in the warships.

Colonel Draper considered this force as just adequate because he did not expect to meet serious opposition. Although far smaller than the Havana expedition it was more of a risk because it would be sailing into almost uncharted waters – not just one dangerous channel – to an almost unknown destination amongst the 7,000 islands of the Philippines archipelago. This expedition, too, would be constricted by the cycle of weather, for those remote seas were whipped by hurricanes towards the end of September and in

October; so Cornish was determined to sail by the beginning of August. Another risk was that Manila might hear of the declaration of war by Britain before they arrived. So, on 19 July, Cornish sent a frigate to patrol between the islands of Singapore and Sumatra to prevent the news reaching the Philippines from the west. There was also a chance that it might come from the east with the next Acapulco galleon so that was another reason for urgency. Yet Cornish was hopeful that surprise would be achieved when Draper's little army was embarked by 31 July and his squadron sailed the next day.

As the British stood for the Straits of Malacca, the city of Manila drowsed in peace. The Spaniards, confident of its invulnerability, had not bothered to fortify it on the scale of Havana. The mouth of the huge, almost landlocked, harbour of Manila Bay was guarded by the fort, naval dockyard and anchorage of Cavite, and, across the water to the north-east, Manila itself lay within its walls; Cornish planned to take Cavite and use it as his base for the attack on the city itself.

Although Anson had been confident that the expedition would not encounter rough weather, because so much of the passage would be through sheltered straits, there was the problem of the ships' seaworthiness. So worn and leaky were they that Cornish reported to the Admiralty that 'nothing but the necessity of the Service … could have justified my Proceeding with them on the Expedition, for during my Passage … every day produced new Complaints, which gave me great Uneasiness'.[3] Malacca was reached safely on 19 August and, although it was nominally Dutch, the British used it 'as a port of their own'.[4] The voyage continued slowly and, 48 days out from Madras, the island of Luzon was sighted; on the evening of 23 September, all but two of the ships sailed into Manila Bay.

Ahead stretched the great, circular bay; dark greenery, tufted with palms; lumpy volcanic hills and, seen through the heat-haze, distant mountain ranges. To the east lay the fort and naval dockyard at Cavite and, farther north, the towers and turrets of Manila. Built in a grid-pattern within its walls – mostly of wood above the first storey for fear of earthquakes, sometimes on stilts for fear of floods – the city and its sprawling suburbs were said to be inhabited by 100,000 Spanish colonists, Chinese and Filipinos.

When the British squadron was sighted from Manila on that evening, they had achieved the same surprise as at Havana. The acting Governor and Captain-General of Manila was, surprisingly, a priest, Archbishop Don

Manuel Antonio Rojo del Reio et Vieria, who, as the senior churchman in the Philippines, had automatically succeeded to the office on the death of his military predecessor. He had concluded, on military advice, that the city could only be defended against attack by a European enemy by 4,000 well-trained and well-armed soldiers; 'Manila never thought it would be attacked by European nations', he complained.[5] In fact, the garrison consisted of something short of 600 regular troops, a few Filipino gunners, 200–300 militiamen and hordes of wild Filipino irregulars from the surrounding country. Even now, he had no idea what was afoot and sent a letter to the senior British officer in the ships, asking whether they were in distress, or what was their business.

Draper had intended to take Cavite first as his base and sent boats to take soundings. Deep water was reported close inshore but he realised that, as his own little army was too small to invest Manila and cut it off from reinforcement, an immediate, direct attack on the city was essential. Rojo's letter arrived next morning, and when the officer who delivered it was told exactly what was their business, 'he smiled, tacitly indicating he thought the enterprize rash and indigested'.[6] In reply, Draper wrote a formal letter to Rojo, informing him that war had been declared and demanding he surrender the city. This was refused.

Sending frigates ahead, Cornish sought a suitable landing beach beyond the range of the Spanish guns on the walls of the city. He found one just over a mile distant and the troops climbed into boats while the frigates opened fire on a crowd of soldiers and sightseers who had gathered ashore to watch the spectacle. The boats formed three divisions, each commanded by a captain, one of them Kempenfelt, another William Brereton, who had lost a year's seniority for lack of initiative in one of Pocock's actions with d'Aché. Several boats capsized, or foundered, in the surf, but by dusk on the evening of 24 September, the 79th Regiment, the marines and the gunners were safely ashore in the heavy humidity. The walls of Manila, built at the end of the sixteenth century, were about 20 feet (6 metres) high, stained green with damp, and looked vulnerable to artillery. However, the principal defence was water: there was no moat, but the west side of the city faced the bay, into which the river Pasig, swift, swollen and muddy after rain, ran past the north wall, while the east and most of the south wall stood behind a swampy creek. At the south-west angle of the city, guarded by the bastion of San Diego, between the creek and the shore of the bay, was about a quarter of a mile of dry land, and it was there that the attack would have to be made.

The landings continued all night, then, since there was no opposition at sea, 700 men were landed from the ships' companies. When all were ashore, the British could muster nearly 1,000 European troops and 800 sepoys and labourers. Draper's headquarters had been set up in the church of the Hermita, half a mile from the city; other buildings were occupied and gave shelter to the soldiers when the first, drenching, warm monsoon rains broke over Manila. The Spanish, hoping to catch the attackers off balance, launched a sortie, which was beaten back; it only resulted in Draper sending another ultimatum to Rojo, couched in threatening language: 'I beg you … to consider Your Situation before it is too late. I have a multitude of most Fierce People, who are unacquainted with the more Humane Parts of War; it will not be in my Power to restrain them if you give us more Trouble.'[7] This, too, was rejected.

While Draper was laying out and building his siege works opposite the San Diego bastion, exciting news arrived from the sea. On 25 September, the frigate *Argo* had captured a small galley with news of what seemed a fulfilment of the most extravagant dreams. She belonged to the Acapulco treasure-galleon, the *Filipina*, inward bound with her silver, which must therefore be within reach of capture. Among the prisoners was Antonio Tagle, who proved to be Archbishop Rojo's nephew, which gave Draper an opportunity to display a flourish of military courtesy. The young man was entertained in the British officers' mess and Draper, sending a note, accompanied by a gift of fruit and wine, to Rojo, told him of his intention to send his nephew into the city. The archbishop was effusive in his thanks, but added: 'It seems a pity that a British officer of such distinction should waste so much time and effort and be the occasion of so much useless suffering.'[8] Accompanied by Draper's secretary, Lieutenant Frayer, and a drummer, young Tagle set out towards the gates of the city. At that moment events assumed an unexpected ugliness. Filipino irregulars – called 'Indians' by the British – saw a small party approaching the city from the besiegers' lines and, without orders, launched a sortie. These were unlike the volatile, dark-skinned Indians the 79th had faced, or fought beside, in India; they were sallow-skinned men with high cheekbones and dark, fierce, watchful eyes, quick-moving and hard-muscled. The sepoys immediately counter-attacked and, in the skirmishing, the Filipinos, seeing Frayer's red coat, went for him. He was killed and shockingly mutilated and Tagle, trying to save him, was mortally wounded. When the battlefield cleared, the furious Draper threatened to hang all his Spanish prisoners until mollified by a letter from Rojo, apologising and admitting that he could not control his irregulars. From this time, the campaign took on a cruelty reminiscent of the fighting in North America.

By the beginning of October, the breaching batteries were ready for action. From one, the muzzles of eight naval 24-pounders aimed at the walls, and work began on a second and another for heavy mortars. At first light on the 3rd, the guns opened fire on the bastion of San Diego 'with such justness, quickness and dexterity that the Twelve Pieces on the Face of the Bastion were Silenced in a Few Hours and the Spaniards drove from them',[9] and this provoked another sortie.

Since the city could not be wholly invested, nearly 2,000 Filipino fighting men had been brought into the city, and at three o'clock in the morning of 4 October, after a heavy rainstorm had cleared, they attacked. Three columns of them, armed with spears, bows and arrows, charged the British, who just had time to form ranks and fire: 'They advanced up to the very muzzles of our Pieces, repeated their Assaults, and died like wild Beasts, Gnawing the Bayonets.' But British volleys had performed their task and, as Draper laconically put it, 'by this means the Indians began to be dismayed'. It had been a close-run fight and the British had lost more than a dozen men to spears and arrows. Draper realised that he had underestimated the Filipinos, confiding in his diary that 'had their skill been equal to their Strength and Ferocity, it might have cost us dear'.[10]

Another council of war was called by Rojo. The British bombardment had continued all day – supported by noisy but ineffective naval gunfire – and beaten a breach in the city wall. More sepoys had been landed from a British transport that had lagged behind the squadron and had just arrived; yet more, the Spanish feared, might be following. A practicable breach had been blown in the walls to the immediate east of the San Diego bastion by the 24-pounder cannon and an assault would follow. On the night of 5 October, Rojo took the precaution of sending an officer, Oidor Don Simon Anda y Salazar, out of the city to the town of Bulacan to organise resistance if Manila should have to be surrendered.

The assault came at dawn on 6 October. The storming parties had filed into the forward siege-works in the darkness and, at first light, all the guns and mortars fired together in an eruption of flame and smoke. The 79th Regiment advanced – 'They all mounted the Breach with amazing Spirit and Rapidity', Draper reported[11] – and swept the defenders before them. There was resistance at the guardhouse of the Porta Real to the east of the breach, where Major More, leading a charge, 'was transfixed with an arrow and died immediately, universally lamented for his good qualities'.[12] When a summons to surrender was refused, the gatehouse was stormed and all the Spaniards and Filipinos defending it killed. As the British infantry, followed by sailors armed with cutlasses, ran through the streets, many of the defenders fled from the northern gate of the city and tried to swim the river; it was said that some 300 were drowned in the attempt. Rojo, his staff and the most resolute of the defenders fell back on the citadel of Santiago in the north-west corner of the city, where the river ran into the bay. But it was in poor repair, the wooden gun-carriages were often rotten so could not be moved, and the archbishop realised that further resistance was hopeless. He sent a message to Draper asking for a meeting to discuss terms for surrender.

Spanish and Filipino losses were counted in hundreds but the campaign had cost the British only five officers and 30 other ranks killed and just over 100 wounded; the last casualty was Commodore Tiddeman, who was drowned but was accorded only a disparaging epitaph by William Nicholson, the master of the *Elizabeth*, to the effect that there was nothing 'so noble or distinguished in his character that deserved to be transmitted down to posterity'.[13] But it was not quite over. While Rojo and his council considered terms, the victors were taking advantage of the custom by which a city taken by storm could be sacked. Half Draper's army was, on his own admission, a rabble, and they ran riot, raping and looting. This continued for four hours – the Spanish claimed it was 40 – until the disciplined 79th restored order.

The Spaniards tried to prolong the negotiations. Draper did not speak Spanish but he had been taught Latin at Eton and that, of course, the archbishop understood. Finally, Rojo accepted Draper's terms that 'All the islands subordinate to Luconia [Luzon] and Manila, its capital … must be ceded to His Britannic Majesty, who must be acknowledged Sovereign 'til the fate of these islands is decided by a Peace …'[14] As at Havana, civil government would carry on under British supervision, the Roman Catholic religion could be practised and commerce continue. The salaries of officials would be paid but all Spanish officers should become prisoners of war on parole. What was, in effect, a ransom for private property of $4 million was to be paid to save the city from further plunder; as this was more than could be found in the treasury, it could be paid later. The document was drawn up and signed the next day, 7 October, 1762.

The naval dockyard at Cavite was occupied immediately and found stocked with all that was needed to refit the British ships. Large quantities of ordnance were discovered there and in the city, including 460 guns. The magazines were stacked with huge piles of roundshot, which were needed since, during the two-week siege, the British had fired more than 2,200 24-pound cannon-balls and 1,000 mortar-bombs. But the conquerors' thoughts still concentrated on the whereabouts of the treasure-ships from Acapulco, one of which was known to be somewhere among the myriad islands of the Philippines.

On 30 October, as Draper was completing his despatch to the British Government, news came that a galleon had been captured. Captain Hyde Parker of the 50-gun *Panther* had chased a huge ship he supposed to be the *Filipina*, inward bound from Acapulco with a cargo of silver. On boarding her, however, he had discovered that she was the *Santissima Trinidad*, which had sailed from Manila for Acapulco just before the arrival of the British, laden with merchandise worth $1 million. Welcome as this prize was, the hunt had to continue for the *Filipina*, but when she was eventually found and taken by Brereton of the *Falmouth*, her holds were found to be empty and the exasperated captors burned her. What had happened to her bullion was more than a huge financial deprivation. It was discovered that her captain, hearing of the surrender of Manila, had made contact with Anda, the Spanish officer who had left the city for Bulacan just before the final assault and had now proclaimed himself Captain-General of the Philippines. He had ordered the galleon to be unloaded and her treasure carried along jungle tracks to the headquarters of the guerrilla army he was assembling to drive out the British.

That problem lay in the future and Draper, content that his mission had been completed, was determined to leave. He realised that he could not hope to capture and dominate the 40,000 square miles of Luzon with his tiny army, let alone undertake an operation against the huge, southern island of Mindanao as had been considered. So, before sailing for Madras, he handed Manila over to a civil governor, Dawsonne Drake, an official of the East India Company, who had accompanied the expedition, and at once new problems arose. Admiral Cornish complained that he had not been fully consulted over the appointment, and Drake himself protested that the booty was not being distributed as agreed: instead of half of it being presented to the East India Company, they had been given a third, and Cornish had allowed regular soldiers, but not Company troops, a share of the proceeds of the *Santissima Trinidad* capture. Also, as in India, there were jealousies between regular officers and those of the Company. At the back of their minds was the thought that, over the horizon in the jungles of Luzon, Anda's guerrillas were gathering strength.

Colonel Draper sailed from Manila in the frigate *Seahorse* with Captain Kempenfelt and Captain Fletcher of the East India Company, who was carrying the official despatch. Draper had left Drake to govern Manila, collect the promised ransom and fight off Anda's guerrillas; he himself had no knowledge of events in India, North America or the Caribbean, nor, of course, in Europe, nor in London at the centre of the strategy he had helped to devise and carry out.

It was not until January, 1763, that the *Seahorse* anchored off Madras and Draper was rowed through the surf to the beach before the ramparts of Fort St George. India was quiet compared with the first four, desperate years of the war. After Clive had returned to England in 1760, Colonel Eyre Coote had defeated Lally at Wandewash, captured Pondicherry in 1761 and himself returned home the following year. Clive had been given a hero's welcome, the thanks of the King, Parliament and the East India Company, and an Irish peerage. He had aroused resentment, too, because of his wealth, having a fortune of nearly a quarter of a million pounds and an Indian annuity of £30,000, and this was wildly exaggerated. 'General Clive is arrived, all over estates and diamonds', remarked Horace Walpole. 'If a beggar asks for charity, he says, "Friend, I have no small brilliants about me."'[15] Meanwhile, the humbled Comte de Lally returned to France in disgrace[*] to face trial, much as Byng had done. The British now ruled Bengal from the new, enormous, star-shaped Fort William at Calcutta and dominated the Carnatic and Coromandel coast from their bases at Madras and Fort St David. There were still tortuous Indian politics to be monitored and manipulated and always the distant possibility of the French trying to return. But there was nothing to detain Colonel Draper and he continued his voyage to England with the captured Spanish colours from Manila in his luggage, planning to present them to his old college at Cambridge[†]. His own part in the twin thrusts at the two hearts of the global Spanish Empire had been an unqualified success.

As Draper's report on the conquest of Manila made its way across the Indian Ocean, around the Cape of Good Hope and northward towards England, other reports for London were crossing the Atlantic from Havana at the other extremity of the great, double offensive. One was from Admiral Pocock, who had, on 9 October, completed his report on the immediate aftermath of the surrender.

Once the army – or what remained of it – had marched into Havana and the fleet had sailed into the harbour, minds had been concentrated upon two overwhelming preoccupations: plague and plunder. While cases of dysentery and heat exhaustion were reduced when the fighting ended, the epidemic of yellow fever showed no sign of abating. Some of the sick were sent to North America, others to the port of Mariel, while, in Havana, the Spanish hospitals and the tents of the British field hospitals were filled and the convalescent were put on board captured Spanish ships in the harbour. But little medical treatment was effective and deaths continued at the former rate. As Pocock reported on 9 October, nearly 800 seamen and 500 marines had already died – only 86 of them in action – and some 2,673 seamen and 601 marines were sick and most seemed unlikely to survive. The army had suffered far worse. The total casualties had amounted to 5,366 dead, of whom 560 had been killed in action, or died of wounds; another 150 had now been posted as missing or deserted. The remaining 4,708 had died of disease or other tropical sicknesses. It could therefore be seen that by the end of the year more than half the army would have died. In an attempt to preserve the health of those still on their feet, precautions taken against sunstroke included the posting of sentries along the waterfront to prevent soldiers from swimming, or fishing, in the heat of the day.

Now came the question of prize-money. This was eventually to be £737,000, which was to be shared in a series of distributions. A third went, as agreed, to the two commanders, who each received about £123,000, while the three Keppel brothers together collected some £200,000. The allocations decreased down through the ranks to the seaman's £314s 10d. and the private soldier's £4 1s 8d. But Lord Albemarle was not content with his share and made a blunt demand to the Bishop of Cuba, writing:

I am sorry yet you oblige me to remind your Excellency of that which you ought to have done some time ago. I mean a present from the Church to the General of a conquering Army. The least your Excellency can think of offering for this Gift is one hundred thousand dollars. My Desire is to live in Friendship with you and the Church, which I have as yet shown on every Occasion. I hope I shall not have to deviate from my Inclinations by any mistake on your side.[16]

The letter followed a personal call by a British artillery officer. Already Albemarle had, at the end of August, ordered him to demand a levy and, when this had been refused, had written to the bishop, 'Illustrious Sir, the payment offered to the officer in command of H.M. Artillery ... is so negligible that I am obliged to demonstrate my disgust.'[17] The officer was now sent in person and the sum demanded was doubled. On 22 October, the bishop wrote to Albemarle, 'Yesterday afternoon, between four and five o'clock, I was visited on behalf of Your Excellency by one whose Christian name, surname and nationality I am ignorant. I only know that he speaks Spanish with a foreigner's bad pronunciation and that he wears little gold rings in his ears as women do.' Finding his visitor disrespectful, the bishop had asked his rank and was told 'that the only privilege he enjoyed was that of firing cannon-balls on behalf of his King. He continued upon this theme at some length and bade me farewell in a loud voice ... '[18]

On the same day, the bishop wrote to Pocock, who had a reputation for fairness, to 'interpose' with Albemarle. This put the admiral in a difficult position since his relations with the Keppel brothers had been good. Realising that there was nothing he could do without jeopardising this, he replied next day, admitting that he knew of 'the orders from the Earl of Albemarle to collect two hundred thousand Dollars on the Inhabitants of the Havana'. In some embarrassment, he continued:

I am not acquainted with the reasons of the Contribution. My sincere wish is that Harmony and good Will constantly reign among all Degrees of People; more particularly that the Earl of Albemarle and your Excellency keep in Friendship ... The Church has nothing to apprehend: the Bishop and Clergy will always be safe under the protection of the British Government; and I think your excellency will think it right and proper to cultivate a good understanding with my Lord Albemarle. Your excellency will now permit me to take my Leave with my best Wishes that God Almighty may preserve your Excellency many years a Worthy Shepherd over an Obedient Flock.[19]

He promised to forward the archbishop's complaint to Albemarle.

Admiral Pocock was planning to leave Havana as soon as possible and hoped that a non-committal response would save him from involvement with Albemarle's venality. But there was more to come because the general, unable to extract the money, manufactured another issue and a consequent threat. He demanded a list of clergy in the diocese so that he could choose whom he wished to promote; the bishop refused. Albemarle wrote angrily to him on 3 November:

> Whereas the Bishop has always in a most disrespectful manner declin'd complying with the said demand of His Excellency and has ... not only absolutely refused to send the list required but has threatened in an illegal and imperious Manner to Complain to the Courts of Great Britain and Spain of the irregularity of the Demand as a breach of the capitulation and has in the same Letter mentioned in a most seditious manner both Courts, both Kings ... and forgetting his being a subject of Great Britain only and Considering himself a subject to His Catholick Majesty notwithstanding the Capitulation ... His Excellency the Earl of Albemarle has therefore thought it absolutely necessary to Remove the Bishop from this Island and to send him in one of His Majesty's Ships to Florida that tranquillity may be preserved in the Town and that Harmony and Good Understanding may be kept up between His Majesty's Old and New Subjects, which the Bishop in so flagrant a Manner has endeavoured to interrupt.[20]

As Pocock put it in a letter to Augustus Keppel, 'The Earl of Albemarle thought it proper and necessary for the quiet of the city to translate his Illustrissimo to the Florida coast.'[21]

It was simple to banish the bishop to St Augustine, but impossible to counter the news that in Cuba, as in the Philippines, opposition to British rule was taking shape. Albemarle had to report to Lord Egremont that the Governor of Santiago de Cuba, nearly 500 miles away at the eastern end of the island, had proclaimed himself Captain-General of Cuba and that several towns, assumed to have been surrendered with Havana, were reported to have declared their loyalty to him. All Albemarle could do was to bluster that he had summoned the magistrates from the rebellious towns 'to receive my commands' and that, if they failed to appear, 'whenever the troops are in Health and the season permits it, I will send detachments into these parts, many of them too far to send troops to by Land and, at this season of the year, it is impossible to venture any ships upon that Coast'.[22]

The time had come for the fleet to depart. Several sailed independently before Commodore Keppel left in September, taking seven ships of the line and two frigates with him to Jamaica, where he was to command. Three ships of the line and two bomb-ketches were to remain at Havana but the rest of the fleet and most of the transports were to sail for England with Admiral Pocock. One ship of the line, the *Stirling Castle*, which had disgraced herself in the attack on the Morro, was so leaky that she was towed to the head of the harbour and scuttled. But Pocock was taking with him five sail of the line, more than 50 transports and three captured Spanish ships of the line to be commissioned into the Royal Navy. On 22 October he departed, sailed into a storm and was lucky not to lose more than three of his ships before struggling back to Havana. On 3 November, the day on which Albemarle decided to banish the Bishop of Cuba, he did get away and steered east in fine weather.

Homeward-bound, Pocock's ships sailed comfortably north-east, past the Florida keys. Then the 70-gun *Marlborough* became separated from the rest, a gale blew and she began to take in water, the leaks spread and she began to wallow, waterlogged. Guns had to be heaved overboard to lighten the ship, and for days all hands worked the pumps and only just managed to keep her afloat; meanwhile, her most senior passenger, Major-General John Lafaussille, died. Two days later, a convoy from Newfoundland was sighted, her crew were taken off and the ship was abandoned and burned.

Three weeks out, when they were 600 miles west of Land's End, the rest of the fleet struck foul weather. The big ships – 'Most of them were leaky and worm-eaten when they left the Havannah', it was admitted – sprang dangerous leaks, easterly gales delayed their passage and provisions and fresh water began to run low. A new ordeal began for men who had already suffered much. 'Reduced by famine and wasted by fatigue', it was recorded, 'the men were in a great measure worn out; many died of thirst, sickness and cold. Coming from a warm climate, their clothes were ill calculated to resist the severe weather they met in the northern latitutudes.'[23] The wind increased to hurricane force, distress signals were sighted from the little, tossing transports and 12 of them disappeared, lost with all hands. Two ships of the line, the *Temple* and the *Devonshire*, foundered but their ship's companies were saved, and the *Culloden* came close to sinking. Beating against strong headwinds, the surviving ships could make no headway for nearly a month after sighting the Scilly Islands.

Finally, on 13 January, 1763, the *Namur* put into Plymouth to report on the terrible voyage. 'The sufferings of those who rode it out are not to be conceived', ran a newspaper report, 'reduced by famine and wasted by fatigue, the men appear like skeletons and more than half have died of thirst, sickness and fatigue ... The continual apprehensions of death were as terrible to many as death itself.'[24] Even in ships that survived there were losses, Pocock reporting to the Admiralty that 'many of the Weak Men aboard the men of War have died in the Passage'.[25] Other storm-battered ships managed to work their way up-Channel, but not always to safety; a fine Spanish prize, the *San Genaro*, dragged her anchor when she tried to shelter in the Downs roadstead off Deal and was lost.

Admiral Pocock and his passengers, General Eliott and Brigadier Carleton, made their way to London on 18 January, the admiral bringing lead canisters of Havana snuff as presents for friends. But although Pocock was formally thanked by Parliament and the City of London, the euphoria had passed and the talk was now of peace. Seven years of war had drained enthusiasm and that over the news from Havana had been dampened by reports of disease and of the extravagant amounts of prize-money awarded to senior officers. Charles Johnstone, a satirical writer, lampooned Pocock and Albemarle – recognisably, but not by name – in his novel *Chrysal, or, The Adventures of a Guinea,* in which he described the progress through many hands, most of them unworthy, of a coin. He described the admiral saying to the general before the attack on an unspecified Spanish colony, 'Now, my dearest friend, you will have an opportunity not only of gaining such glory as will add lustre to the dignity of your birth but also of acquiring a fortune to support that dignity properly. But what is the matter? You do not seem affected at the happy prospect! Are not you well?' The general replies, 'Yes, I am well enough as yet; but I know not how long I shall continue so in this damn'd place, the heat of which seems to set you on fire.'[26]

Even Horace Walpole added his customary flippancy:

The booty – that is an undignified term –I should say the plunder, or the spoils, which is a more classic word for such heroes as we are, amounts to at least a million and a half. Lord Albemarle's share will be about £140,000. I wish I knew how much that makes in *talents* or *great sesterces* ... What an affecting object my Lady Albemarle would make in a triumph surrounded by her three victorious sons![27]

Even among London crowds, news of the victory had become stale and lost amongst more familiar memories, attitudes and prejudices. One night in December, James Boswell was at a Covent Garden theatre to see a new comic opera, *Love in a Village*, and recorded in his diary:

> Just before the overture began to be played, two Highland officers came in. The mob in the upper gallery roared out, 'No Scots! No Scots! Out with them!', hissed and pelted them with apples. My heart warmed to my countrymen, my Scotch blood boiled with indignation. I jumped up on the benches, roared out, 'Damn you, you rascals!'... I went close to the officers and asked them what regiment they were of. They told me Lord John Murray's and that they were just come from the Havana. 'And this,' said they, 'is the thanks that we get – to be hissed when we come home ...'[28]

Those remaining in Havana settled down to garrison life of guardmounting, church parades[*], inspections, parades, the firing of salutes on royal birthdays and ceremonial punishment. In December, a private of the 34th Regiment was sentenced to be flogged and received 500 lashes on the Grand Parade for 'taking a Haversack of flower (*sic*) from the provisions Magazine', and, a month later, another suffered 1,000 lashes for 'sleeping at his post'.[29] It was the same routine as would have been followed by regiments stationed in Madras, Jamaica or Gibraltar.

Yet trade was beginning between Britain and the new colony, with large quantities of Cuban mahogany being shipped from Havana to meet the new demand for furniture in that wood, which had already exhausted stocks in Jamaica. The soldiers settled down to garrison life and soon the Cubans were reciting a doggerel:

Las muchachas de la Habana
No tienen temor de Dios
y andan con los Ingleses
e los bocoyes de arroz[30]

['The girls of Havana have no fear of God; they go with the English in the rice barrels.']

As the British read their newspapers, the scale of their conquests was difficult to comprehend. Success in Europe had been immediately reflected in the resumption of trade and the ability to travel on the Continent. But, as yet, there was little tangible to confirm that these distant, vast and exotic territories had been acquired. In conversation with James Boswell at the Mitre tavern in Fleet Street, Dr Johnson even used the conquest of Canada as a parable to illustrate religious faith.

'I deny that Canada is taken,' he declared, 'and I can support my denial by pretty good arguments. The French are a much more numerous people than we; and it is not likely that they would allow us to take it.'

'But the ministry have assured us, in all the formality of the *Gazette*, that it is taken,' replied Boswell.

'Very true. But the ministry have put us to an enormous expense by the war in America and it is their interest to persuade us that we have got something for our money.'

'But the fact is confirmed by thousands of men who were at the taking of it.'

'Ay, but these men have still more interest in deceiving us. They don't want that you should think the French have beat them but that they have beat the French. Now, suppose that you should go over and find that it is really taken, that would only satisfy yourself; for when you come home, we will not believe you. We will say you have been bribed.' Then Johnson concluded, 'Yet, sir, notwithstanding all these plausible objections, we have no doubt that Canada is really ours. Such is the weight of common testimony. How much stronger are the evidences of the Christian religion!'[31]

The Earl of Albemarle sailed at the beginning of 1763, leaving his brother, General Keppel, as Governor. He returned to England shortly before Colonel Draper arrived from Manila with his despatches on 16 April; the two horns of the global assault on the Spanish Empire had finally been withdrawn. Despite Draper bringing the first news of the capture of Manila and Albemarle being the first Governor of the King's new possession, Cuba, their arrivals also proved an anticlimax. Unknown to both, a peace treaty with France and Spain had been signed in Paris on 10 February and the seven years of war had ended.

William Pitt's grand strategy of maintaining the balance of power on the Continent – particularly the security of Hanover – while achieving dominance in North America and on the trade routes and trading stations around the world – notably in India and the Caribbean – had succeeded. Britain had nothing more to gain and could afford to agree on generous terms for peace. In North America, Britain took Canada from France and Florida from Spain, so that the entire east coast became British; the Mississippi was recognised as the western border of the British colonies; and France also ceded Grenada in the Caribbean and Senegal in West Africa. In return, Britain returned to France the Indian trading ports and territory the French had occupied in 1756 – although these were now puny compared with the Indian Empire founded by Clive with the assumption of direct rule in Bengal – and Goree [Dakar] in West Africa. But in exchange for Florida, Britain promised to return Cuba to Spain. News of the capture of Manila having arrived after the treaty had been signed, it was not even considered at the peace conference, but it came into the category of conquests that would not be kept by the conqueror and was to be returned to Spain.[*] The last British troops left Havana on 6 July, 1763, and Manila on 1 April of the following year. One of the first acts of the Spaniards on reoccupying the former was to build a colossal fortress on the heights of La Cabaña to prevent a repetition of the siege.

As the surviving soldiers and sailors drifted back from Cuba and the Philippines, they had the satisfaction of knowing that their efforts and suffering had added rich territories to King George's domains – only to learn that this was not to be the case;[†] in fact, it was soon forgotten that both countries had briefly been part of the British Empire. The conquerors of Havana retired into comfortable obscurity. Albemarle aroused a brief flicker of interest on his return in a flowery verse:

Brave Albemarle bright wreathes of glory crown,
Due to his conduct in the scenes of war;
Ages unborn shall speak his high renown,
And sires shall tell it to their infants' ear.[32]

He soon retired to Quidenham Hall, a house he had bought in Norfolk to live in comfortable, rural obscurity. He never fully recovered from the rigours of the campaign, although he had experienced it in relative comfort; he was made a Knight of the Garter in 1771 and died the following year.

At the end of 1763, Admiral Pocock married Sophia Dent, the widow of a naval friend and heiress to two East India Company inheritances through the Drake and Pitt families. There were to be no further commands and when, in 1766, Sir Charles Saunders, a more junior admiral who had made his name at Quebec, was appointed First Lord of the Admiralty, Pocock was affronted but was persuaded by Admiral Hawke to join him in congratulations; even so, he resigned his commission and retired to the house belonging to his wife's family on the river at Twickenham[*] and a town house in Mayfair. He died in 1792, leaving a son and a daughter; his son's baronetcy became extinct in 1921.

Augustus Hervey, who had so often appeared at the vortex of events, became member of Parliament for Saltash and a courtier and he, too, never held another command at sea. He did, however, sit on the Board of Admiralty, succeeded to the earldom of Bristol in 1775, was promoted vice-admiral and died in 1779.

Another volatile officer, George Townshend, came into titles and rank, becoming the fourth Viscount Townshend. Later he became the first Marquess and finally a field marshal; he was appointed Lord Lieutenant of Ireland, took controversial decisions and was finally recalled, retiring to Raynham Hall, his country seat, to become Lord Lieutenant of Norfolk and dying in 1807.

Townshend had succeeded Wolfe, who, together with Clive, remained a popular hero of what became known as the Seven Years War. Wolfe had been buried in his parish church at Greenwich, while Lord Clive returned to India to become Governor of Bengal. After instituting reforms in the civil and military administration, he returned to England the following year, faced a Parliamentary enquiry into his finances and, while taking opium to relieve stress, committed suicide in 1774.

The last of the conquerors, William Draper, tried and failed to wrest 'The Manila Ransom' from Spain, but despite this he received a knighthood. On the death of his first wife he visited America, where he married Susannah de Lancey, the daughter of the Chief Justice of New York, and he became involved with the Loyalist cause as the movement for American independence gathered momentum. Returning to England, he lived at Manilla Hall near Bristol, where he set up a memorial to the 30 officers and 1,000 men of his 79th Regiment who had died in India and the Philippines. On the death of his second wife, active duty took him abroad again. Now a lieutenant-general, he was appointed Lieutenant-Governor of Minorca under the governorship of one of Wolfe's brigadiers, now Lieutenant-General the Honourable James Murray, who had subsequently been Governor of Canada. In an echo of the past, Minorca was again attacked by the French in alliance with the Spanish, and in 1781, after a siege of six months, Fort St Philip surrendered. Another echo followed with a public and acrimonious quarrel between the two generals on their return home. Draper retired to Bath and died there in 1787.

Looking back seven years, the trial and execution of Admiral Byng illustrated a vanished world. Whether or not this had, as Voltaire had joked, encouraged the others, there was a new spirit about. The Royal Navy had become efficient at deploying its fleets and squadrons, running convoys and, above all, mounting combined, amphibious operations with the Army. The soldiers, in turn, had learned (if they were not always to remember) how to fight in wilderness, forest and the tropics, even though the problem of disease remained unsolved. New standards had been set and senior officers recognised that lacklustre performance could lead to a court-martial, public outrage, or both. The British were supreme at sea and, on land, could, with the help of the Navy, concentrate overwhelming force at any point within reach of the sea.

As Pitt had foreseen, North America had been the great prize. The shared burdens of war might seem to have forged new links of friendship and mutual dependence across the Atlantic. Americans had fought beside the British at Ticonderoga, Quebec, Montreal and Havana, and their provincial troops had suffered heavily. Regular soldiers from Britain had also gone to the American colonies to recuperate after the trials of Cuba. 'A Letter from a Gentleman in New York to his Friend in London', quoted in an English newspaper at the time of the signing of the Treaty of Paris, told a familiar story: 'The Royal Highland Regiment are now in our neighbourhood; they, with some others, were sent back after the Havannah was taken, being unfit for any service, and reduced to less than one-third of the number that went from New York last November; and those that returned appear dejected and enfeebled with little hopes of recovery.'[33] They had returned in time for the ferocious North American winter.

As both Pocock and Albemarle had admitted, their magnificent fleet and army was unfit for further active service, but, despite the peace treaty, they were required sooner than could have been expected. The disappearance of the French from North America, except as settlers under British rule, had left their Indian allies confused and restless. Three years earlier, one of their most forceful chiefs, Pontiac of the Ottawa tribe, had met Major Robert Rogers, who was still one of the most active American officers with the British Army, on the march to occupy forts surrendered by the French near the Great Lakes.

Pontiac had agreed to the passage of Roberts's rangers on condition that his tribal rights were respected. This was agreed but the Indians were soon disillusioned: the French had been traders and trappers with whom the Indians had established an understanding; the British and Americans seemed less friendly and brought settlers in their wake, hungry for land. Encouraged by the French in his fear of losing more land, Pontiac began plotting with other chiefs throughout 1762, while the British were preoccupied with the campaign in Cuba. Just as the British had launched the coordinated attacks on Havana and Manila, so Pontiac organised simultaneous assaults on British forts from Lake Superior to the mouth of the Mississippi for May, 1763. He himself was to lead the Ottawa in an attack on the fort at Detroit.

In the spring of 1763, just as warm weather was beginning to bring hopes of recovery to those who had survived the Havana campaign and the North American winter, terrible news began to reach the garrison towns reminiscent of the first reports of the massacres at Fort William Henry, Fort Duquesne and Ticonderoga. Twelve forts, deep inland, had been attacked and all but four had fallen and their garrisons been slaughtered, together with the settlers living under their protection. Detroit had managed to hold out but elsewhere were smoking ruins and scalped corpses. Relief columns, hurriedly assembled and marched into the forests, were ambushed and several almost wiped out.

The survivors of Havana were in no state to fight. A report, reaching London from America via Paris at the end of the year, was alarming: 'Forty thousand savages of 84 different nations have conspired against the English to cut them all off and had actually made themselves masters of all the forts on the Great Lakes, massacred the garrisons and butchered the inhabitants.' General Amherst, the French reported, had sent an ultimatum to Pontiac demanding his submission to King George. Pontiac, it was said, had replied: 'Answer me, Englishman, can a child have more than one father? All these nations have long ago made choice of the great Onontia [the Indian name for King Louis XV] for theirs. How pretendest thou that we now have another?'[34]

Lord Albemarle's fine army had been destroyed by yellow fever during the long and, some said, unnecessary siege of El Morro. Had it survived, Pontiac's rebellion could probably have been extinguished quickly. As it was, reinforcements had to be shipped from England and gradually, over more than a year, the fire-power of disciplined infantry, guided by American rangers, beat back the Indians. It was not until 25 July, 1765, however, that Sir William Johnson, the veteran superintendent of Indian affairs, concluded a peace treaty with Pontiac[*].

Pontiac's rebellion achieved one concession. This was the British proclamation under which territory west of the Appalachian mountains was reserved for the Indians; this antagonised those American colonists who looked westward for new land to farm. The unrest among the colonists, the Indians and, indeed, the French still living in what had once been New France, required the establishment of strong garrisons of British and provincial troops throughout the North American Empire at an annual cost of about half a million pounds. The British, who had been the most heavily taxed of all Europeans, since they had been subsidising their Prussian allies as well as fighting a global war, strongly objected. As it was the North American colonists who would benefit from this expensive protection, it was surely right that they should pay for it, concluded British politicians. Therefore, Parliament in London decided to tax them through the Sugar Act and the Stamp Act of 1764, which aroused even stronger objections from the colonists, particularly those directly engaged in trade. This combined with other resentments, notably against the impressing of men for the Royal Navy in the Atlantic ports, and discontent grew to antagonism and then into civil disobedience and rioting.

From this point, the pace of discord mounted and it escalated into violence and war. The outcome of the American Revolution, or War of Independence, was inevitable, particularly since Generals Howe and Wolfe were not there to command the British Army in North America and fight their former brother-officers, George Washington, Charles Lee, Horatio Gates and the rest. Had Howe or Wolfe survived to command at Havana and taken the city within a week, as would probably have been the case, their army would have survived intact. Pontiac's rebellion would have been quickly extinguished, the punitive taxation for defence expenditure made unnecessary, and history might have taken a different turn. It is conceivable that liberal attitudes and diplomacy might have kept all the North American colonies within the British Empire, which might also have included Cuba and the Philippines.

As it was, the British Empire had been founded and would survive until transformed into a shrinking Commonwealth in the twentieth century. When war had been declared in 1756, Britain had possessed the 13 North American colonies, Nova Scotia, Newfoundland and Jamaica, together with the strategic bases Gibraltar and Minorca; trading islands, among them the Bahamas, Bermuda and Barbados; and trading ports in India. Now Britain ruled a global empire. Clive is remembered for creating the expanding Indian Empire, Wolfe[*] for the creation of Canada, where it would be more than two centuries before the ghost of New France stirred in Quebec to threaten its future as a united nation. At the end of the twentieth century, the United States of America looks back at more than two centuries of independence and, 20 years before that, to a time when the Americans and British fought as allies in the very first world war, as they were again to fight victoriously in the twentieth century.

A Short Bibliography

Archivo Nacional de Cuba. *Papeles Sobre la Toma de la Habana por los Ingeles en 1762*. Havana, 1948 and 1951.

ASPINAL-OGLANDER, CECIL. *Admiral's Wife*. London, 1940.

BARCLAY, JULIET. *Havana: Portrait of a City*. London, 1993.

BEATSON, ROBERT. *Naval and Military Memoirs of Great Britain*. London,1804.

BELLICO, RUSSELL P. *Sails and Steam in the Mountains: A Maritime and Military History of Lake George and Lake Champlain*. New York, 1992.

BENCE-JONES, MARK. *Clive of India*. London, 1974.

BRADLEY, A.G. *The Fight with France for North America*. London, 1900.

CAMBRIDGE, RICHARD. *An Account of the War in India*. London, 1767.

CLOWES, WILLIAM LAIRD. *The Royal Navy*. London, 1890–95.

CONNELL, BRIAN. *The Plains of Abraham*. London, 1959.

CORBETT, JULIAN. *England in the Seven Years War*. London, 1907.

ERSKINE, DAVID, (ed.). *Augustus Hervey's Journal*. London, 1953.

FEARNE, CHARLES. *The Trial of Hon. Admiral John Byng*. Dublin, 1757.

FORREST, GEORGE. *The Life of Lord Clive*. London, 1918.

FORTESCUE, J.W. *A History of the British Army*. London, 1899.

GUITERAS, PEDRO J. (ed.). *Conquista de la Habana por los Ingeles*. Havana, 1932.

HAMILTON, EDWARD P. *Fort Ticonderoga: Key to a Continent*. Boston, 1964.

HART, FRANCIS RUSSELL. *The Siege of Havana*. London, 1931.

HIBBERT, CHRISTOPHER. *Wolfe at Quebec*. London, 1959.

HILL, S.C. (ed.). *Bengal in 1756–7*. London, 1905.

HOLMES, MICHAEL. *Augustus Hervey: A Naval Casanova*. Durham, 1996.

IVES, EDWARD. *A Voyage from England to India and an Historical Narrative of the Operations of the Squadron and Army in India....* London, 1773.

JOHNSTONE, CHARLES. *Chrysal, or, The Adventures of a Guinea*. London, 1764.

KEEGAN, JOHN. *Warpaths*. London, 1995.

KEMP, PETER. *The Oxford Companion to Ships and the Sea*. London, 1976.

KEPPEL, SONIA. *Three brothers at Havana, 1762*. London, 1981.

KEPPEL, THOMAS. *The Life of Augustus, Viscount Keppel*. London, 1842.

KIELMANSEGGE, FREDERICK. *Diary of a Journey to England, 1761-2.* London, 1902.

LANGFORD, PAUL. *A Polite and Commercial People: England, 1727-83.* Oxford, 1989.

LAWFORD, JAMES P. *Clive: Proconsul of India.* London, 1976.

LOSTY, L.P. *Calcutta, City of Palaces.* London, 1990.

MANTE, THOMAS. *The History of the Late War in North America and the Islands of the West Indies.* London, 1772.

MIDDLETON, RICHARD. *The Bells of Victory.* Cambridge, 1985.

MINNEY, R.J. *Clive.* London, 1931.

MOWL, TIMOTHY. *Horace Walpole: The Great Outsider.* London, 1996.

ORME, ROBERT. *A History of Military Transactions of the British Nation in Indostan.* London, 1861.

PARKMAN, FRANCIS. *Montcalm and Wolfe.* London, 1884.

POPE, DUDLEY. *At 12, Mr Byng was Shot.* London, 1962.

REILLY, ROBIN. *The Rest to Fortune.* London, 1960.

RODGER, N.A.M. *The Wooden World.* London, 1986.

SYRETT, DAVID. *The Siege and Capture of Havana.* London, 1970.

TOWNSHEND, C.V.F. *The Military Life of Field Marshal George, First Marquess Townshend* London, 1901.

TRACY, NICHOLAS. *Manila Ransomed* Exeter, 1995.

TURNBULL, DAVID. *Cuba.* London, 1840.

WALPOLE, HORACE. *Memoirs of the Reign of King George II.* London, 1846.

WALPOLE, HORACE. *The Letters of Horace Walpole.* London.

WARNER, OLIVER. *With Wolfe to Quebec.* London, 1972.

WILLSON, BECCLES. *The Life and Letters of James Wolfe.* London, 1909.

WINDHAM, WILLIAM and TOWNSHEND, GEORGE. *A Plan of Discipline Composed for the use of the Militia of the County of Norfolk.* London, 1759.

WOOD, JAMES. *Gunner at Large: The Diary of James Wood R. A., 1746-65.* Ed. Rex Whitworth. London, 1988.

WRIGHT, ROBERT. *The Life of Major-General James Wolfe.* London, 1864.

Acknowledgements

The publishers would like to thank the following for their permission to reproduce photographs and illustrations:

©The British Museum: Plate 1
Courtauld Institute of Art: Plate 16;
The McCord Museum of Canadian History, Montreal: Plates 7 and 9;
Arquivo Nacional de Fotografia- Instituto Portgues de Museus, Jose Pessoa and Martin Charles: Plate 13;
National Maritime Museum, London:
Plates 1, 2, 3, 8-9, 9, 10, 14, 15;
By courtesy of the National Portrait Gallery, London: Plates 2, 5 and 7;
The Pennington-Mellor-Manthe Trust and the Courtauld Institute of Art: Plate 4;
Courtesy of St Edmundsbury Borough Council (Manor House Museum): Plate 12;
Private collection: Plates 2, 6, 11 and 12-13.

Whilst every effort has been made to trace the owners of copyright material, in a few cases this has proved to be problematic and so we take this opportunity to offer our apologies to any copyright holders whose rights we may have unwittingly infringed.

and silver to the right and left and these crowned with jewels, by God, at this moment do I stand astonished at my own moderation.'[64]

[*] A magnificent monuments was erected over the grave, with a pediment on each face and an obelisk rising from the roof, that still stands in the churchyard.

[*] Built on the future site of Pittsburgh.

[*] The first President of the United States of America; other officers to escape included Horatio Gates and Charles Lee, who both became generals in Washington's army in the War of Independence, and Daniel Boone, the pioneer of westward expansion.

[*] Her wreck was discovered in 1979 and much of her armament, equipment and stores salvages.

[†] Now part of the Royal Anglian Regiment.

[*] His gravestone can be seen at Hudson Falls, New York State.

[*] The historian Christopher Hibbert wrote in his *Wolfe at Quebec* (p. 10): 'There was much in his temperament suggestive of the latent homosexual. The suppression and sublimation of homosexual tendencies is undoubtedly a reasonable explanation for the neuroses which complicated his character. That they were suppressed seems certain.'

[*] Forty years to the day before Nelson came up with an anchored French fleet in Aboukir Bay and destroyed it at the Battle of the Nile.

[*] Draper would write the definitive *Laws of Cricket* in 1774.

[*] The chosen sculptor was Peter Scheemakers (1691–1770), who showed Pocock, life-size, in a Roman soldier's dress with the star of the Order of the Bath on his breastplate. The statue was placed in an alcove in the General Court Room of East India House near to a matching statue of Clive, to be followed by others of Stringer Lawrence, Eyre Coote and the Governors-General Warren Hastings and Lord Cornwallis. The fate of Pocock's statue is described in the Introduction to this book.

[†] Pocock's three actions with d'Aché would be criticised by naval tacticians as unimaginative and illustrative of the crippling strictures of the Admiralty's *Fighting Instructions*. They must have seemed so in the light of Nelson's dazzling tactical coups, but it is difficult to see what else he could have done. He was always outnumbered and outgunned; his captains were of variable quality, both personally and in training; some were commissioned in the Royal Navy, while others belonged to the East India Company, so they lacked the zestful cohesion of Nelson's 'Band of Brothers'. The French practice of firing at an enemy's masts and rigging so that they could not be pursued achieved that aim, while the British fired into their enemies' hulls, inflicting enormous casualties and achieving victory thus, and not by the more spectacular feat of destroying, or capturing, enemy ships. The historian Sir Julian Corbett wrote of Pocock's final victory in his *England in the Seven Years War*: 'It was indeed the death-blow to the French position in India … the end might be far or near, but if the English were left in control of the Indian seas there could be but one end … What d'Aché, the sailor, could not see, Lally, the soldier, saw too well; and Pocock saw it, too.'

[*] The future explorer of the Pacific Ocean.

[*] Two and a half centuries later, British cannon-balls were still being found on building sites in the Old City.

[*] One of his officers was Captain Charles Lee, the survivor of Ford Duquesne and Ticonderoga, who was then promoted major; as a lieutenant-colonel, he later served in Portugal.

[*] Created a baronet in 1765.

[*] A court-martial held me next month sentenced Campbell to be dismissed me service bur did not specify whether his behaviour had been due to cowardice, drunkenness, or both.

[*] Ever since, a warship in the Spanish Navy has been named *Velasco* in his memory.

[*] The leader of a slaves' revolt against Rome. 73–1 BC

[*] As a rear-admiral and one of me most promising senior officers in me Royal Navy, Kempenfelt died in 1782 when his flagship, the *Royal George*, capsized while being heeled for repair at Spithead.

[*] He was imprisoned and finally executed in 1766.

[‡] They hung in King's College Chapel until they finally mouldered.

[*] The church of San Francisco de Asis was taken over as garrison church and Roman Catholic services have never been held there since, it being used as a post office and then as a concert hall.

[*] The Manila ransom was never paid because the Spanish maintained it had been agreed under duress.

[‡] Yet the loss of both territories could later be seen as the beginning of the decline of the Spanish Empire, just as the loss of Singapore in 1942 began the extinction of the British Empire in Asia. Both Cuba and the Philippines were ruled by Spain for 135 years until they were lost during the war with the United States, which most of the British North American colonies had become.

[*] Later named Orleans House, when the admiral's son sold it to me Duc d'Orléans.

[*] Three years later, Pontiac was murdered by a fellow-Indian and inter-tribal warfare followed.

[*] When R.A. Butler was appointed Education Minister in Winston Churchill's post-war Government, he asked me Prime Minister for advice and was told, 'Tell me children how Wolfe took Quebec.' (Butler to Michael Charlton in an interview)

[1]

Notes to the Text

Abbreviations used in the Notes

BL   British Library
BM   British Museum
HL   Huntington Library, California, U.S.A.
NAM   National Army Museum
NMM   National Maritime Museum
NPG   National Portrait Gallery
NYPL   New York Public Library
PRO   Public Record Office

Chapter One

[1] Pope, p. 262.

[2] Aspinal-Oglander, p. 136.

[3] Navy Records Society. *A Naval Miscellany*, Vol. 4, p. 228.

[4] Erskine (ed.) p. 203.

[5] Walpole, *Letters*.

[6] Boscawen Letters, *Naval Miscellany*, Vol. 4.

[7] Walpole, Horace *Reign of King George II*, Vol. 2, p. 216.

[8] Pope, p. 161.

[9] Walpole, *Letters*.

[10] Erskine (ed.), p. 231.

[11] BM. Satires 18.3360.

[12] Erskine (ed.), p. 242.

[13] Fearne, Vol. 1, p. 125.

[14] Aspinal-Oglander, p. 239.

[15] Fearne, Vol. 2, p. 477.

[16] Ibid., Vol. 2, p. 478.

[17] Erskine (ed.), p. 239.

[18] Ibid., p. 237.

[19] Parliamentary History XV; Add. 35895, f. 53.

[20] Erskine (ed.), p. 242.

[21] Ibid.

[22] 22 Walpole, *Letters*.

[23] Erskine (ed.), p. 242.

[24] Ibid.

[25] Walpole, *Letters*.

[26] Ibid.

[27] Pope, p. 298; *A Letter from a Gentleman to his Friend in the Country*, pamphlet.

[28] Pope, p. 299.

[29] Ibid., p. 247.

[30] *Candide*, 1760, Chapter 23.

[31] Walpole, *Letters*.

[1]*Chapter Two*

[1] Ives, p. 179.

[2]Ibid., p.177.

[3]Ibid.

[4]Powis Collection, Box VII, BL.

[5]Wood, p. 96.

[6]Ibid., p. 98.

[7]Ives, p. 80.

[8]Ibid.

[9]Ibid., p. 82.

[10] Wood, p. 99.

[11] Ives, p. 83.

[12] Ibid., p. 84.

[13] Ibid., p. 85.

[14] Cambridge, p. 98.

[15] Wood, p. 104.

[16] Ives, p. 87.

[17] Forrest, Vol. 1, p. 267.

[18] Ives, p. 89.

[19] Wood, p. 107.

[20] Losty, p. 21.

[21] *London Chronicle*, 9 June, 1757.

[22] Ives, p. 96.

[23] Hill, Vol. 2, pp. 70–1.

[24] Ibid., p. 76.

[25] Ives, p. 100.

[26] *London Chronicle*, 9 August, 1757.

[27] Ives, pp. 100–1.

[28] *London Chronicle*, 6 August, 1757.

[29] Ibid., 9 August, 1757.

[30] Hill, Vol. 2, p. 77.

[31] Ives, p. 102.

[32] Hill, Vol. 2, p. 96.

[33]   Ibid., p. 97.

[3]34   India Home Office Records, Home Miscellaneous Series, Vol. 193, 3 February, 1757.

[35]   Hill, Vol. 2, p. 176.

[36]   Ibid., p. 213.

[37]   Forrest, Vol. 1, p. 366.

[38]   Ibid., p. 105.

[39]   Hill, Vol. 2, p. 175.

[40]   Ibid., p. 200.

[41]   Hill, Vol. 2, p. 253.

[42]   Orme, Vol. 1, p. 143.

[43]   Hill, Vol. 2, p. 279.

[44]   Ibid., p. 277.

[45]   Ibid., p. 300.

[46]   Ibid., p. 311.

[47]   Ibid., p. 278.

[48]   Hill, Vol. 3, p. 9.

[49]   *Edinburgh Evening Courant,* 6 October, 1757.

[50]   Ives, p. 133.

[5]51   Ibid., p. 129.

[52]   Hill, Vol. 3, p. 27.

[53]   Hill, Vol. 2, p. 300.

[54]   Ibid., p. 290.

[55]   Ives, p. 131.

[56]   Hill, Vol. 2, p. 27.

[57]   Hill, Vol. 3, p. 27.

[58]   Ibid., p. 28.

[59]   Hill, Vol. 2, p. 307.

[60]   Hill, Vol. 3, p. 372.

[61]   Watts, William. *Memoirs of the Revolution in Bengal.* 1757, p. 61.

[62]   Orme, Vol. 2, pp. 17–34.

[63]   Orme, Vol. 2, p. 178.

[64]   Ibid., Vol. 23.

[65]   Powis Collection, Box 6.

[66]   NMM. MS 9956.

[67]   NMM. MS 9956.

[68]   India Office Library. Watson Letterbrook, MSS EUR. D1079.

[69]   Ives, p. 177.

[7]70   Ibid., pp. 177–8.

[71]   Ibid., p. 178.

[72]   Orme, Vol. 3, p. 124.

[73]   NMM. MS 9956.

[74]   PRO. ADM 1/161/223.

[75]   PRO. ADM 1/161/235.

[1]*Chapter Three*

[1] Kemp, p. 98.

[2]*Journal of Gen. Rufus Putnam*, ed. E.C. Dawes. Albany, NY, 1886, p. 66.

[3]Quebec House.

[4]*Boston Evening Post*, 12 June, 1758.

[5]Willson, p. 392.

[6]Beatson, Vol. 2, p. 128.

[7]Warner, p. 38.

[8]NAM. Lee MS, Archives, 780318.

[9]Connell, p. 102.

[10]   Parkman, Vol. 2, p. 95.

[11]   Fort Ticonderoga Museum. *Bulletin*, Vol. 10, No. 3, pp. 192–220.

[12]   Fort Ticonderoga Museum. *Ticonderoga: A Legend of the West Highlands*. 1947, p. 9.

[13]   Bellico, p. 64.

[14]   Knox, J. *An Historical Journal*. Freeport, NY, 1970, Vol. 1, p. 190.

[15]   Ticonderoga *Bulletin*, Vol. 10, pp. 192–220.

[16]   *Journals of Major Robert Rogers*, pp. 113–4. 1765; reprinted 1966, Ann Arbor, USA.

[17]   Perry, David. *Recollections of an Old Soldier*. Ticonderoga, 1981, p. 5.

[18]   Ticonderoga *Bulletin*, Vol. 10, pp. 192–220.

[19]   Pell, S.H.P. *Fort Ticonderoga: A Short History*. Ticonderoga, 1978, p. 9.

[20]   Parkman, Vol. 2, p. 102.

[21]   Mante, p. 147.

[22]   NAM. Lee MS.

[23]   Ticonderoga *Bulletin*, Vol. 10, pp. 192–220.

[24]   *Tradition*, Vol. 4, No. 19, p. 2; 'The Black Watch at Ticonderoga' by Lt. Col. J.B.R. Nicholson.

[25]   Stevenson, R.L. *Ticonderoga: A Legend of the West Highlands*. Scribners' Magazine, 1887.

[26]   Mante, p. 147.

[27]   Parkman, Vol. 2, p. 107.

[28]   NAM. Lee MS

[29]   Ibid.

[30]   Ticonderoga *Bulletin*, Vol. 10, pp. 192–220.

[31]31 Mante, p. 149.

[32]   Perry, *Recollections*, p. 6.

[33]   Pennsylvania Archives, 3/474.

[34]   Bellico, p. 69.

[35]   MacLaughlin, the Revd Thomas. *A History of the Scottish Highlands. Highland Clans and Highland Regiments Etc*. London, 1852, Vol. 2, p. 340.

[36]   *Tradition*, Vol. 4, No. 19, p. 2.

[37]   NAM. Lee MS.

[38]   Kimball, J.S. (ed.). *Correspondence of William Pitt*. New York, 1906, Vol. 1, p. 300.

[39]   *Tradition*, Vol. 4, No. 19, p. 2.

[40]   Perry, *Recollections*, pp. 6–7.

[41]   *Diary of Abel Spicer*, p. 407. From Meech, S.S. and Meech, S.B. (eds), *The History of the Descendants of Rita Spicer*. Boston, USA, 1911.

[42]   Perry, *Recollections*, p. 7.

[43]   Bellico, p. 72.

[44]   Ticonderoga *Bulletin*, Vol. 10, pp. 192–220.

[45]   NAM. Lee MS.

[46] Parkman, Vol. 2, p. 116.

[47] NAM. Williamson MS, 7311-85-2.

[48]48 Hibbert, pp. 2–4.

[49] Reilly, p. 53.

[50] Warner, pp. 19–20.

[51] Reilly, p. 89.

[52] Warner, pp. 19–21

[53] Hibbert, p. 3.

[54] Ibid., p. 4.

[55] Wright, p. 388.

[56] NAM. Williamson MS

[57] Reilly, p. 181.

[58] NAM. Gordon MS 8001-3/807-131.

[59] NAM. Williamson MS.

[60] Parkman, Vol. 2, p. 68.

[61] NAM. Townsend MS diary, 8001-30.

[62] Ibid.

[63] NAM. Williamson MS

[64] Parkman, Vol. 2, p. 73.

[65] Ibid., p. 77.

[66] Ibid.

[67] Warner, pp. 50–1.

[68] Parkman, Vol. 2, p. 80.

[69] Ticonderoga *Bulletin*, Vol. 10, pp. 192–220.

[70] *Annual Register*, 1759, p. 433.

[1]*Chapter Four*

[1] University of Minnesota Archives.

[2] Bence-Jones, p. 169.

[3] Orme, Vol. 2, p. 300.

[4] PRO. ADM 1/161/262.

[5] *Naval Review*, 1939, Vol. 27, pp. 294–300.

[6] NMM. MS 68/29.

[7]PRO. ADM 1/161/5297.

[8]PRO. ADM 1/161/261–2.

[9]Ibid.

[10]　Ibid.

[11]　*London Chronicle*, 20 March, 1758.

[12]　Dreaper, James. Biographical notes.

[13]　Orme, Vol. 2, pp. 390–1.

[14]　Forrest, Vol. 2, p. 103.

[15]　Orme, Vol. 2, p. 455.

[16]　NMM. POC/1d. MS 9956.

[17]　PRO. ADM 1/161/261–3.

[18]　*Gentleman's Magazine*, May, 1760.

[19]　PRO. ADM 1/161/356.

[20]　*Gentleman's Magazine*, May, 1760.

[21]　NMM. POC/1e. MS 9956.

[22]　Ibid.

[23]　NMM. POC 1f. MS 9956.

[24]　Beatson, Vol. 2, p. 219.

[25]　*Gentleman's Magazine*, December, 1760.

[1]*Chapter Five*

[1]　Warner, p. 50.

[2]McCord Museum, MG/18/L6.

[3]Warner, p. 60.

[4]Ibid., p. 33.

[5]Ibid., p. 66.

[6]Ibid., p. 65.

[7]Windham/Townshend, p. 111.

[8]Ibid., p. xii.

[9]Ibid., pp. 20–1.

[10]　Ibid., p. 61.

[11]　Warner, p. 130.

[12]　Reilly, p. 196.

[13]   NAM. Townshend Papers, 6806/41.

[14]   Beatson, Vol. 3, p. 267.

[15]   NAM. Townshend Papers, 6806/41.

[16]   Warner, pp. 96–7.

[17]   Ibid., p. 95.

[18]   Parkman, Vol. 2, pp. 214–16.

[19]   Beatson, Vol. 3, pp. 268–9.

[20]   Ibid., p. 232.

[21]   Parkman, Vol. 2, pp. 216–17.

[22]   Beatson, Vol. 3, p. 234.

[23]   Parkman, Vol. 2, p. 216.

[24]   NAM. 7311/85/3.

[25]   Reilly, p. 243.

[26]   McCord Museum. Wolfe's journal transcript.

[27]   NAM. Williamson MS, 7311-85-2.

[28]   Ibid.

[29]   Warner, p. 109.

[30]   NAM. Townshend Papers, 6806/41.

[31]   Warner, p. 113.

[32]   Reilly, p. 260.

[3]33   Parkman, Vol. 2, p. 244.

[34]   Reilly, p. 263.

[35]   McCord Museum. Wolfe transcript.

[36]   Reilly, pp. 263–4.

[37]   Ibid., p. 265.

[38]   McCord Museum. Townshend caricatures.

[39]   Reilly, p. 276.

[40]   Ibid., p. 284.

[41]   Townshend, p. 210.

[42]   Ibid., p. 155.

[43]   Raynham Hall Archive.

[44]   Reilly, p. 285.

[45]   Ibid., pp. 284–5.

[46]   Ibid., pp. 289–90.

[47]   Ibid., pp. 293–4.

[48]   Warner, p. 146.

[49]   Connell, p. 204.

[50]   Parkman, Vol. 2, p. 297.

[51]   Connell, p. 206.

[52]   Walpole, *Letters*.

[53]   Connell, p. 209.

[54]   Ibid.

[55]   Reilly, p. 311.

[56]   Hibbert, p. 156.

[57]   Reilly, p. 312.

[58]   Connell, p. 215.

[59]   *British Magazine*, April, 1760.

[60]   Walpole, *Letters*.

[61]   *British Magazine*, February, 1760.

[62]   *Gentleman's Magazine*, June, 1760.

[63]   *British Magazine*, February, 1760: 'An Ode to the Ever-Memorable Year, 1759'.

[64]   *Gentleman's Magazine*, January, 1759.

[1]*Chapter Six*

1   Duke of Devonshire's Diary. Chatsworth, 6 January, 1762.

[2]BL. Add. MSS 32/933, ff. 179–82.

[3]Sedgwick, Romney (ed.). *Letters from King George III to Lord Bute, 1753–66*. London, 1939, p. 78.

[4]Hart, p. 18.

[5]Kielmansegge, pp. 227–8.

[6]Walpole, *Letters*.

[7]*British Magazine*, February, 1762.

[8]Kielmansegge, pp. 251–4.

[9]Ibid., pp. 256–7.

[10]   Boswell, James. *Life of Johnson*, (20 July, 1762). London, 1791.

[11]   Kielmansegge, pp. 258–9.

[12]   Ibid., p. 262.

[13]   *London Magazine*, March, 1762.

[14]   Mante, p. 402.

[15]   Walpole, *Letters*.

[16]   PRO. ADM 1/237.

[17]   *British Magazine*, March, 1762.

[18]   HL. HM/1000.

[19]   PRO. WO 34/55, ff. 139–40.

[20]   Boswell's *Johnson*, 21 December, 1762.

[21]   Walpole, *Letters*.

[22]   Phillips' MSS Catalogue, 2 July, 1981.

[23]   Walpole, *Letters*.

[24]   HL. Pocock Papers.

[25]   Ipswich and East Suffolk Record Office. Albemarle Papers.

[26]   HL. HM/1000.

[27]   HL. NMM. MS 62/060.

[28]   NMM. N/N/18.

[29]   NYPL, Rare Books Department.

[30]   Johnstone, Charles. Vol. 3, p. 25.

[31]   *Journal of the Society of Army Historical Research (JSAHR)*, Vol. 51, p. 8.

[32]   Duro Fernandez. *Armada Espanola*. Madrid, 1895–1903, Vol. 7, p. 46.

[33]   Mante, p. 419.

[34]   HL. Pocock Papers.

[35]   Ipswich RO. Albemarle Papers, HA67: 973/A5.

[36]   HL. PO/862.

[37]   Ibid., Pocock Papers.

[38]   *JSAHR*, Vol. 51, p. 9.

[39]   HL. Pocock Papers.

[40]   Ibid.

[41]   Ipswich RO, Albemarle Papers, HA 67: 969/E99.

[42]   *An Authentic Journal of the Siege of Havana, 1762*. London, 1762, p.

13.

[43]   Urrutia y Montoya, D. Ignacio Jose de. *Teatro Histórico, Juridico y Politico Militarde la Isla Fernandina de Cuba.* Havana, 1931, Vol. 2, p. 153.

[44]   Public Archives of Canada. Amherst transcripts, 54.

[45]   HL. PO/952.

[46]   *Journal*, pp. 13–14.

[47]   Mante, pp. 425–6.

[48]   *JSAHR*, Vol. 51, p. 9.

[49]   Moseley, Dr Benjamin. *A Treatise on Tropical Diseases and on the Climate of the West Indies.* London, 1787, pp. 407–10.

[50]   HL. Pocock Papers.

[51]   Ibid., PO/892.

[52]   *British Magazine*, August, 1762.

[53]   HL. Pocock Papers.

[54]   Lady Hervey to Augustus Hervey, 14 December, 1761. Transcript in author's archive.

[55]   HL. PO/886.

[56]   PRO. ADM PO/795.

[57]   PRO. ADM 50/12.

[58]   Ibid. ADM 1/5301.

[59]   Ipswich RO. Albemarle Papers. HA: 461/118.

[60]   PRO. ADM 1/5301.

[61]   Mante, p. 425.

[62]   Ibid., p. 424.

[63]   PRO. CO 117/1, f. 79.

[64]   Ibid.

[65]   Mante, p. 461.

[66]   Phillips Catalogue, 2 July, 1981.

[67]   HL. PO/962.

[68]   Turnbull, pp. 518–19.

[69]   Ibid., p. 519.

[70]   *British Magazine*, November, 1762.

[71]   Turnbull, pp. 520–1.

[72]   Beatson, Vol. 3, p. 190. *Mackellar's Journal.*

[73]   Ipswich RO. Albemarle Papers. HA67: 969/E74.

[74]   HL. PO/938.

[75]   Ibid. Pocock Papers.

[76]   Ibid., PO/969.

[77]   *Gentleman's Magazine*, February, 1763: 'Letters from New York'.

[78]   HL/NMM. MS 62/060.

[79][79] William L. Clements Library Archive, University of Michigan.

[80]   Keppel, Thomas. *Life of Augustus, Viscount Keppel.* London, 1842, Vol. 1, pp. 361–2.

[81]   HL. PO/790.

[82]   PRO. ADM 50/12.

[83]   Ipswich RO. Albemarle Papers, HA67: 969/D23/1.

[84]   Ibid. HA67: 973/A27.

[85]   Beatson, Vol. 3, p. 388.

[86]   PRO. ADM 1/237.

[87]   Ibid. WO 34/55, ff. 200–1.

[88]   Walpole, *Letters.*

[89]   Ibid.

[90]   Ibid.

[91]   *Memoirs of the Marquis of Rockingham.* London, 1875, Vol. 1, pp. 123–4.

[92]   *British Magazine*, October, 1762.

[93]   Walpole, *Letters.*

[94]   Boswell's *Johnson*, fn. March, 1752.

[1]*Chapter Seven*

[1] PRO. CO 77/20.

[2] Ibid. WO 1/319, p. 353.

[3] Ibid. ADM 1/162 (2), f. 60.

[4] Nicholson, William. *Sundry Remarks and Observations made in a Voyage to the East Indies, 1758–64.* London, 1773, p. 7.

[5] Archbishop Rojo's Journal, quoted in *Manila Ransomed* by Nicholas

Tracy. Exeter, 1995, p. 12.

[6]India Office. Orme MSS 27, p. 78.

[7]Cushner, N.P. *Documents Illustrating the British Conquest of Manila*, No. 35. London, 1971.

[8]Ibid. No. 39.

[9]PRO. CO 77/20. Draper's Journal.

[10]   Ibid.

[11]   Ibid.

[12]   Draper's despatch quoted in *Gentleman's Magazine*, April, 1763.

[13]   Nicholson, William. *A Treatise of Practical Navigation and Seamanship*. London, 1796, p. 284.

[14]   PRO. CO. 77/20.

[15]   Walpole, *Letters*.

[16]   HL. Pocock Papers.

[17]   Valdés, Antonio José. *Historia de Cuba*. Havana, 1987, p. 81.

[18]   Ibid., p. 84.

[19]   HL. Pocock Papers.

[20]   *Papeles sobre la Toma de la Habana por Los Ingleses en 1762*, Vol. 11, p. 100.

[21]   HL. Pocock Papers. Pocock to Keppel, 8 November, 1762.

[22]   Ibid., p. 93.

[23]   Beatson, Vol. 2, p. 571.

[24]   *Gentleman's Magazine*, January, 1763.

[25]   HL. Pocock Papers.

[26]   Johnstone, Vol. 3, p. 27.

[27]   Walpole, *Letters*.

[28]   Boswell, James. *London Journal*. London, 1950, pp. 71–2.

[29]   NAM. Havana Garrison Orderly Book, MS 9212/73.

[30]   From Juliet Barclay's research in Havana.

[31]   Boswell's *Johnson*, 14 July, 1763.

[32]   *Gentleman's Magazine*, May, 1763.

[33]   Ibid., February, 1763.

[34]   Ibid., December, 1763.

Printed in Great Britain
by Amazon